D1222559

Escape From Plauen

A True Story

iBooks
Habent Sua Fata Libelli

iBooks
1230 Park Avenue
New York, New York 10128
Tel: 212-427-7139
bricktower@aol.com • www.ibooksinc.com

Library of Congress Cataloging-in-Publication Data

Stoever, Renate
Escape From Plauen, A True Story
p. cm.

1. Nonfiction—Biography 2. Worlds War II—Nonfiction
3. Cold War—Nonfiction 4. East Germany—Nonfiction
Nonfiction, I. Title.

ISBN: 978-1-59687-981-2, Hardcover

January 2014

Cover art by Renate Stoever

Escape From Plauen

A True Story

Renate Stoever

Acknowledgements

I want to thank my husband, all my friends, and especially Ghost Bear. Without their support and encouragement, this book would not have been written.

Dedication

To my parents and grandparents, whose courage gave me a chance for a better life, and to our son and our grandchildren, so they may understand the past and always cherish the value of freedom.

Table of Contents

THE WEST

THE UNITED STATES

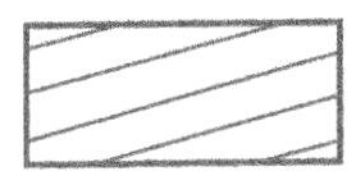

Former East Germany

Chapter 1

The Golden Heart

Baltimore 1936

On a cold blustery day in March, an elderly woman sat by the window looking at the mail delivered a short time ago. Among the bills a letter with foreign stamps and postmarks drew her attention. She held it up to view it in a better light.

It was a letter from Germany, a country she had left a long time ago to find a better life in the United States. She was a young girl then, but now she was nearing the end of her life. Settling herself comfortably in her chair, she began to read the letter. News from what had been home was always welcome. What she read was happy news indeed. Her nephew and his wife had become the proud parents of a little girl, a tender new branch on the family tree.

She couldn't think of what to give the baby girl for her journey through life. But then, on one of her errands, she saw a delicate gold necklace with a small golden heart beckoning to her from a jeweler's window. This was it, she decided. Never married, and earning her living as a maid in a wealthy household, she couldn't really afford it, but her heart told her otherwise. She entered the store and bought the necklace, regardless of its price. Lovingly wrapped in tissue paper, she sent it on its journey across many miles of ocean to the baby girl in Germany.

The heart necklace found its way to the little girl's neck when she was about four years old and didn't leave its place there for many years to come. It was with her when she played, dancing with joy around her neck when she skipped rope or ran to catch a ball. It took part in her happiness in the flower-laden meadows and blue skies of spring and the wonder of winter's first snow. Swimming in cool lakes in the summer, it shared her pleasure in the water's caress. The necklace and the girl were inseparable, and soon became as one.

Then war, the great destroyer, swept over the land and the girl's world turned dark, extinguishing all lights of joy. Communication with the woman in Baltimore ceased, because now the United States was enemy land.

It was the beginning of a terrible time for the girl wearing the heart necklace. During the darkness of that terrible war, when the little girl sat trembling in basements, as exploding bombs tore the air and death hunted for victims, the necklace felt her terror, and did its best to absorb her fright. When the girl's fear became unbearable, she would take the necklace's little gold heart in her mouth and bite down on it to stifle the screams surging in her throat. Patiently bearing the marks of her teeth, the heart soothed her hunger pangs when she was starving, and there was nothing to eat. After the war, during the country's occupation by foreign troops, the little gold heart trembled with her when Russian soldiers prowled their icebound house, and she was so afraid that she almost stopped breathing.

The memories of many terrible things happening in those years of misery were faithfully stored in the necklace's golden links, along with past joys and the love with which it was given. Her companion, friend and talisman in good days and bad days throughout her young life, it gave the girl comfort with its golden embrace. She loved the little necklace, not only because it had become part of her, but also because of the selfless love of the woman who gave it to her.

When the war was over, the girl learned that the woman in Baltimore had died after a simple life of hard work in a foreign land. How could she ever thank her now? The woman never knew how treasured her generous gift was to a little girl she had never seen. Her gift had made a world of difference to a little girl who learned that gifts, large or small, given freely with a loving heart, made even miserable dark days shine brighter.

When the girl became a young woman, the little necklace still graced her neck. She was often teased about wearing a child's necklace by the young men she met, but she only smiled. How could they ever know what the necklace meant to her? This gift of love crossed an ocean and transcended time, for more than half a century later, the generosity of a woman in a faraway land is still remembered with gratitude. The woman with the heart of gold was my father's aunt, Marie Gross, and I was the little girl.

The golden heart witnessed the events, which shaped my life. Some of my recollections were of wonderful, if not miraculous, incidents, reaffirming my faith in a higher power, while others were so horrifying, they were relegated to the pit of forgetfulness. If only the little heart could speak, it would have many stories to tell. But since the heart is mute, I have recounted events as I remember them, beginning with a peaceful early childhood, followed by the harrowing years during and after the war in Plauen, a once-upon-a-time beautiful city in the German state of Saxony.

* * *

Chapter 2

My Childhood Plauen

Plauen's municipal building

I was born in Plauen, a bustling eastern German city of 130,000 people with a worldwide reputation for the manufacture of laces and embroideries.

Looking back over the centuries, Plauen's fate has been destruction by war and fire, time and time again. In its one thousand year history, it has been resurrected repeatedly following decimation by wars and the Black Plague. After Plauen was laid waste by war in AD 1430, it came under the sovereignty of the Princes of Saxony, with Dresden as the capital. That's where my great-grandfather was Secretary of the Judiciary for Saxony's last monarch, King Friedrich III, who abdicated in 1918 after 829 years of House of Wettin family rule.

Following the Lutheran Reformation, in AD 1525 Plauen was completely burned down again during the religious wars between Protestants and Catholics. Even Napoleon and his great army left their mark of destruction when they passed through on the way to Russia in AD 1812. But ever tenacious, the city always rebounded from whatever destiny had ordained.

Plauen is situated in the foothills of a mountain range called the Erzgebirge, which means "mountains of ore." Serbs and Slavs populated the area until around AD 900, when German settlers came in covered wagons from Bavaria and Franken, and the population became a mixture of these different groups. Plauen's original name was Vicus Plawe. The word "plawe" is derived from a Slavic word meaning "place of floods," and the word "au" (as "au" in Plauen) is the German word for flood plain. So the White Elster River, which winds its way through the city, must have flooded the area often enough to earn the same name in both languages.

The heart of town lies in a valley where the White Elster finds its way through Plauen's granite hills. The St. Johann's Church, consecrated in 1122, stands near the municipal building, which was constructed during the fourteenth century at the edge of the old cobblestone marketplace. I fondly remember the festive Christmas markets held there every year. The square became the fantasy world of every child's dream, where the smell of roasting chestnuts and pretzels permeated the frosty air. Toys, candy, and sugar-frosted cookies hung in the many booths. Christmas trees decorated with candles and tinsel appeared like fantasies from a storybook, making the anticipation of Christmas all the greater.

We lived at 7 Annen Strasse, not far from the heart of town and close to bustling Bahnhof Strasse with its elegant stores, movie theaters, and restaurants. Streetcars and automobiles added to its lively atmosphere as they drove noisily up and down the hill. But our street, where we had a nice, second-floor apartment only half a block from all the activity, was relatively quiet. It was a great place to live, especially for a child, since most of the area inside our block consisted of lawns, trees, and bushes. There was a sandbox and a swing set for the kids, and there were quite a few of us in the same age group. The area was enclosed, so we couldn't run out into the street, but we were allowed to freely roam the park-like interior of the block. There we played to our hearts' content, while our mothers took care of their chores. I remember playing there from early in the morning until dark. When we got hungry, we would line up under our mothers' kitchen windows and call to let them know that we wanted something to eat. The windows opened, and it didn't take long for the wrapped sandwiches to come sailing down. Soon we were all sitting in the grass, munching our mother's tasty missiles.

On nice days we would visit Plauen's huge city park to feed the ducks and the swans that made their home in a large pond. I was particularly impressed by the stately elegance of the swans gliding over the pond's smooth green surface. It was a long walk to the pond, but there were many interesting things to see on the way. Birds, red squirrels, and other small animals crossed our path, and a profusion of acorns and chestnuts waited to be picked up for my collection.

An afternoon visit to my father's parents was another thing I always looked forward to. Their spacious apartment, which included grandfather's design studio, took up the entire second floor of the apartment house they owned. Plauen was the center of the lace and embroidery industry in Germany, and my grandfather had his own design firm, with a diverse clientele from as far away as New York. As a three-year-old, I was fascinated with all the strange things in his studio. A large drawing table covered with lots of pencils, pens, and charcoal sticks took up a good part of the room. I loved looking at the many books full of beautiful designs, but what really intrigued me was a machine surrounded by black curtains hanging on one of the walls. I thought that it was a movie projector and that maybe Grandfather would let me see some movies. But to my lasting disappointment the machine only enlarged grandfather's patterns in preparation for his clients' embroidery machines.

To entertain me, Grandfather would sit me on his lap and show me all the fun things that could be done with a pencil. He would hold my hand, and together we drew smiley faces, flowers, and trees. I was always fascinated with the results of our joint efforts, and I became very proud of my newly acquired skill. To my mother's delight, pencils and paper became my best friends, because they kept me occupied, and she rarely heard me say, "I'm bored."

Then in late August of 1939 we went on vacation. I dimly remember a brooding, dark-green lake fringed with reeds, surrounded by lush meadows and a tall, dark pine forest. Little did I realize that this was to be our last vacation for a long, long time. I just knew that our vacation was suddenly cut short, and all the adults, including my parents, were very upset because war had broken out. What was a war? I didn't know, but the way everybody acted as we made our way home frightened and puzzled me. I remember the train stations full of upset people and the coaches jammed with excitedly talking crowds. The atmosphere was charged, crackling with excitement and dark foreboding. Young men sang old German songs, which spoke of a people's love for their country, and even at my young age I could tell that the songs came from the heart and soul. I could sense people's unity in the face of calamity as I absorbed the tumultuous feelings and all the strange things happening around me. When we finally got home, my head was spinning!

For a while the only evidence that there was a war were ration cards, but they weren't of much concern to a three-year-old. Quite a few friends and family members, including my two uncles, became soldiers and were sent away. My mother's parents came home from the United States, where they had been visiting my other two uncles. My grandparents actually caught the last boat from America to Germany, and they too were extremely worried and upset. This thing called "war" seemed to be very bad indeed.

Grandmother told me that Mother and I were supposed to go on that trip to faraway America, but Mother was expecting a visit from the stork, who was going to bring me a brother or a sister, so we had to stay home. Of course I knew all about the stork. He made his home high up on rooftops and church steeples, where he could be seen standing on one leg, guarding his nest. I wondered whether this was where he kept the babies, and if my future brother or sister was in one of them. According to what I was told, you put salt on the windowsill if you wanted a boy, so in preparation for the stork's visit, I put a pinch of salt on the windowsill every night before going to bed. Since I always wished for an older brother, the salt would inform the stork of my preference. Sugar was placed outside if you wanted a girl, so I was extremely careful not to put out sugar by mistake.

Imagine my surprise when on January 24, 1940, my mother introduced me to Margit, my baby sister. I was terribly disappointed, and thought the stork had made a mistake. Not only had he forgotten to bring me an older brother, he brought me a younger sister instead. What kind of a stork was this? Didn't he see all the salt I put outside our kitchen window night after night? How the stork could make such a mistake was beyond my comprehension.

Mother tried to console me. "The stork must have been out of boys, but look, you have a beautiful little sister."After more of my complaining, she finally told me, "No, we can't give her back. No, the stork doesn't make exchanges." I definitely wasn't happy with this outcome, and my faith in the stork was badly shaken. I suspected foul play.

I wasn't crazy about life with a baby sister. For one thing, I had to share my mother's attention with her, and for another, she got all the pudding and milk. Rationing meant that milk was scarce, and since Margit was an infant, she had priority claim on whatever we got. I took it personally, because I was too young to connect it to the war and the rationing. Mother seemed to fuss with Margit constantly, which left less time for me. Eventually I got used to it, and I spent more time with my friends in the yard. That made me more independent and self-reliant, which was to serve me well in the stormy times coming my way.

Not long after the stork dropped off my little sister, I was happily excited on the day my mother fastened a gold necklace with a little heart around my neck. "It's a present from your Aunt Marie in America," she told me. I was puzzled. I didn't know any Aunt Marie. Mother explained, "America is very far away; that's why you have never met her." I accepted her explanation, and thought of Aunt Marie as my fairy godmother. After all, according to the fairy tales Mother read to me, most lucky people had one, and mine even lived in America, a beautiful place across a large pond. So I was delighted and proud to wear Aunt Marie's wonderful gift. I liked the way it hugged my neck and made me feel special and loved. Was I ever lucky to have such a nice aunt.

As time passed, we children started opening the doors to the street, which became a new and interesting playground. Our mothers' worry-free years were over. Of course we were told to stay in the yard, but it went in one ear and out the other. The minute our mothers' backs were turned, we were back on the street.

One day I found a rather odd booklet on the sidewalk. It had drawings of some strange-looking people with huge noses, long black beards, and long curls over their ears. They wore funny black hats and long black coats. Since I had never seen people like that, the book aroused my curiosity. There was writing under the pictures, but since I couldn't read yet, I didn't know what it said. It didn't look like any book I had ever seen, and I didn't know what to make of it. Looking for an explanation, I took it upstairs to show it to my mother. She took one look at the booklet, tore it up, and shoved it into the fire she had going in the stove. She was very angry and told me in no uncertain terms to never look at a book like that again, let alone bring one home. I had never seen her so furious. She didn't explain, and it left me wondering about the people in the book, and why she was so irate. Not wishing to anger her any further, I went back downstairs to play with my friends. I never saw anything like it again, and I soon forgot all about it.

Summer weekends were spent at our garden in Joessnitz, a three-acre piece of property with a small cottage about seven miles outside of Plauen. It was our summer retreat as far back as I could remember, and we always referred to it as "the garden." Just going there was a pleasure, even though it was a rather long walk. Mother and Father took turns pushing my little sister Margit in a stroller while I trotted alongside wishing that I too could get a ride, because by the time we reached the city limits, my legs began to tire and my feet started to hurt.

Once we left Plauen's outskirts, narrow paths led us through a tall pine forest. Birds flitted busily from tree to tree, their voices breaking the silence of this shadowed world of green. The sun breaking through the dense growth of tall pines made ever-changing patterns on our path. Strawberries, raspberries, and blueberries grew in little clearings where shafts of sunlight penetrated the deep shadows of the forest. By the time we left the cool shade of the woods and reached the open meadows, my mouth was usually smeared red and blue from all the berries I had eaten.

The meadows were colorful carpets of all kinds of wildflowers. There is nothing like the wonder of a meadow in the spring. The warm sun shining in a clear blue sky, gold, blue, purple and white flowers exuding their scent, and bees humming their way from blossom to blossom was pure delight! The flowers bent their little heads gracefully and swayed in a languid dance whenever a gentle breeze wafted over them, giving the meadow the appearance of a multihued sea. I waded through its knee-high abundance and picked as many flowers as my hands could hold. A little brook meandering through the fields of flowers went gurgling over small rocks and rootlets, dislodging a stone here and there and sweeping it along on a short-lived trip. I took pleasure in letting the brook's cool clear water flow through my fingers, until Mother called to me that it was time to go: "If you keep playing around like this, we won't get to the garden until the afternoon. So let's go." I would leave the brook reluctantly and run to catch up.

The garden property was completely fenced in, and was entered through a wide gate off a dirt road. A path bordered by flowerbeds led up to the cottage, which was surrounded by meadows full of wildflowers.

The cottage with only a tiny foyer, a kitchen, and a bedroom, had no heat, no electricity, no plumbing, and no running water, but it was like heaven for us. Climbing purple clematis and a vine with little sour grapes covered the outside of the little house, giving it a charming, romantic look. Inside it always smelled of good things like fresh apples, pears, and plums that grew on the garden's many fruit trees. There were also strawberries, raspberries, fresh vegetables, and potatoes, depending on the season. The scent of grass, flowers, and growing things came through the open windows and doors on gentle breezes.

In late summer the kitchen became a very busy place. The wood-burning stove was crowded with large pots in which all the season's fruits and vegetables bubbled and cooked for hours before they were put into preserving jars for the winter. The process made the kitchen look like an alchemist's workshop, where my mother and grandmother, swinging long-handled spoons with practiced ease, filled the jars with the garden's wonderful gifts. The garden was our little paradise. Usually my cousin Inge was there with her mother. Inge and I would get into all kinds of mischief and have a marvelous time while our parents and grandparents were digging, weeding, planting, and watering.

Toward the back of the property were two large barns, one of which was filled to the top with hay, making it an ideal playground for Inge and me. Our escapades usually earned us a scolding with dire warnings, because we always messed up Opa's neatly stacked hay. Not that those scoldings and warnings did any good; we were back in the barn the minute Grandfather was out of sight. Jumping off the top of the stacked hay, sliding down in a cloud of dust and dried grass to land in a soft pile at the bottom, was just too much fun to forego. It was worth a scolding or two. The other barn was used for storage and had an outhouse attached to it. That was one place it was wise not to visit at night. Inge told me some grisly stories about it, and since she was older and smarter, I was sure that she knew what she was talking about. Her tales of malevolent, nightmarish creatures waiting to pounce upon unwary prey at night were enough for me to avoid it after dark.

At night, after the adults had finally struggled us into bed, Opa would tell us stories of all his exciting adventures with the Indians in the United States. Never at a loss for words or ideas, he made those yarns up as he went along. We couldn't hear enough of his fantastic tales. We always clamored for more, with the added benefit of gaining a bit of extra time before going to sleep. If we were lucky he would tell us another story, but since we never knew when enough was enough, he always had to put an end to it with, "No more now! Go to sleep!" And I drifted off to sleep, dreaming of Indians in the wilds of America.

The weekends were always over too quickly, and it was time to go home again. I remember those magical Sunday nights when we made our way back to the city through the dark sleeping forests and meadows, with a cart full of fruits and vegetables. The darkness of the night held a strange quiet, which had a sound of its own. Only the trees whispering to each other as gentle breezes wafted through them, the creaking noise of the handcart, and the occasional rustle of a nocturnal animal or the hoot of an owl would break the stillness.

Crossing the open meadows, we could see the dark, velvety sky stretching over us with millions of sparkling stars, and the Milky Way arching across its vault like a glittering necklace. The moon shed its pale light, silvering the meadows with their grasses and flowers, giving them an appearance of haunting beauty. Opa would tell us about the stars, the Milky Way, and the moon. He would keep us spellbound as he pointed out the constellations while telling us stories about them. He told us that if we were real quiet, we could hear the stars sing. So we were quiet, because we wanted to hear the song of the stars, and sometimes we thought that we could hear them. When we kids got too tired to walk any further, we were allowed to climb up on top of the wagon. There we sat among all the cabbages, beans, carrots, and apples, looking up at the glittering sky, wondering about its incredible beauty and the magic of the night.

Back in Plauen we hardly noticed that there was a war going on. Occasionally there would be a drill. The alarm was sounded, and everyone had to go into the basement. Then the "all clear" was sounded, and we would come out. It was taken as an occasional annoyance, and we soon forgot about it. Of course the windows now had to have light-proof shades so the enemy couldn't detect a glittering city below. But these were all minor inconveniences. Aside from that, life went on as it did before, and everything seemed all right with my world.

My grandmother and grandfather
(informally Oma and Opa in German)

Then in late 1941, two years into the war, my father was drafted into the army. He hadn't been called earlier because he was already thirty-eight years old. Too young to have a concept of time or the meaning of war, I accepted our father's becoming a soldier like a necessary change of jobs. Life continued as before, only without our father. But then, Inge's father and all the other children's fathers were gone too, so it didn't seem unusual. We now went to the garden without Father, but thank God Oma and Opa were still there.

* * *

Chapter 3

The Calm Before the Storm

In the fall of 1942 I started my first year of school, which was a big event in Germany. To sweeten the first day of school, the novices were traditionally picked up by their mothers, who presented them with large colorful cones filled with cookies and candy. To my delight, my mother surprised me with a two-foot cone. However, I soon found out that it was mostly stuffed with tissue paper, and only had a few cookies on the top. But I wasn't the only child whose hopes for lots of sweets were dashed. Because of the war, things like cookies and candy were very hard to come by, but our mothers did their best to make it a happy day for us. This was my first inkling that this thing called war, which happened at a mythical place called "the front," was worse than I thought.

My school was a few blocks away, and after crossing busy Bahnhof Strasse with some of the older kids the first few times, I soon navigated it all by myself. School wasn't as much fun as I expected it to be either. I had to sit still for long periods of time and talk only when spoken to, which was really hard to do. There was also lots of homework, even for first graders. When the teacher entered the classroom, we had to stand, raise our right arms, and greet him with "Heil Hitler." I couldn't imagine what was wrong with the normal "Guten Tag," which I liked much better. My teacher was a very strict man, and any fooling around in his class of about thirty-five children was not tolerated. I remember getting a sharp slap on my hand just for turning around to see what the girl behind me was doing.

At home, Mother would sit knitting while I did my homework. Since clothing was also in short supply, Mother unraveled old sweaters and stretched the wool to take out the curls. That's how she created new sweaters from the old ones, and thanks to her skill I wound up with some very colorful sweaters. While her knitting needles were busily clicking away, I practiced writing the alphabet and memorizing the multiplication tables without much enthusiasm. But Mother held me to the task. "How much is five times six, what is six times eight?" she kept asking me, going through all the tables until I got it right. She also inspected the letters I had written in script. A little later, we learned how to use pen and ink, which was difficult, but progress was swift, because instruction wasn't interrupted with playtime. It was serious business throughout, and our parents made sure that we did our homework. Of course I would have preferred running around outside, playing catch or hide and seek as I used to, but my friends were all inside doing their homework too. So like it or not, I kept my nose in the books.

Despite the war, we still made frequent trips to Markneukirchen, a small town near the Czech border where my mother's cousin and other relatives lived. We were always welcome there, because my Aunt Traudl was very hospitable and her large house could easily accommodate us. My cousin Ursula and I got along famously and we always had lots of fun together. Ursula and I liked to sneak into her grandfather's workshop, where violins and bows were made. The room always smelled of wood, glue, lacquer, and other indefinable things, and had a lot of tools lying around. There were violins in various stages of completion, bows and strings, all very interesting things, which begged to be touched. It was a fascinating place, but unfortunately we weren't able to investigate it thoroughly, because we were always chased out. So our excursions into her grandfather's inner sanctum were of short duration, and most of its treasures had to remain unexplored.

But we had our most enjoyable times when Aunt Traudl, Mother, Ursula, and I left early in the morning to go deep into the forest to pick mushrooms and blueberries. The sun had barely risen above the horizon as we made our way through the dew-laden meadows to the forest. Narrow mossy trails between towering trees led us ever deeper into a world where reality and fantasy seemed to be one and the same, blending into a delightful whole. The forest gave me the impression of a huge cathedral, its shimmering green roof upheld by columns of tall pines with their tops seemingly disappearing in the sky. Their dense growth shut out the sunlight, immersing the forest in a perpetual hushed twilight. Shafts of light penetrated here and there, creating patterns of bright light and deep shade. Tiny dust motes and insects with gossamer wings reflected within the streams of light like shimmering clouds between the trees. Occasionally a red squirrel scampered among the branches, harvesting pinecones for its nest, or a rabbit scooted for cover among the ferns. Mossy rocks, ferns, blueberries, and mushrooms hid in the shadows of the forest floor. It was an entire universe unto itself with its own set of rules, where humans were tolerated intruders. I remember small clearings full of blueberry patches and raspberry bushes, which hummed with the activities of bees and other insects, with iridescent wings flashing in the warm summer sun. Birds were flitting about, adding their sweet voices as they scooped up insects in flight or feasted on berries. Fireweeds growing in profusion lent their vibrant colors to contrast the somber green of the surrounding forest.

Ursula and I, only slightly intimidated by the majesty of our surroundings, practically ate our way through the woods. A lot of berries were eaten before they reached our baskets, but the forest provided more than enough to fill our stomachs and our baskets. The mushrooms didn't interest us since they couldn't be eaten on the spot. So we left them for Mother and Aunt Traudl, who were experts at culling the poisonous ones from the many different species growing on the forest floor. The only one we recognized as poisonous was one of exceptional beauty. It had a white stem, crowned with a bright red hat covered with white raised dots, which resembled pearls of all different sizes. We preferred to spend our time in the clearings with the berries under a brilliant blue sky and the bright sunshine, where we sat in the high grass to snack on our gathered delicacies.

When the trees started to throw long shadows, dimming the vibrant colors of the fireweeds, and the air cooled, silencing the bees and the birds, we knew it was time to leave this paradise. Only clouds of tiny gnats danced in the last rays of a waning sun, signaling the end of a beautiful day. As the twilight of the approaching night slowly crept over the land, the winged and four-legged inhabitants of this world settled down in an ever-deepening silence. Mysterious shapes and shadows appearing between the trees gave rise to fanciful thoughts as we made our way home through the gathering night. It wasn't difficult for me to believe the tales of dwarfs, giants, fairies, and witches dwelling in the shadowy depths of the forest. I had fleeting glimpses of the shadows coalescing into all kinds of fantastic forms as my imagination ran amok. I thought them manifestations of animals, gnomes, or fairies, their shape-shifting silhouettes moving swiftly as I spied them from the corners of my eyes. Fireflies winking like fiery red eyes in the darkness lent credence to my perception of the forest's ephemeral forces.

Ancient lore told us that the mythical denizens of this world who bedeviled or delighted mere humans were very shy and rarely seen. I thought it a real pity, for I would have loved to meet one of those fabled creatures. Of course to my disappointment, what often looked like a gnome turned out to be a small bush or a rock, and strange-looking animals unmasked themselves as twisted branches in the undergrowth. Yet there were other mysterious things I couldn't explain, which left me wondering. As far as I was concerned, the forest was full of mysteries as yet untold.

Stars twinkled in the night sky by the time we cleared the forest and made our way back home through open meadows by the light of a rising moon. We would come back home with our nostrils still full of the pine scent and our stomachs and baskets filled to the brim with the forest's gifts. We were tired and dirty, but always very happy. The next day we took our treasures and our beautiful memories back to Plauen with us. As usual I didn't want to leave, and Mother had her hands full distracting me on my teary train ride home.

* * *

Chapter 4

Christmas 1942

The sunny days of childhood gone forever, the storm clouds of war began to shadow my life. Once again Christmas arrived, but without the joys of past times. It was not much of a Christmas in Plauen that year. The war was now in its third year, but in spite of the grim times and general feeling of anxiety, it was a Christmas I remember to this day.

Of course there were no presents, no Santa Claus, no Christmas tree—there was nothing! Instead it felt as if an ominous, all-encompassing darkness had descended over our world. That Christmas my father was stationed in a town not too far away, so my mother was able to take a train to visit him. She took my two-year-old sister with her, while I had to stay behind with my grandmother. I would have much preferred to go see my father. Oma was rather strict and taciturn. I rarely saw her laugh or smile anymore.

To my shock and surprise, she woke me at 5 a.m. that Christmas morning to go to six o'clock Christmas Mass. I wasn't happy to be pulled out of my nice warm bed to brave my grandmother's cold kitchen. I was still half asleep when she made me sit on a table, where she struggled to get me dressed. But when she tried to put those hated itchy homemade woolen stockings on me, I was suddenly wide-awake. I could have sworn my mother had used glass wool to knit them. I fought my poor grandmother tooth and nail to avoid the horrible stockings, but she won in the end. Not even my tears deterred her.

It was still dark and bitter cold that Christmas morning when we set out for the centuries-old church about three blocks away. No streetlights or even a glimmer from a window lit our way. Stars still shimmered in the velvety black sky like glittering tears, and the moon shed its silvery light over the otherwise dark dismal streets, throwing long shadows over glistening ice and snow. The fresh snow crunched loudly under our feet, and our breath seemed to freeze as soon as it left our mouths. I was a very cranky, unhappy little girl as my grandmother pulled me along the snow-covered sidewalk. Then suddenly the church bells began ringing, breaking the stillness. Their rich, full sound echoed far and wide over the snowy streets and rooftops, filling the air with the call to prayer. Their magic dried my tears and made me all but forget my hated itchy stockings.

When we entered the church through its huge doors, we were greeted by a vision of enchanting, dreamlike beauty. The only light came from two thirty-foot-tall Christmas trees on either side of the altar, lit by hundreds of wax candles, which glimmered in the darkness like living things, bathing the altar in their golden light. The organ was playing, its rich, powerful sound reverberating through the nave, sending shivers down my spine.

The church was bursting with people wrapped in dark clothing, their breaths hovering like shimmering clouds in the bitter cold. The service started, and the people sang the familiar old hymns as if with one voice, their fervent prayers resounding in the nave with heartfelt anguish. All was very solemn, reflecting the perilous times in which we lived. The candlelight mirrored itself in the glistening tears that spilled from many eyes, leaving glittering tracks on cheeks. My grandmother was crying too, for she worried about her two sons, who were fighting somewhere in a cold country called Russia. Many tears and many prayers rose to heaven for the missing, the wounded, and the dead. I hoped that God and the angels were listening.

Imagination merged with reality when an angel in a flowing white gown and golden wings seemed to slowly float down the center aisle through the mist of incense, carrying a tall candle. Its flame threw dancing shadows as the angel moved gracefully within the glowing light. It sang the announcement of Christ's birth, its beautiful voice echoing through the church and from its high vaulted ceiling with crystalline clarity, proclaiming the joyous tidings.

I let the solemn beauty of the service wash over me, and I soaked it up like rays of the sun. I was filled with the sound of the organ, the glitter of a myriad of candles, the aroma of incense, and the melodies of the beautiful old Christmas songs. This symphony of sight and sound suffused my whole being and coalesced into a harmonious, mystical experience. It all felt unreal, like a beautiful, once-in-a-lifetime dream, never to be forgotten.

When it was over, and we walked back home, I knew that I had been given a truly wonderful Christmas gift after all!

* * *

Chapter 5

Harsh Realities

By 1944, the bombings had taken a heavy toll on German cities and their inhabitants. Despite the deteriorating situation, Plauen had remained unscathed by bombs, so we children were blissfully unaware of the harsher realities of war. We heard about the bombed cities of course, but it was beyond our scope to imagine what that meant. Death was an unknown quantity for us. Our childish brains weren't able to fathom the concept of an eternal sleep. But time cruelly taught us the meaning of all those things, ending our childhood all too soon.

My father

The summer of 1944 also brought a very unpleasant surprise for me. When my mother took me for my annual checkup, the doctor found that my bones were so soft from lack of calcium that my rib cage was bent. Not only that, I was also severely underweight for my age. To fatten me up, he decided to send me to a children's home in Bad Harzburg. I was rather apprehensive about this turn of events, because I was only eight years old, and it was the first time I would be away from home with complete strangers.

To get there, Mother and I took a train to the collection point in Halle where the home's staff awaited the arrival of children sent to them from all different parts of the country. It was already dark by the time we pulled into the station. The place looked so scary that I was afraid to get off the train. Halle, including the train station, had already been bombed, and the damage was visible everywhere. The huge dome that used to cover the station was missing. All that was left was the skeleton of twisted girders that had once supported it. My eyes registered it with the mixed emotions of astonishment and horror. This was when I had my first shock to see firsthand that war was very serious business indeed! Due to the bombings there wasn't any electricity, so the cavernous hall of the train station was dark, and it smelled of fire and soot. People quietly huddled in groups, sitting on their luggage or on the ground. Others wandered around, looking for friends or relatives among the new arrivals. There were candles and kerosene lamps sitting around on the floor in this very spooky atmosphere, which had the feeling of a funeral in the murky depths of purgatory. I wouldn't have been surprised if horned, clubfooted devils with pitchforks appeared to harass this sad-looking assortment of humanity.

Scared and unhappy, I sat on my suitcase like a little heap of misery while Mother went to look for the group from the home. "You wait here," she told me, "and don't wander off. I'll be right back." Sitting there, I could see the stars through the lacework of the twisted steel girders. The stars were twinkling in the inky darkness of the sky, competing with the flickering candles on the ground. The scene was surreal in its eerie beauty, and I was shocked to the depth of my soul.

Finally my mother found the group I was supposed to go with, and she took me to where several frightened-looking children clustered around two women. I was more than a little scared! It was a trip into the unknown for me, and the appearance of the train station wasn't at all reassuring. This was the place where my mother had to leave me with complete strangers. After all the mothers said their tearful good-byes, all the food lovingly packed by them was confiscated. It was redistributed later among all the children to ensure that even those who brought nothing would have their share. Sadly, my mother's few cookies were also taken.

Once all the children were assembled we boarded another train, which brought us to Bad Harzburg, where once upon a time Europe's nobility went for their health and to socialize with one another. It was an absolutely beautiful place in the Harz Mountains. Old tales told of the yearly celebration of "Walburgisnacht," when witches, devils, and warlocks from all over the universe met on the Brocken mountain for their sybaritic bacchanal, which was later immortalized in Walt Disney's "Fantasia."

My spirits were lifted when the children's home turned out to be an old villa on the side of a hill surrounded by deciduous woods in a charming setting. There were four of us to a bright, cheerful room where we were forced to take a nap after a healthy lunch. That definitely didn't work for me. There was no way I could sleep in the afternoon. If my mother never succeeded in getting me to nap when I was younger, their chances of success were between zero and nil. To while away this very boring enforced rest, I snuck books out of their library to read under the covers. Of course I was caught, and my punishment was a whole afternoon in bed without books, which wasn't my idea of an interesting day. After our nap we were usually taken for long healthy walks in the wooded mountainside. We collected acorns and chestnuts, which we turned into little men and women that we placed into villages of bark and leaves. So our days were spent in a relaxed, quiet atmosphere.

Aware of all the old tales of "Walburgisnacht," I looked for evidence of the veracity of those stories when we went up to the Brocken on our afternoon outings. Even though I gave the big rocks ringing the mountaintop a thorough inspection, I couldn't find any signs that anyone, let alone a coven of witches and warlocks, had celebrated there. It all looked very peaceful, with only a few squirrels scurrying around the rocks looking for acorns. This was very disappointing of course, and I felt cheated. But then, maybe they cleaned up after themselves when they were done, or maybe it was the wrong time of the year. So much for old legends, I thought.

Other times they took us to the spa, where my sisters in misery and I endured what seemed like hours in large vats of warm mineral water. Warm mud baths were another specialty of the spa to which we were subjected on several occasions. I don't know if all this did any good, but after two months of good food, naps, and a few afternoons in bed for various misdemeanors, I had gained seven pounds and my rib cage had straightened out, which made the staff very happy.

Some time in August, news trickled down to us that the war was going very badly, and more of our cities had been bombed. A lot of distraught parents arrived to pick up their children, and their tales of horrendous conditions in the cities were enough to give me nightmares. After what I had seen in the Halle train station on our way to Bad Harzburg, I feared the worst. Did Plauen get bombed too? Did I still have a home, a mother, and a sister?

There were only three of us left at the home, and I felt very insecure and extremely worried. Why didn't my mother come to get me? Was she dead or injured and couldn't come? My mind conjured up all kinds of scenarios—none of them good.

Finally a soldier in uniform arrived, causing quite a stir. It was my father who came to get me. Was I happy to see him! He looked very handsome in his uniform, and it didn't escape my notice that the home's female staff was all smiles. I hadn't seen them smile so much in all the weeks I had been there. My father informed me that while I was away, Plauen had been bombed too, but that Mother and Margit were fine. He told me that I would have to be very brave in the days to come, and help my mother as much as possible, since he had to leave again that same night. Little did I know that this was the last time I would see him for a very long time.

The train ride home was a little less scary because my father was with me, although there was an oppressive feeling of panic in the air. People were tense and nervous, their faces wearing harried, anxious expressions. Something was definitely very wrong. The pervading sense of gloom and doom transmitted itself to me, and left me feeling fearful and confused. That's when it really dawned on me that the situation was very serious.

Back in Plauen, I didn't see any evidence of its first bombings, so I was somewhat relieved. Unfortunately that didn't last long, because soon the sirens started to howl with an urgency, which told us that an attack was imminent. That sound alone, which I'll never forget as long as I live, was like all the demons of hell screaming with malicious delight to announce the dark angel's arrival. It permeated every cell in my body, causing an immediate rush of adrenaline to run or fight for life. To this day I have intense feelings of danger and an overwhelming urge to run whenever I hear a siren, even though the sound is innocuous compared to what I remember.

The sirens were still howling when we rushed into the basement. The thunder of low-flying, heavily loaded planes was already over us, vibrating the ceiling and walls around us. Fear of what was to come constricted my throat. When the explosions started, I thought the house was collapsing around us, for everything shook. The lights flickered and went out, leaving us in darkness, raising my already high level of terror a few more notches. Black smoke and soot came billowing down the window chutes with a ghastly whooshing sound. It felt like I was caught in an earthquake, and I expected the earth to open up and swallow us as we tumbled screaming to our doom. I was so petrified that I held my breath and it felt like my heart was doing somersaults.

Luckily it was over fairly quickly, and the sirens' even tones informed us that it was over. The bombers, having emptied their bomb bays over Plauen, were gone for now. When we came out of the basement, we saw that an area two blocks away was on fire. We could see all the sparks and the black smoke, hear the roaring flames and the crashing of collapsing roofs and walls. But thank God, except for minor damage our immediate neighborhood was untouched. I stood there openmouthed and crying hysterically. It was difficult for me to grasp how my familiar, secure world could suddenly come apart and become such a frightening place.

This was the first time I experienced a bombing, and it left me in shock and struck dumb with fright, unable to voice the terror I felt. All I could do was cry. I had my mother so worried over the effect the bombing had on me that she sent me to our relatives in Markneukirchen that same evening. I remember sitting on the train curled up with fear, afraid of the locomotive's sparks, which flew by my window like armies of hostile fireflies. Fear was an almost palpable presence sitting beside me, whispering of death and destruction. I hid deep within myself in an effort to shut out the fear, and I fought its insidious attempts to claim me by replaying the images of the day's horrible experience over and over in my mind.

My stay with my aunt in Markneukirchen lasted one week. With nostalgic longing my thoughts returned to past visits and the wonderful times when my aunt, mother, Cousin Ursula, and I left early in the morning to go deep into the forest to pick mushrooms and blueberries. What wonderful memories they were. What a stark contrast to what life had become.

During that week my mind worked tirelessly to adjust itself to my new circumstances. I realized that, like it or not, I had to accept whatever life had in store for me, and deal with it as best I could. I remembered my father's words to be brave. If I hadn't before, I fully understood their meaning now. I instinctively knew that our world would never be the same again. Tears and fear would be a waste of the energy needed to survive what was coming.

When I returned to Plauen, my mother found a different child. I had grown up and hardened in one week. Never again would I cry and cringe with fear. The many subsequent bombings left me stoic and in control of myself, which didn't mean that I wasn't afraid. Fear became my constant companion but it was with me, not part of me. It had lost the power to stampede me into mindless panic as it had done before. Now it advised caution and calm when all seemed lost. So life went on, even though it had acquired a decidedly frightening and nightmarish dimension.

I still went to school sporadically for a short time. We were shunted from school to school, always with different children and different teachers, as bombs destroyed one school after another. Finally the city of Plauen gave up its efforts to keep the schools open. The alerts and bombings became too frequent to maintain any semblance of normalcy. What was normal now was to be constantly on the run and to hide in basements.

I learned a lot in an incredibly short span of time. I became a seasoned veteran in a dangerous and strange existence, viewing it with fatalistic acceptance. The peaceful years of my early childhood seemed to belong to someone I barely recognized. The memory of a normal life had faded away like the morning mist; the war, the bombs, the terror, and the effort to stay alive was all there was.

It wasn't unusual to be caught away from home during an alert or a bombing. Seeking shelter with strangers in the closest basement became a necessity. This happened to me several times when I was doing errands for my mother. Each time, sitting with strangers in a strange basement, I worried about the safety of my mother and sister at home. Would I find them alive when I got home? Would I still have a home? Would I be an orphan?

One afternoon when I was on my way to see my grandfather, I was caught out in the open, because the warning was too short to seek adequate shelter. I hid in the doorway of a burned-out building as the sirens kept howling. I was watching the beautiful reconnaissance planes, glittering silver in the blue sky like mythical birds, draw crosses with their exhaust, making the sky look like an otherworldly graveyard. But how could anything so beautiful be so deadly, a little voice inside me asked?

We had learned from past experience that these crosses were a very bad omen indeed. Their meaning couldn't have been clearer. I crawled further back into the charred rubble, hoping that they would not bother to waste any more bombs on this already devastated area. The reconnaissance planes were quickly followed by an armada of heavy bombers, their terrible throbbing sound vibrating the air. This was a faceless, impersonal enemy against whom there was no defense, except to pray that it would pass you by. The metallic-gray winged monsters dropped their deadly loads, almost breaking my eardrums. Their job done, they left behind their calling card of fire and smoke, obscuring the graveyard in the sky with veils of red and black. Luckily for me, their deadly gifts were dropped in another part of town this time. Otherwise I could have become part of the rising black smoke mingling with the blue of the sky.

To my mother's great relief I returned unhurt, but full of dirt and soot from my hideout in the burnt building. I was grateful that the strike hadn't taken place in our neighborhood, and that my mother and sister were alive. There seemed to be nothing haphazard about the methodical way they went about destroying the city section by section, but nobody knew where the next strike would be.

By late 1944 the city was destroyed to such an extent that no more warnings could be given, because there was no electricity for the sirens. That meant we had to be constantly on the alert to listen for the drone of bombers and be ready to run.

Christmas 1944 passed unnoticed as we sat in our dark, cold basement waiting for the next strike. All I remember about that Christmas is the dark, the cold, and the smell of fire. Life had become a constant cycle of trying to survive the next day and the next attack. It wasn't much of a life, but it was better than the alternative!

* * *

Chapter 6

Surrounded By Fire

By early 1945 the daily and nightly bombings had increased dramatically from the year before. Air raids became so frequent that all normal life ceased to exist. School was just a memory for me and all the other children. I had already missed most of the third grade because we spent our days and nights in the basement, only venturing out in search of food and water when it seemed safe to do so.

Fear and panic spread in Plauen after the destruction of Dresden, which was one of the closest large cities—about seventy miles to the northeast. Often called "Florence on the Elbe," Dresden had been one of Europe's most beautiful cities. People came from all over the world to see its magnificent baroque architecture and its historically and culturally significant treasures. But all its beauty and fame couldn't protect the doomed city from the horrible fate it was to suffer.

From February 13th through the fifteenth, repeated air raids by thousands of American and British bombers inundated the defenseless city with thousands of tons of firebombs and explosives. During those fateful days and nights we heard the thunderous roar and felt the vibrations of thousands of heavily loaded bombers flying over us as we sat huddled in our basement. It took forever for the countless airplanes to fly over us, as they came and went in wave after wave, keeping us in a state of wrenching anxiety. The destination of the endless bomber formations was unknown to us at the time, and we wondered and worried about the unfortunate recipients of their deadly cargo, but we were also glad it wasn't us. Death, ever capricious, played games with us. It was as though he kept us suspended over a yawning chasm, threatening to drop us at a sudden whim. Fear sat in the basement with us the whole time, its loathsome company choking us. Our hearts beat in our throats waiting for the moment when our luck would run out , and the bombers would decide to unload their deadly cargo on us. Later, on their way back to England, they dropped a few bombs on Plauen, just to let us know that they hadn't forgotten us. But as we were soon to find out, Dresden had been their designated target.

When we were finally able to leave our basement, we saw a huge black smoke cloud hovering over a blood-red sky in the northeast. We stood in awe, not yet realizing the full extent of what had happened until the completely devastated and traumatized survivors, horror still glazing their eyes, began to arrive in Plauen in the days that followed. They gave absolutely horrific accounts of catastrophic events that would make your worst nightmares pale by comparison.

They told us that Dresden's normal population had more than doubled to well over a million with all the refugees, mostly women and children fleeing the advancing Russian army. They choked Dresden's streets and alleys, camping out under bridges and in railway stations, because there wasn't enough shelter available for the hundreds of thousands of unfortunates. All those poor souls, already traumatized by their flight and Russian depredations, were caught out in the open during the bombing raids, and most of them were roasted alive or blown to bits. I listened to their accounts with mounting horror.

We heard from them that the enormous heat generated by the fires created a firestorm with hurricane-force winds. Thousands of people were incinerated and reduced to the size of small dolls; they were impossible to identify. There was no way to count or identify the charred and blown-apart bodies strewn all over the city, with some even hanging in the scorched trees. Women and children were sucked into the raging fires by the hurricane; others were trapped in liquefied asphalt or boiled alive in the city's fountains where they tried to save themselves. Those with shelter were no better off, as the tremendous heat melted untold thousands into a thick liquid of flesh and blood in their basements. They said that those who managed to escape the city between attacks were hunted down by low-flying fighter planes and mowed down with machine guns. The doctors and nurses rescued patients from the burning hospitals, placing the wounded and sick in rows on the banks of the Elbe River, where they too were machine-gunned by American fighter planes. My mind in turmoil, I tried to grasp the enormity of what had happened in Dresden. It was an unimaginable nightmare and more than I was able to comprehend.

The adults tried to keep the news of Dresden's horrible fate from us children, but their efforts were in vain, because the red glow of the fires could be seen for more than 100 km. They couldn't hide the blood-red sky and the massive columns of black smoke, which was visible from Plauen for days, nor could they plug our ears to prevent us from hearing all the gruesome details from those who escaped to Plauen. Fear in their voices, they talked about all the horrors in hushed tones, as if normal speech would bring us the same fate and an oppressive, all-consuming feeling of doom spread its noxious poison among us.

Days and weeks later we heard that they used pitchforks and shovels to make huge piles of mangled corpses and body parts, which were soaked with gasoline and burned. Estimates of the number of fatalities ranged as high as 250,000. At age nine my knowledge of numbers was limited, but I knew that it was an incredibly huge amount. I couldn't even imagine so many people dying in such a short time. Thinking of all the children burning like torches with their little feet stuck in melted asphalt made me shudder and cringe. Winding up as a charred little doll wasn't something I wanted to contemplate. It was too scary to even think about, yet it was always on my mind, and a terrible fear of such a ghastly death invaded my days and nights. I vaguely wondered where God was, and why he didn't put an end to this horrible war. Since there was no answer that made sense, I had no choice but to accept the fact that I too might die in a reality I couldn't have imagined only a year ago.*

After the annihilation of Dresden, we began to get so many bombing raids that one flowed endlessly into another. Plauen's population consisted almost entirely of women and children, the old and the infirm. All able-bodied men, including my father, had been drafted into the army. But even though the Allies knew that Plauen was

---

*Twenty years later I read an article in the November 1965 issue of *Esquire* magazine that completely verified the hysterical depictions I heard from those who managed to escape from Dresden. "Apocalypse at Dresden; the long suppressed story of the worst massacre in the history of the world," by R. H. S. Crossman, who was part of a secret department attached to the British Foreign Office, stated, "This conventional air raid was far more devastating than either of the two atomic raids against Japan that were to follow a few months later."

of no military importance whatsoever, it was all but obliterated during several months of almost continuous bombing. There was no respite. American planes bombed us during the day, British planes bombed us at night. The only breaks came when the sky was overcast and clouds obscured their targets, so we constantly prayed for rain! A clear day brought long columns of pretty silver birds glittering like jewels in the sky. But their appearance was deceptive, for when they descended, they morphed into hideous winged predators carrying a deadly cargo, which they disgorged on us, leaving chaos, death, and destruction. Ultimately, 80 percent of Plauen was reduced to twisted steel girders, broken concrete, charred building facades, and rotting corpses.

We lived in the center of Plauen, but even after many air raids our apartment house still stood with relatively minor damage. Incendiaries had smashed through the roof several times, but my mother and the other women were always able to put the fires out before they did too much damage. Of course all of the windows were blown out and some of the inside walls had collapsed, but at least the outside walls remained. Several huge concussion bombs had fallen into the children's playground in the center of our block, but luckily they hadn't detonated. They lay there sleek and innocent, some of them very close to our house, until a team came to defuse them hours later. In the meantime we waited, holding our breath, afraid to as much as sneeze.

But the rest of Plauen wasn't so lucky. Since Plauen's infrastructure had been destroyed, there was no more electricity, and consequently no sirens to warn us of impending attacks. Instead they started to ring church bells to warn us, but they were also silenced when the churches fell victim to the bombs. Now we had to be on constant alert, listening for the sound of approaching bombers, and be ready to run for shelter. Often uncertain as to whether an attack was over or not, we simply stayed in the basement, waiting for the next strike. One day's bombings merged into the next, but there was one particular night I'll never forget!

After surviving another harrowing day and night in the basement with the other women and children while it rained bombs, my mother decided to take a chance and try to sleep in our apartment. Optimistically, we hoped that our tormentors would give us at least one night's rest. We hadn't seen a bed for days, so we were totally exhausted and badly needed sleep. We went to bed with all our clothes on after we cleaned chunks of plaster, glass and wood splinters off the bed. My sister Margit, who had just turned five, slept between me and my mother.

Suddenly the droning of heavy bombers flying low overhead woke me up! I could tell from the sound that they were fully loaded. I had become expert in being able to tell whether they flew empty or with a belly full of death. Frantic, I tried to wake my mother. I shook her and yelled, "Bombers are over us! Wake up, Mother! Wake up!" But she was in an exhausted stupor, and I couldn't rouse her. She only groaned and refused to move. Then the bombs started falling! The sharp, whistling sound of their rapid descent was quickly followed by the sound of many explosions. The noise of close impacts almost broke our eardrums. That finally woke her up! We jumped out of bed, grabbed a few things, and stumbled down the dark, rubble-strewn stairs as fast as we could amid the deafening noise. Flashes of exploding bombs lit the staircase eerily in red, white, and yellow. There were so many explosions that they almost seemed like one never-ending one. Unfortunately we had to go outside to reach the basement entrance, which was on the other side of the building. Bomb blasts lit our surroundings with a glaring white light, blinding us momentarily as we ran along the side of the building, fighting the concussion waves that tried to pin us to the wall. We ran for our lives! Mother carried my sister Margit, wrapped in a blanket, and a small bag with important papers. I struggled behind, dragging a first aid kit and our gas masks. In my haste and fright I fell on a heap of glass left over from the afternoon attack. My hands and knees were badly cut, but I quickly got up and kept running as the bombs fell without pause!

We finally made it, and just in time. We had barely run down the cellar steps when, like vengeful spirits pursuing their prey, the cellar door and all kinds of debris came flying down, missing us by seconds. The force of the explosion blew us deeper into the basement and knocked us to the floor, depositing parts of the basement door and pieces of masonry on top of us. But we picked ourselves up again to find a safer place among the other women and children who were there already. They had lit some candles, but the air pressure blew them out. So we were in the dark, which only intensified our terror. It soon became very difficult to breathe, because the oxygen was sucked out to feed the fires, causing our breath to come in labored gasps.

Most of the mothers, including mine, were sitting at a long, low table along one of the walls, holding the small children in their protective arms. They screamed at us over the hellish noise to keep our mouths open, so the air pressure wouldn't blow out our eardrums. I had managed to crawl to a corner of the basement, where I lay on the stone floor with some of the older children. Some cried, some screamed, and some prayed. I did neither. Utterly terrified, I was curiously calm. I was in a place where terror had lost its meaning.

There was one detonation after another. Smoke, debris, and soot came billowing down the window chutes, filling our lungs and burning our eyes and throats. The foundation shook, the floor heaved, the ceiling threatened to come down on us, and the walls writhed like living things in pain. Glued to the pitching floor by the air pressure, we endured while time stood still. The whole basement rocked like a ship in a storm, its shrieking winds hurling us into the chasm of a terrifying netherworld, drowning us in its sound and fury. The explosions momentarily lit up the dark basement, revealing its occupants huddled there with ashen faces, the mothers clutching their little ones, covering them with their own bodies as chunks of mortar fell from the ceiling. We didn't think we would make it out alive this time! Death was in that basement with us, waiting impatiently to begin his harvest. I saw him in the terrified gray faces around me, in the whirling dust and smoke that clutched at us with greedy fingers, enveloping us in an acrid shroud. All the terrible stories we had heard about Dresden came alive. Thoughts were flitting through my head about what death would be like, when I wasn't even old enough to know what life was. I only knew that I didn't want to die.

Finally, after what seemed like an eternity, it was over and we were still alive. We had cheated death once again! After clearing the stairs of debris and the shattered basement door, we groped our way up, half deaf and covered with soot. What we found was awful! The only houses on our block that were still standing were ours and the houses on either side of us. The rest of the neighborhood was on fire, the roaring flames banishing the darkness of the night, bathing everything around us in a flickering red light. Hell had opened up, the gleeful howling of its denizens mingling with the sound of the raging fires and collapsing walls and roofs. We stood frozen in horrified silence, staring at the infernal chaos around us with uncomprehending eyes, not wanting to believe what we saw.

Then suddenly we heard that people in a burning house across the courtyard were trapped and screaming for help. That shocked everybody out of their daze and got people moving. All the women, including my mother, ran to see if they could help. Of course there was no fire department to come to the rescue, because there was no way for them to negotiate the bomb-cratered streets. Besides, most of the city's water mains were broken and under rubble.

Margit and I stood in the courtyard hugging each other, frozen with fear amid the roaring of flames and the crashing of disintegrating walls and roofs. Live sparks and flaming debris rained down on us, and the trees held charred and glimmering things in their scorched branches, some of which flared and fell hissing to the ground. Margit was screaming for Mother, afraid she wasn't coming back, afraid she would be swallowed up by the flames all around us or buried under a collapsing wall. She was holding on to me for dear life as I tried to comfort her. "Mother is coming back! Don't cry! She'll be back!" I kept assuring her, even though I wasn't so certain myself. I was terribly afraid too, but I was able to keep calm and console my little sister, who was only five years old and didn't really understand what was happening. The only world she had ever known was fear, hunger, and running for shelter. This was normal, everyday life for her. At my wise old age of nine, I knew better. I remembered playing in this same courtyard with my friends when our world was whole. She had no memories of those charred trees when they were full of green leaves and nesting birds. I was the older one, and the only thing my little sister could hold on to.

When Mother returned we saw that tears had left white streaks on her soot-blackened face. There had been nothing they could do. The people trapped in that burning building died horribly, like so many others that night. God and our guardian angels had been looking out for us for sure! Grateful to be alive, but thoroughly shaken with the terror of the last few hours still reverberating within us, we went back upstairs to our wrecked apartment for what was left of the night. There was nowhere else to go. Leaving the city was impossible because of the many fires and late-exploding bombs. We appeared to be trapped for now!

After Mother managed to get Margit to sleep, she and I sat at our shattered kitchen window, watching the houses burn and collapse.

The fires were frightening, yet awesome in their murderous beauty. Whenever a wall collapsed, huge flames would shoot high into the night sky and showers of sparks fell like stars. Awestruck, we watched without speaking as the fires burned undisturbed.

When morning came, the fires were still burning, but now black smoke obscured some of the destruction. The sun shone balefully through this black haze, illuminating our surroundings in a strange half-light, giving it a surreal appearance. It reflected our perilous existence in a frightening world shrouded in the murky twilight of uncertainty.

In an effort to diminish the impact that night had on me, I did my best to shut off my feelings and to close my eyes to things too painful to see. Like a battle-hardened soldier, I went through what passed for life, only flinching now and then.

* * *

Chapter 7

The Caves

March 1945

The next day Mother decided that the basement wasn't safe enough anymore, so we sought refuge in caves, which had been blasted into the hillside in two places to serve as bomb shelters.

One cave was only two blocks away, so we tried that one first, but unfortunately that tunnel was very crowded and extremely narrow. We were jammed in there like sardines, giving us a severe case of claustrophobia, not to mention black and blue feet from being stepped on, for it was standing room only.

So the next time we decided to try the other cave about four blocks away. This cave went straight in for about fifty feet and then branched off into two tunnels, which went much deeper into the hillside. It was very crowded there too, but the tunnels were wider, and therefore it was more bearable. Compared to the cave we tried first, this one was definitely an improvement. We even had oxygen pumped in by machines from somewhere on top of the hill. Other than that, bare rock walls and a dirt floor was all the cave had to offer. The toilet facilities were impossible to reach through the tightly packed crowd. You just had to hold it for the duration, which wasn't always easy, especially for the younger children who were scared half to death.

We spent most of our days and nights there with hundreds of other women, children, and old people. Whenever the bombers had gone and it was over for the moment, everyone streamed outside to see what was left standing, and to get some fresh air. Even though the air was filled with grit and soot, it was better than the stuffy air in the cave.

The days and nights passed in a haze, numbness alternating with fear. We only went home occasionally, climbing over rubble and skirting the bomb craters to see if our house was still there, and strangely enough it was. On the way back to the cave we stopped at a bakery operating out of its basement. Bread was the only food still available, and only those who brought bread to the caves with them had something to eat. After picking up the bread, we went back to sit on the ground in front of the cave entrance with our few belongings, waiting for the next wave of bombers to arrive. We joined a lot of other women and children waiting there to get the coveted wall spaces when it was time to go back inside. Those who were lucky enough to get wall space could sit on the ground and lean against the rock wall. It also gave you a little more breathing space.

At the first droning of planes, everyone rushed back into the cave where we could hear the thunder of the explosions somewhat muffled by the tons of solid rock above and around us. Whenever there was a close hit, the rock walls would tremble and groan in protest. The lights would flicker and go out, leaving us in darkness and multiplying our fright. There was a collective moan of fear, and then a sigh of relief when the lights came back on. Mothers were hugging their little ones tightly and speaking softly to them in an effort to calm their fears. The old endured stoically.

As the situation took a turn for the worse, and the attacks became more frequent and closer together, I could feel an increased sense of panic building up around us. More and more people came to the cave to seek safety, making it more crowded than ever. Occasionally there were arguments over a wall space claimed by one person and coveted by another. "I was here first."—"No, I was, so move!" was usually settled by both cramming into the same space. Many were sitting on the ground along the walls while others who had come too late to get wall space stood tightly packed in the center for hours on end. Tension and fear were palpable. Some sat quietly, their eyes dulled by fatigue, resigned to whatever fate had in store. Maybe death would come as a savior for them, not as an enemy. In others, the fires of life burned with fierce determination to outwit death.

Conversation was subdued and sporadic. "God, will this ever be over? How much longer will we have to endure this?" Someone in the crowd answered: "Be glad you're in here and not out there, so stop your complaining."

An elderly woman sitting next to us aired her feelings. Bitterness in her voice, she muttered, "Two wars in a life time—I've had it. Enough is enough. First WWI, after which the English blockade nearly starved us to death, and now this! I can't take any more." Mother could only agree with her. It was the second war for her too, and she remembered the first one only too well.

Sometimes, when a child cried incessantly, you heard: "Can't you please keep your child quiet? My nerves are frazzled enough already." Then there were occasional angry outbursts, "Get off my foot!" or "Stop pushing me! Do you need to take up so much room? Who do you think you are, the Queen of England?" But to their credit, people remained reasonably well mannered, which wasn't easy under the circumstances, especially since everybody was overtired, hungry, and cranky.

Then came a day when the oxygen pumps on the hill above us received a direct hit. The lights went out and it was pitch-dark for a long time while the thunder of explosions continued, assaulting the rock walls of our sanctuary with incredible ferocity. Death was howling outside, prowling the mountain in pursuit of our lives. Deprived of our sense of sight, the darkness increased the terror we all felt. Fear moved among us like a malignant entity, which made our hearts beat like drums and made our blood run cold. Would the rocks be strong enough to protect us and hold this beast at bay? Not even screams of anguish could be heard over the noise of the bomb blasts.

After what seemed like an eternity some emergency lights came on, shedding their pale half-light over the people crouching there, but unfortunately the oxygen pumps did not come back on! There was no more oxygen coming into the tunnels, so it wasn't long before hundreds of people were gasping for air. Fear returned with a vengeance, clouding everyone's mind as reason fled under its onslaught. The ensuing pandemonium was horrendous. People panicked! In their distress and inability to breathe, they were trampling one another and elbowing their way through the tightly packed crowd trying to get to the entrance, bombs or no bombs. They fought death from asphyxiation any way they could. It was survival of the fittest! Civilized behavior was shed and disappeared like the mask it is. And the bombs kept falling! People were screaming and children were crying, all fighting for air! The situation was so precarious that teenage Hitler Youth were sent in to restore order and to carry the children closer to the entrance. That included my sister Margit and me. I still remember looking over the young man's shoulder as he lifted me over the crowd. It was like looking over ocean waves in a howling storm threatening to engulf and destroy everything in its wake. I felt like the survivor of a shipwreck watching others desperately trying to stay afloat, while I was carried to safety by friendly waves.

I was terribly worried about my mother, who had to stay behind in that airless tunnel among the tightly packed, panic-stricken crowd. I still see her standing there pressed against the bare rock wall, buffeted by the human waves pushing in on her. Her face was beet red from her strenuous effort to breathe air, which had become dangerously low in oxygen. I was very afraid for her, and I felt guilty leaving her in this perilous situation. But I had no choice in the matter.

Margit and I, together with a lot of other children, were deposited close to the entrance, where the impact from the explosions was heard and felt much stronger than farther back in the cave. The ground under our feet shook and the air itself seemed to be torn apart. My eyes perceived everything in fractured bits and pieces. Some of the bombs exploded so close that the concussions almost broke my eardrums. I didn't know what was worse: being asphyxiated in the tunnel, or the possibility of being blown up only twenty feet from the entrance. Panicked, screaming people were pressing in on us from behind, and only the terror raging around the mountain prevented them from forcing their way outside. They had no alternative but to stay where they were and endure.

I felt suspended in time, caught in the maelstrom of an endless nightmare from which there was no waking up, no matter how hard I tried. Submission to its madness and shutting down emotionally was the only choice as the bombs fell relentlessly.

When it was over for the time being and we could go outside, we saw that the City Theater diagonally across from us was hit. It had been a nice neoclassical building with a small park surrounding it, where people could go during intermission. I sadly remembered the many times my mother had taken me there to see fairy tales. Now the theater park was littered with the remnants of colorful costumes. Glittering tiaras and shreds of fabric were hanging in the trees in a macabre display. It had the look of a party gone awry, except that this party was one arranged by malevolent forces that ended in death and destruction. A row of badly hit buildings on fire behind the theater was barely visible through clouds of pulverized debris.

The crowd, anxious to flee the cave, pushed Margit and me along, out into the smoke and soot-filled street. We had no idea what had become of our mother or where we were going. It was pure chaos! Gray-faced, worried mothers were looking for their children, their anguished voices echoing in the billowing smoke. Children like Margit and me, dazed and crying, were looking for their mothers in the twilight of the attack's aftermath. Smoke surrounded us like a heavy fog, burning our eyes and making it difficult to see. People looked like ghosts in this nebulous, dust-laden place, which appeared foreign and unrecognizable. That and the encroaching darkness made me wonder if we were still alive or if we had entered a different and more menacing dimension. Maybe we were all dead and on our way to hell. But I was somewhat reassured when I saw no clubfooted devils herding us with pitchforks, nor did I see a fire-breathing chimera thrashing its serpent's tail to fan the flames bleeding crimson through the thick smoke.

Margit and I were holding hands so we wouldn't become separated. We kept looking for Mother and calling for her, but the crowd just kept pushing us along. It was early evening now and darkness started to settle in. Poor little Margit was crying, and I didn't know how to console her or what to do. So we sat down on some chunks of broken concrete a few blocks away, where Mother finally found us. We clung to each other with tears of joy and relief at finding each other alive. We fought our way over and around the rubble to find out what had become of our home, and to see if we could salvage a few things. Amazingly our house was still standing—at least the outside walls were. We had to climb over all kinds of debris to get to our apartment on the second floor, where Mother managed to find a few useful things, which were added to the other stuff we carried around with us.

Then it was back to the cave to wait for the next wave of bombers to arrive. As usual, we joined many others in front of the cave entrance, too tired and too numb to feel anything—not even fear. There we sat in silence, withdrawn deep within ourselves, removed from a world that had become a very frightening place.

A mother holding her two young sleeping children in her arms sighed: "This is so hard for the little ones. Look at them, they're exhausted. Thank God they are sleeping a little. I can't remember the last time we slept in a bed." That was true for all of us of course. We all longed for a night in a bed. Only most of us didn't have a bed anymore.

"Yes" Mother said. "This is bad enough for grown-ups, but it's even worse for the children. I feel so sorry for them. No sleep, nothing to eat, and constantly on the run from bombs."

"The little ones don't understand what's going on, and it's difficult for a mother to deal with their misery and their fear. What do you tell them when they are crying with hunger and you have nothing to give them, or when they are afraid because the world is blowing up around them? What's a mother to do?" The woman continued, struggling to hide her tears.

"I don't know, but we're all in the same boat. We have to be strong for the children and do our best to keep them safe. All we can do is hope and pray that this war will be over soon and that we survive," was Mother's weary response. With that, they fell silent again, each lost in her own worrisome thoughts.

The row of houses beyond the theater that had been hit in the afternoon was ablaze and burning uncontrollably. One house still partially standing had its whole side missing, with the furniture and appliances hanging precariously on the downward sloping floors. Electrical wiring and plumbing were grotesquely exposed, going from nowhere to no-where. Shredded draperies fluttered in the updraft created by the raging fires, which bathed everything in an eerie red glow. The only sound to be heard was the hellish symphony of the roaring flames accompanied by the crashing of walls and roofs as they collapsed in plumes of soot.

I watched in a trancelike state, with a feeling that this was not real. Even though it was! The smell of fire was everywhere and in every breath we took. We watched as the flames consumed everything. Collapsing floors and walls were shooting flames high into the night sky, their sparks mingling with the stars. Sparks swirled around us like millions of fireflies on a warm summer night, raining down on us as we sat on the ground in front of the cave. Ashes covered everything around us with a soft gray blanket, which glimmered here and there with the glow of dying embers. We were so tired and emotionally depleted that we barely roused ourselves to shake off the ashes accumulating on us. Only when live sparks burnt us, or when our clothes started to smoke, we would come alive and frantically beat the sparks out. That kept us very busy.

However, it didn't take long for the heavily loaded metallic-gray monsters to return, causing a frantic push back into the cave. It was a little less tightly packed than it had been. The afternoon's experience when the oxygen pumps failed had filled many people with so much dread that they had gone elsewhere to seek shelter. Again the mountain above us was heavily bombed. Again the lights went out and fear imprisoned us in its steely grip. The rock walls trembled and shook, freezing everyone in a state of complete terror.

This time one of the tunnels towards the rear collapsed, and huge boulders and rocks fell on the women and children huddled there. Everybody watched in shocked silence as badly injured, bleeding people, including children, were carried toward the front entrance. Some were unconscious, some were horribly mangled, and others were probably already dead. We watched horrified, thankful that we had not been in the back of the cave. Our guardian angels had protected us once again.

* * *

Chapter 8

Armageddon

Plauen Germany at war's end in 1945
(The most prominent structure was my neighborhood church.)

Plauen, April 1945

Night was approaching when we left the cave after another heavy afternoon bombardment. That's when Mother decided that if we wanted to survive, we had to leave the city immediately for our little country cottage in Joessnitz. But getting out of the city was easier said than done. Progress was arduous and slow because we had to help Margit climb over and around chunks of concrete as we passed ruin after smoldering ruin. Smoke and soot veiled the once-familiar streets in a spooky twilight, blessedly obscuring some of the devastation. Mother did her best to shield us from the sight of bodies and body parts, but her efforts weren't very successful. The bloodied arms and legs among the rubble were hard to miss, but I registered them with the saving grace of detachment. After months of bombings and several close escapes, I had become desensitized to the horrors around me.

Even though I was barely nine years old, death was very real to me. I saw that death was often cruel in the way he snatched his victims, and it was a great mystery to me why he took some and passed others by. I thought of death as a hideous wraith, cloaked in swirling clouds of black smoke reeking of human carrion and decay, which hovered over my city and ruled it without pity. His all-pervasive presence grinned at us from empty window openings of charred buildings, his long bony fingers poised to pluck more victims from our midst. I felt him watching our efforts to escape his domain with malicious amusement. But I didn't fear him anymore, and if Mother was afraid, she didn't show it. Mother was courage personified, setting a wonderful example for us as she struggled to shepherd us to safety. Little Margit looked scared and confused as we stumbled on as fast as we could. Until we reached the safety of the surrounding woods, we had to be wary of low-flying fighter planes looking for targets. So whenever we saw or heard a plane, we hid and flattened ourselves to the ground, which further prolonged our journey. Finally, after hours of grueling struggle, we made it safely to the protective cover of the forest. Taking little-used paths and always mindful of cover, we managed to reach the relative safety of our country cottage.

Thank God we had our small cottage in Joessnitz to give us refuge! We arrived filthy and completely exhausted but unharmed. My maternal grandparents, who had fled earlier, received us with tears and open arms. They had been terribly worried about us, so "Thank God you are here! Thank God you aren't hurt!" was all they could say. After they helped us settle in, we finally allowed ourselves to relax a little in the garden's familiar surroundings. That our refuge had no water, heat, electricity, or plumbing was a minor inconvenience compared to what life in Plauen had become. The important thing was that we were alive, had a roof over our heads, and a little to eat. Nothing else mattered. We were safe for now!

Shortly after our arrival at the cottage, it was clear that Mother's decision to leave the city was more than timely, for there was much worse to come.

The end of the world seemed to be upon us that unforgettable night of April 10th. It is indelibly ingrained in my memory as a horrendous event, a grand finale, which eclipsed everything that had gone before, and destroyed what was left of my hometown.

That day most of our small family also fled the city and arrived at the cottage. Like us, they were destitute. They not only came to find refuge, but also because all their homes in Plauen were either rubble or uninhabitable. We were all homeless. Consequently the two rooms of our little cottage were quite crowded, with my grandparents, my cousin Inge, age thirteen, Aunt Else, my elderly Aunt Frieda, my mother, my sister Margit, and I sharing them.

April 10th was a beautiful spring day. The sun was a brilliant disk in the deep blue sky as the first flowers were beginning to emerge from the ground. The trees were budding and the birds had come back from their winter homes in the south. It was a day full of the promise of spring, but it was also perfect bombing weather. What we didn't know that sunny morning was that Plauen was to receive the "Dresden Treatment." We were all slated to die with our city that night, but luckily we weren't there. Thank God!

By late afternoon the azure sky was marred by white crosses painted there by reconnaissance planes with their exhaust to warn that doomsday was at hand. Their job completed, they circled high overhead as if perusing their artwork. The meaning of those crosses was an extremely ominous one. Everyone, young and old, knew their meaning. In this instance the Christian symbols of hope and salvation presaged the coming of hell on earth. Death, our old nemesis, was on his way in the form of hundreds of gray-winged raptors carrying heavy loads of murderous weapons. There was nothing to impede their progress. All of our antiaircraft guns and fighter planes had been destroyed a long time ago, so they could deliver their deadly cargo with impunity. Plauen was completely at their mercy, and they showed none.

Many people still in the city heeded the warning of the crosses in the sky, and thousands fled the city to seek refuge in the surrounding woods. Others sought shelter in the caves or in the basements of solidly built, large buildings. More than twenty of my grandparents' friends and neighbors came to find safety with us. We put them up in the barns because our small cottage was already overcrowded.

We gathered next to our cottage in small groups, looking with trepidation at those crosses in the sky. Many voices expressed the same thoughts: "I don't like the looks of this. This is going to be bad. Are they going to bomb the ruins now? Aren't they ever satisfied? Dear God in Heaven, we beg you, please protect those still in Plauen from what is coming!"

Waiting uneasily for what was to come, we anxiously listened for the first sound of approaching planes. We were very scared! Would we be safe enough in the cottage only seven miles from Plauen? Often they even dropped a few bombs in the countryside. It seemed like they just wanted to keep us in a constant state of terror. No place was completely safe. Even Inge and I were very subdued for once. We could read the signs of approaching death, but we couldn't imagine how bad it was going to be.

The first drone of arriving aircraft started after dark, around 9 p.m. British planes began setting their many yellow flare bombs high in the night sky, where they broke apart and fell like holiday fireworks in large clusters to light their targets. This was followed by a spectacular display of marker bombs, which turned the heavens into a riot of reds, and, yellows..The whole night sky was aflame with their terrible beauty. We called this "setting Christmas trees" because the sight was as beautiful as it was terrifying, but it had nothing at all to do with Christmas. Its beauty was deceptive, because it was the precursor of death, and heralded the imminent arrival of the dark angel. Having seen it before, we knew very well what followed. But this was the most spectacular display of flares we had ever seen. Though it was night and we were seven miles away from the intended target, it was as light as day—bright enough to read a newspaper.

We stood stunned in the flares' eerie light, which surrounded everything in their harsh unnatural glare. It was very spooky, for it transformed our garden into a sinister, alien world full of unspeakable menace. Every tree and every bush seemed to have changed its character from one of familiar benevolence to one of creepy malice. We had entered the anteroom of hell. I saw fear reflected in all the faces around me, which did nothing to lessen my fear.

Her voice trembling, my sweet, hunchbacked Aunt Frieda whispered: "Oh my dear God in heaven, this is the end. We won't survive this. Maybe they'll drop bombs on Joessnitz too this time."

Grandfather said, "I don't think they are going to waste any bombs on Joessnitz—They are after Plauen, not us," which calmed her down a bit.

"After this, there'll be nothing left of Plauen but a huge pile of rubble. This time they'll wipe out the sections of the city they missed before, and pulverize the ruins of the inner city," remarked Aunt Else. "But why? Plauen has no military importance whatsoever, and they know that. So why would they do this?" We all wondered about that, but the answer eluded us.

A short time later, the dark angel's armada arrived, its enormous bulk darkening the sky. The motors of the gray-winged monsters strained to carry their heavy loads of death, emitting a low, menacing roar, drowning out all other sounds. They came like a threatening swarm of locusts to obliterate everything in their path, leaving nothing but burning, smoking ruins behind. Our bodies trembled and the ground under our feet vibrated from the hundreds of fully loaded bombers flying very low overhead, all headed in the direction of Plauen! They were flying so low that I'm sure that they could see us standing there in the bright light of the flares. But they weren't interested in us. Plauen was their objective, and their numbers kept coming and coming. Hundreds of bombers thundered over our heads. Terror closed our throats as we stood rooted to the spot, struck dumb with fright and awe.

Our visitors made a mad dash for the barn as grandfather yelled at us over the earsplitting drone of the bombers: "Get into the house quickly! This is going to be terrible! Hurry! Run!" Scared to death, we all ran for the door, jostling each other in our haste to get inside. We barely made it into the house when it began. There were continuous detonations as a hailstorm of bombs rained down on Plauen. Like an apocalyptic thunderstorm raging over our cottage, everything around us shook and trembled. Wave after wave of British bombers dropped thousands of tons of explosive and incendiary bombs, including the feared phosphor canisters, on this defenseless city of women, children, the old, and the infirm.* Since our cottage didn't have a basement, Margit, Mother, and I were on our knees in front of the bed, our heads and backs covered by a feather bed, while Mother held her arms around us protectively as bombs kept falling on Plauen. In her innocence, little Margit was praying that God would spare the woods and all the life in them. She was praying for the mushrooms and our berry patches, and for the birds, the rabbits, and the trees. Only it was not God bombing us, it was the British! I prayed too; we all did! "Dear God in Heaven, please help us!"

How can you describe what it was like? It was a taste of hell. All rational thought stopped; all senses were occupied with the task of sheer survival. I felt like I was lost in a dark valley where barren trees with grasping branches held me fast, preventing my desperate attempts to reach safety in a sunlit landscape just over the horizon. But there was no escaping.

Despite the feather bed, and despite holding our mouths open as in a silent scream to equalize the air pressure, it felt as if our eardrums would burst. The windows came crashing in, with glass flying in all directions. The room was lit with the ghastly, flickering light of the dying flares and exploding bombs, flashes of red and white penetrating even the thickness of our feather bed. The air pressure made breathing difficult even though we were seven miles away. I felt like I was suffocating as I struggled to get out from under the confines of the feather bed, but nothing changed. I still could barely get enough air. My mother forced me back under the feather bed to protect me from the flying glass, plaster, and wood splinters. Mother's loving arms around us gave me some measure of comfort. Should death find us, at least we would be together.

---

*What we called phosphor canisters were actually napalm bombs, that had been invented in the United States in 1943. We didn't know that at the time. We only knew that when it got on you it seemed to burn forever.

When the bombardment finally ended after about 40 minutes, an eerie quiet descended on us. Our tears started to flow in relief and gratitude for being alive. Dazed and disoriented, we took a quick head count. Everyone was there except my grandfather. In our panic and rush to get inside the cottage, we hadn't even noticed that he was missing. We thought that he was right behind us when we ran into the house. Where was he? What had happened to him? Frantic, we called his name: "Opa, Opa, where are you? Answer us!" But there was no answer.

Half deaf and very worried, we ran outside to look for him. There we found him, standing next to the shattered door, leaning weakly against the wall. He had not made it into the house in time, and the air pressure from the exploding bombs had thrown him against the house wall. Like a fly stuck on flypaper, he was kept there for the entire attack. Even though he was right next to the door, he had been unable to move to reach it. Luckily that wall was facing away from Plauen, giving him some protection, so aside from being thoroughly shaken, he survived the ordeal unscathed. We hugged each other, crying with relief. "We're alive! Death passed us by!" Our guardian angels were with us once again.

Opa's friends came staggering from the barn, glad to be alive. One of them exclaimed: "This time they really did it. Do you think that there's anybody left alive in Plauen?"

"We were lucky to be able to hide out here," said another. "Just look at all the stuff on the ground and hanging in the trees."

Only then did we take notice of our surroundings. The trees were festooned with flaming and glimmering debris. They held unidentifiable glowing things in their poor scorched branches. The ground around us was littered with all kinds of charred and shredded items that the firestorm had carried the seven miles from Plauen to our sanctuary. The air had a horrible acrid smell, burning our nostrils and stinging our eyes. Live sparks danced in the air, showering us with a glowing rain before settling softly on the ground.

The monster planes, having divested themselves of their deadly cargo, were gone, and the explosions we heard now were sporadic. The only other sound was a low, angry roar coming from the direction of Plauen. It was the sound of the roaring fires, which engulfed the city. We could see deep red flames licking the horizon, shooting high into the night sky. Everything around us was bathed in their ghastly crimson light as Plauen went to its death clothed in the spectacular beauty of a fiery conflagration. We could only stand and watch in horrified silence. Jittery, with terror and fright still reverberating within us, we were too afraid to go to sleep that night, but that wasn't unusual. Sleepless nights had become common for us.

When morning came, Plauen was still burning, and it did so for many days to come. Black smoke began to mingle with the flames. It was a fearsome sight! We were grateful that we hadn't been in Plauen the night before, and that we had our garden cottage to shelter us. We felt very sorry for all those poor souls who did not have a safe place outside the city where they could have gone to seek shelter. It cost many of them their lives.

Thousands of people who sought shelter in what were thought to be safe basements of large buildings all died there. Those basements had become death traps where nobody survived. Death was dancing in what had been Plauen's streets, gleefully celebrating a bountiful harvest.

* * *

Chapter 9

In the Aftermath of Armageddon

Joessnitz, April 1945

Thank God we were in our small country cottage on the night my city was all but annihilated by intense carpet-bombing. A red sky and black clouds of smoke hovered over what had been Plauen for many days. All that was left of it were smoking ruins and thousands of rotting bodies under mountains of rubble. Even from seven miles away in Joessnitz, it was an event never to be forgotten.

We were so terrified after the awful night of April 10th that my grandfather decided that even our little country house might not be safe enough. He thought that a large area of spruce trees adjoining our property would be a better place to hide during the day. So he loosened a few slats in the fence at the end of our property, where we could squeeze through the opening, sprint across a small meadow, and disappear into the woods. We crawled on all fours under the low branches of the trees until we came to a small clearing where my grandfather dug pits for us, which we lined with branches of spruce. Luckily the weather was dry and the sun felt wonderfully warm. It shed its brilliance over fields and woods in equal measure, reawakening new life and new hope. But there was little hope for us.

Reclining on cushions of pine boughs in those pits, I passed the time watching the white clouds drifting lazily across the blue sky become dogs, swans, ships, and monsters with wide-open mouths that formed, dissolved, and reformed constantly, only to morph into something ever new. My thoughts drifted with them into a land of fantasy populated by strange creatures, far removed from the ugly present. We stayed in our green sanctuary off and on for the next couple of days. Whenever planes flew low over us, we would take extra branches and pull them over us like a blanket so we couldn't be seen from the air. It was like lying in a fragrant green coffin, which we left only when the danger of being detected by circling planes had passed.

Except for sporadic explosions, artillery fire, and the drone of heavy bombers over Plauen, it was quite peaceful. Small animals, insects, and birds went about their lives oblivious to the carnage outside their green world. In a strange way we had become as one with them and like them in our struggle to survive. Never was I so aware of my relationship with the natural world as when I sat in my pit in the middle of the woods, afraid of what the next few days would bring. The revelation that I was part of the earth, its child, made me look with wonder at the beauty of the world around me. I felt the enigmatic forces of nature closing around me and calming my fears. My whole being seemed to merge with the earth, the woods, and its all-encompassing essence, giving me a sense of safety and belonging as a small part of this world. The pine's wonderful scent surrounding us like a protective mantle gave me comfort, and I snuggled deeper into my softly cushioned pit. I was in a cherished friend's domain where I felt sheltered from all harm.

The next few days were simply chaotic, with quickly moving, overlapping events. So much was happening that I only remember the last tumultuous days of the war as a pile of jigsaw puzzle pieces waiting to be assembled. Even with pieces missing, the remainder showed a rather dismal picture. Since we, along with everybody else, had no electricity, we had no official news. Whatever news came our way was by word of mouth, but we could take little comfort from what we heard.

Every now and then we left our hideout in the woods and went to the garden's front gate to assess our situation. The news we gathered from friends and passing fugitives was more than grim. It was horrific. By this time my mother and grandparents had given up trying to withhold bad news from me. My eyes and ears always on the alert, I overheard most, if not all, of what the overloaded grapevine related. To our horror, we learned that low-flying US fighter planes used machine guns and splinter bombs to hunt down and kill Plauen's fleeing survivors. Most were women, some pushing baby carriages or pulling hand wagons with their meager belongings, as they tried to escape from the burning city. Mercifully there were no more bombing raids after April 10th. There wasn't much left to bomb.

Adding to the general chaos were countless fugitives from Germany's eastern states fleeing the advancing Russian army and crowding the main roads around Plauen. They were all fleeing west because nobody wanted to be caught by the Russians, whose reputation for cruelty preceded them. Some of the fugitives were on horse-drawn wagons loaded with children, the old, and the handicapped, along with their few possessions. Even more women and children trudged along on foot, carrying bundles with all they owned. In their attempt to find safety, these survivors of interminably long treks had endured all kinds of depredations, only to find more of the same. No one knows how many lost their lives in Plauen's last bombings, or how many were shot by roving aircraft on Plauen's roads.

Heaping more misery on all these wretched human beings was the lack of water, which had become a huge problem, because most of the water mains were broken and under rubble. Everyone was so desperate for water that some people even used the contaminated water that had collected in the deep bomb craters, making them susceptible to the spreading scourges of typhus and cholera. But standing in line for water in the few isolated places where some was available made them inviting targets for American planes circling overhead.

We were told that the situation in Plauen defied description. It was absolutely horrendous! So many bodies lay piled up in great big heaps at the cemetery that its greenhouse and the reception hall had to be used to store the overflow of dead bodies. Without refrigeration they deteriorated quickly in the unusually warm spring weather, their horrible stench mingling with that of uncontrollably burning fires. The torn and charred bodies of countless other victims were lying all over the city, decaying quickly in the heat. Since the cemetery personnel were completely overwhelmed, many families faced the heartbreak of searching for and collecting their own dead from among the smoking ruins, to bring what was left of them in hand wagons and wheelbarrows to the cemetery. Since bombs had also fallen on the cemeteries, the survivors had to brave the stench of open graves and their strewn-about contents. They had to dig the graves and bury their loved ones themselves. Of course there were no coffins and none of the usual ceremonies accompanying a burial. Only their family's tears went into the earth with them. Hearing all this from haggard fugitives passing our gate, we thought it safer to stay in our garden property as much as possible, only venturing out when it was absolutely necessary.

This circumstance arose when we ran out of food. The entire food distribution system, which had already been extremely precarious, had completely broken down. Food just wasn't available anywhere for any amount of money or ration cards, and people survived on whatever and however they could. Even bread was extremely difficult to get, because even the undamaged bakeries on the outskirts of town had no flour. Opa took a chance and biked to the village of Joessnitz with our ration cards to try to get some bread or potatoes. Since he was well known and well liked, he was more successful than somebody else might have been. What he brought home wasn't much, but it was enough to keep us alive. From a friend who had two goats, he was occasionally able to get a little goat's milk for us. From another he bartered for a few potatoes with the promise of some of our fruit later on. Opa's organizational talents were priceless. What would we have done without him?

The food situation became so desperate that many women and children, including my mother and I, went to the POW camp outside of town. Word got around that the POWs, mostly Russians, Poles, and Czechs, had enough food to barter for valuables. I was rather puzzled and vaguely wondered why they had more food than we did. It must have been due to Geneva Convention regulations, the International Red Cross, and packages from home, which supplied them generously enough to be able to spare some for barter. At the camp, a lot of women and children stood on one side of the fence, while the POWs were lined up on the other side. It was quite a strange, thought-provoking sight. I saw women begging for food with tears in their eyes, because they were unable to feed their children.

A lot of haggling was going on along the fence. Food was exchanged for whatever few valuables people had left. A silver fork, jewelry, or much-sought-after watches, might have bought a few slices of bread or a small sausage. It was a situation I observed with great interest, especially since I noticed a young, good-looking Russian who spoke broken German regarding my mother with fond looks. I could tell that he liked her. Even though there were many things I didn't understand, not much passed by me. I don't remember what Mother exchanged for the small sausage we brought home, because I was much too busy observing all that went on. Of course the sausage was shared among the five of us, with everybody getting only a tiny slice. But it was better than nothing.

Next we heard from one of Opa's friends that the desperate population had broken into a government food depot on the outskirts of Plauen, which was stuffed to the ceiling with food. From what we heard, hundreds of people rushed the depot and took all the food that could be carried away. It was a free-for-all because there was nobody to stop them. All authority had ceased to function in what had become pure pandemonium. It was survival of the fittest, the strong triumphing over the weak.

By the time Opa and I got there with our hand wagon, most people had already left with their loot. It looked like nothing much would be left. Even outside, the place was a mess. Spilled flour and torn packaging littered the area around the building. There were people milling around looking for food that might have been overlooked, or bargaining with each other for items like flour, margarine, or smoked meat. It was sad to see ordinarily law-abiding people behaving like vultures, picking and squabbling over the remains of a kill. It wasn't a pleasant scene, and it made me feel very uneasy. Nevertheless Opa went into the building to see if there was anything the crowd had missed. I stayed outside guarding our wagon, which was a prize in itself under the circumstances. He was gone for what seemed like a long time, and I started to worry about his safety. He finally came back with a sack of flour and a round thing, which looked like a wheel.

My eyes like saucers, I asked: "What is that, Opa?"

"It's a Swiss cheese," he explained. "It's something absolutely delicious. Just wait until we get home and I'll let you taste it."

I didn't really know what cheese was. Never having seen or tasted anything like it, I wasn't even convinced that it really was something that could be eaten. Maybe Opa was telling me one of his famous fibs. I couldn't wait to get home to taste the yellow wheel and see if it was as delicious as Opa said it was. We were extremely pleased with ourselves as we carted our booty home.

When Oma and Mother saw us return with our treasures, they were more than happy; they were elated. They handled the cheese as if it were made of gold. To have a little food in reserve removed some of the worry about what to eat for the next few days and weeks.

Then came the big moment when Opa cut some small pieces from the cheese, just enough to give everybody a taste. I thought it tasted just heavenly and I would have liked more, but he said: "No more now. We have to save it for when your father comes home, for he'll certainly need food."

I could see the wisdom of that and stopped asking for more. I thought of my father often, and prayed that he was safe and would soon come home. So we saved our prize for my father's return, even though we didn't even know where he was, or if he was still alive. The cheese and the flour were then hidden in the root cellar under a trapdoor in the kitchen. At least we now had some flour, so Oma and Mother could make a flour soup for us that consisted of water, flour, salt, and pepper. It wasn't gourmet fare, but nourishing enough to keep us going. So we muddled along as best we could.

* * *

Chapter 10

A Visit to Hell

A few days later, Mother decided to risk going back into the city. Not even the warnings issued by the authorities to stay away from Plauen deterred Mother from her plan. Since we fled Plauen with nothing but the clothes on our backs, we were badly in need of clothing. I was to come along to help, in case there was anything left for us to salvage.

When we prepared to leave the next morning with our old wooden hand wagon to help us retrieve anything we could use, gray clouds covered the sky, which meant that we were relatively safe from Allied bombing attacks. Nevertheless Mother knew that venturing into the devastated city would be a very dangerous undertaking, so my little sister Margit had to stay behind with my grandparents. I clearly remember my grandmother struggling to hold Margit, who was screaming and fighting to go with us. Oma's "Stop it! They'll be back soon!" could hardly be heard over her screams. Oma had her hands full trying to prevent her from running after us. I felt very sorry for my little sister, but I knew we couldn't take her. She was only five years old, and it would have been much too dangerous. I was a battle-hardened nine, and not afraid of anything anymore. Only God knows what went through the mind of this little five-year-

A trip into devastated Plauen, 1945
(Photo Credit: Seventy-Five Days Only, *Laser/Mensdorf, ISBN 3-928828-18-5, 2000)*

old. She had already experienced so much horror and misery in her short life without being old enough to understand that this life wasn't normal. For her the world was a very cruel and frightening place. But we had to ignore her screams and continue on our way. We could still hear Margit screaming as we entered the forest, which was a good distance from the cottage. I guess she was afraid that we would be killed and not come back, which of course was a good possibility. But life on the edge was normal for us. It was the only life we had known for a long time. We were guardedly optimistic, although I don't know why. It took a lot of courage to go back into the hell we had escaped only a few days earlier, but fear was a luxury we could no longer afford.

We wound our way through the forest on narrow paths, avoiding the open country roads. Spring held sway in the forest, but preoccupied with our dangerous plan, we were oblivious to the tender greens of a reawakening earth. It was the somber dark green of the pines that reflected our mood. After we left the safety of the woods, we traveled through the outskirts of the city, where we passed my grandparents badly damaged large corner house. I sadly remembered the nice afternoons I spent there in what seemed a lifetime ago. The entrance to their apartment was on the side of the building, opposite a pen full of turkeys. Even though I used to be quite intimidated by their size and the strange gobbling noise they made, I found them of great interest, and always liked to tarry there to watch these odd-looking creatures strutting about. Nevertheless I was glad that they were penned up, so I could safely watch them from the other side of the fence. The turkeys were gone now, and what remained of the house looked haunted and forlorn.

As we went farther into the city, it was like entering the Gates of Hell. Black clouds of smoke and soot from the final obliterating bombing hung in the air, filled with minute dust particles that felt gritty in the mouth and throat. Smoke curled around the ruins, embracing them in a languid dance. I was horrified and awed at the same time. It felt like we had entered an alien dimension, where malignant forces hostile to all living things held sway. Aside from the rats that had found a new food source in the buried bodies, the two of us seemed to be the only living things around. This once-bustling city felt dead and spooky, a realm inhabited by the ghosts of its former inhabitants. Sometimes I thought I could see them take form in the smoke wafting through the ruins, their insubstantial fingers clawing at the rubble. I dismissed my disquieting thoughts with a shiver as we continued to struggle though the maze of ruins. The deeper we penetrated into the city, the worse the destruction became. Most streets ceased to exist. They were completely covered with mountains of wreckage, interspersed with thirty-foot-wide, water-filled bomb craters staring like filmy dead eyes into a gray sky. The few walls still standing leaned precariously, like ancient grave markers in an old, neglected cemetery. There was hardly anything recognizable in this field of rubble to tell us where we were. We were lost in our own city!

So we kept going in the general direction of where we thought our house would be. We had to fight our way through this maze of rubble and ruins, lifting and carrying the wagon over the broken bricks and concrete until we finally reached our house in the center of Plauen. To our amazement it was still standing! It was badly damaged, but at least it was recognizable. Our house and the one next to it were among the few in a wide area that had not received direct hits. Since the wall separating our apartment from the hallway had disintegrated, we were able to walk right in. Our home looked like a tornado had passed through it, but what else could be expected, when the whole city lay in ruins? We considered ourselves extremely lucky to be able to access our apartment at all.

Once inside, we found that the kitchen wall had fallen into the bedroom onto the beds, and large chunks of the bedroom wall were in the living room on top of my father's beautifully carved desk. Broken glass and wood splinters were everywhere. We dug the bed out from under what had been the kitchen wall. Lifting large chunks of the thick plaster walls was not easy for a five foot two, skin-and-bones woman and a nine-year-old, malnourished little girl. After we had cleaned all the grit and glass slivers from the bed, we carried the mattress downstairs. Luckily it consisted of three separate pieces, so we were able to manage. Back upstairs, we strained to move a large part of the wall that leaned against the wardrobe and the dresser so that we could pull out some of our clothing. Protected by the sturdy furniture, the clothes were still in fairly good condition. So we took what we needed most, like underwear, woolen stockings, shoes, and warm sweaters. This was not the time to tarry or to be too selective, because there was always the danger of more walls collapsing. After several arduous trips up and down the barely passable stairway, we had the wagon fully loaded with the mattress, bed boards, and clothing. I don't know how we thought we would get this fully loaded wagon over all the rubble, around the bomb craters, and out of the city. Mother surely underestimated the danger when we set out on this trip. But how could anyone imagine such destruction? It was beyond the scope of anyone's comprehension. Yet I felt neither anger nor hatred toward the perpetrators of this devastation; I only felt an abysmal sadness.

It was late afternoon when we started the seven-mile trek back to our garden cottage. We decided to take a different route, hoping that it would be easier, so we chose Bahnhof Strasse, which had been Plauen's main traffic artery and a more direct way out of the city. Unfortunately that way wasn't much better than the one into the city. It was hard to believe that this was the same street I had known so well. In my mind I could still see Bahnhof Strasse as it used to be. Strangely, like a double exposure, its image existed side by side with what it had become. However, only the present image mattered, and I was forced to face the heartbreak of a painful reality, but I refused to cry. Tears wouldn't bring back my city, or all the people who had died. It was what it was! At least we were still alive when many others were not.

Yet, the memory of what my beautiful city had been was difficult to banish. Where was the laughter of children playing hopscotch on the wide sidewalks or weaving in and out on their scooters? Where was the ice cream store that was the favorite haunt of children? Where was the chatter of people and all the life that once existed on this street? It was all gone, as though it never existed. Once Bahnhof Strasse had been a very busy thoroughfare, where trolley cars went clanging up and down the hill, with a few automobiles adding their voices to the symphony of traffic. The wide sidewalks used to be crowded with people visiting the many fine stores, restaurants, and movie theaters. Young girls strolled here on weekends to meet their beaus. Maybe they would have gone to the famous Café Trömel, where an orchestra played for the enjoyment of its patrons. People would sit outside, reading newspapers and magazines supplied by the establishment or chat with friends over a glass of wine. Only a block away was the City Theater, where my love for the theater was born. Professionally performed fairy tales always left me entranced and full of wonder. That too was only a memory.

Now the street was deserted and devoid of all the life it once possessed. It was covered with rubble and flanked by ruins, most of which had collapsed onto the street. Other buildings remained as shells, their empty window openings yawning menacingly like open, toothless maws, warning us to keep our distance. They seemed to say, "Don't come too close, or we'll swallow you whole and make you part of the rubble in our belly!" So we tried to stay in the middle of the street, skirting the charred trolley cars, which sat amidst the wreckage like sentinels presiding over an alien wasteland. Its desolation bore an uncanny resemblance to nightmares of forbidding, bizarre landscapes in which we are stalked by vague fears of dark forces preying on us, only to wake with the grateful realization that it was just a bad dream. Only this was not a dream. It was real!

Getting an empty wagon into this devastated city was difficult enough, but getting a fully loaded one out, was much more exhausting! Ignoring our aching muscles and groaning with exertion, we pushed, pulled, and lifted with grim determination. We struggled with all our might to get the wagon with its precious cargo over the remains of buildings. When I lacked the strength to lift the back of the wagon over the debris, Mother would stop and say: "Let's switch; you pull in the front and I'll lift in the back." So whenever necessary, I pulled and Mother pushed and lifted in the back until we had the wagon over the obstacle, only to be confronted by the next one. We skirted the craters very carefully, because falling into one of them would have been disastrous. Many people who fell in were unable to get out, and drowned in their murky depths.

When I complained, "I can't go on; I'm too tired and my arms and feet hurt," Mother spurred me on with "Just a little further. You can do it. I know you're tired, but we have to move on. It's too dangerous to stop in the city. We can rest when we are in the forest." With the vision of the forest before me, I plodded on, doing my best to help get us out of Plauen and away from its many dangers. Other hazards we hadn't considered when we set out on this journey now hovered in the back of our minds. Unexploded bombs hiding in the rubble could be set off by the slightest disturbance, and partially standing buildings could collapse as we passed. To this day I don't know how we managed to escape the city unharmed. But manage we did! Our guardian angels had been with us every step of the way!

Having mastered our exit from the city with the wagon and its precious contents, we decided to take the open country road at least part of the remaining way. It was dark by then, so there was less of a chance of being seen by Allied aircraft. Nevertheless we took the precaution of hiding in roadside ditches whenever we heard a plane. We were incredibly relieved to reach the protective cover of the forest, where the mantle of darkness and deep silence enveloped us. Once safe in the forest, we stopped to rest often. We were completely worn out, especially my poor mother, who had done the lion's share of the work. After each stop, it became increasingly difficult to raise the energy to move on. We had to grit our teeth and call on our last reserves to keep going. Mother looked haggard and dead tired, but her eyes burned with fierce determination. Again and again Mother had to use her powers of persuasion to keep me going whenever I wanted to prolong our respite. "We're almost there. You know it's not far now. You have been very brave and a big help to me; you can't give up now." At that I would rouse myself again for the last stretch of our journey.

We didn't make it back to our garden cottage until long after midnight. My grandparents, who had been anxiously waiting for us, were greatly relieved when we finally arrived safe and sound with all our treasures. Even though we had gone with little food and water all day, we were too tired to eat what little my grandparents had prepared for us. We collapsed into bed immediately and fell into an exhausted, dreamless sleep. Unloading the wagon would have to wait until the morning.

* * *

Chapter 11

War's Final Days

April 16, 1945

Our hard-won treasures safely stowed in the barn, and wearing fresh clothes so that the ones we had been wearing since our flight from Plauen could be washed, we waited with bated breath for what the next few days would bring. After what I had seen and experienced in Plauen the day before, I felt dead inside; I couldn't imagine anything good coming our way. None of us believed anymore that a miracle weapon would turn the tide in our favor and save us.

The events of the last few days, especially our trip into what had been my beloved city of Plauen, made me realize that the end was near. There was an indefinable something in the air. Our world seemed to be holding its breath, waiting with tense anticipation for whatever would come next.

My uncles:
Oskar and Arthur in the German army
Carl and Rudy in the American army

Life had become so precarious that the end of the war couldn't come soon enough. I saw that my mother and grandparents were only skin and bones, looking haggard and completely worn out. With their faded old clothes, which made no pretense of clinging to well-fed bodies, they looked more like scarecrows than the people I remembered from better days. Even though they appeared outwardly calm, they couldn't hide the pain and anxiety I saw in their eyes.

Their dogged struggle to get us through all the hard times made me think of them as almost superhuman. Watching them deal with impossibly difficult situations, I felt love, awe, and respect for them. Margit and I were lucky to have such a mother and grandparents, whose unflagging spirits guided us through Germany's death throes. Brave and tenacious as they were, I couldn't help but wonder how much more they could endure without breaking. Just the thought of losing one of them gave me daymares.

My thoughts wandered to the time when our garden with its cottage was our little paradise, an escape from the city in the summer months. My mother and grandparents used to glow with health and looked happy as they went about growing and harvesting our own vegetables and fruit. I thought of the harmonious evenings after supper when glowworms sparkled in the darkness outside, and when Grandfather wasn't too tired to tell us bedtime stories. Where did those days go? My thoughts in a tangle, I couldn't fathom the changes time had wrought. How much longer would it be before peace returned?

Then news reached us that the American army was closing in on Plauen. The increasing noise of artillery fire told us that it was only a matter of time before the first American tanks would roll into Plauen. We could only wait and hope for the best. Our prayers may not have been answered in the way we would have liked, but Oma, who had a proverb for every occasion, said: "Better a horrible end, than horror without end," which fit our situation perfectly. It was like having to undergo an operation with an uncertain outcome, which would nevertheless end the unrelenting pain one way or another.

As far as I was concerned, whatever the end would bring, it couldn't be worse than what had gone before. Yet, now that it finally came, it was a shock just the same, because it signaled the end of everything I had ever known. The old world gone in a cloud of dust and debris, sunk in an ocean of blood and tears, I sensed that it was the beginning of a new world, which hovered somewhere in a nebulous future. Unable to project my thoughts past the present, I drifted on the apprehension of uncertainty. Like a ship without a rudder, I had to allow the waves of fate to deposit me on whatever shores they chose.

On April 16th, which was only six days after the last horrendous air attack on Plauen, the 347th US Infantry Regiment, which was part of the 87th Infantry Division's "Golden Acorn" under George Patton, took possession of Plauen and its surroundings. The terrible tension and fear of the approaching unknown, which held us in its grip, gave way to hope, slim as it was.

Even though the war didn't end in other parts of Germany till May 8, it was all over for us.

At last the artillery fire slowly came to a halt. Even though I kept listening for the sound of approaching bombers, I noticed with relief that the skies had become unusually quiet, which seemed very strange after they held nothing but menace for months on end. The adults could finally repair some of the worst damage to our cottage, and Margit and I helped clean the yard of all the debris the firestorm had deposited there on April 10th. It was good to pretend that it was just an ordinary day, which kept our minds off what was happening in the world outside our little sanctuary. But we couldn't hide from life forever. It demanded that we acknowledge and deal with its vagaries, whether we liked it or not.

Our emotions ran the gamut from hope to despair. Now occupied by five hundred thousand American troops, we once again faced a very uncertain future.

We asked each other what would happen to us now after we had managed to live through hell. How would the victors treat us? What would they do to us? Judging from the Allies' actions in the last few days and weeks, we expected no mercy. Would they rape, maim, and kill us like we heard the Russians did as they advanced in the east? There was no way to tell what a conquering army would do. We were numb with dread.

Grandfather did his best to calm us down: "I can't imagine the Americans behaving like the Russians. So stop worrying." That was of course easier said than done.

The terrible stories we heard from those fleeing the advancing Russians from Germany's eastern states were so horrible that they made our flesh crawl and our hair stand on end. We heard eyewitness accounts of wholesale murder of unarmed civilians; people being beaten to death, tortured, and mutilated; and women gang-raped and killed, no matter what their age. We also heard that some women even killed their own children and committed suicide, preferring death to falling into Russian hands.

There were reports of pregnant women, their wombs sliced open, nailed to crosses with their fetuses floating in the river entering Germany. The Elbe River brought untold numbers of mutilated bodies from across the borders, which were fished out on the German side not far from us. That in particular scared me more than the bombs had, because bombs were mindless artifacts without a human face, which killed without malice. But these were acts of insane hatred performed by humans upon other humans, which absolutely terrified me. So much hate was beyond my capacity to understand. My mind went into hiding with the horror of it all. So one terror was replaced by another. Had our bitter struggle to stay alive been in vain? What new trials did life have in store for us?

The end of the war and an occupation by victorious foreign troops would bring many new challenges for my mother and grandparents, and I wondered how Mother and my grandparents would deal with this new situation. But I trusted them implicitly and instinctively knew that they would somehow manage to get us through this dangerous period. They would grit their teeth as they had always done and do whatever was necessary for us to survive.

I remembered my mother crying bitterly when we heard the news of our defeat. Undoubtedly she remembered the aftermath of WWI, which she experienced as a child, and knew what we were facing. I cried with her, only dimly sensing the depth of her grief. The only other time I had seen her cry was when we were informed of the deaths of her two brothers. One died in Stalingrad. The other, who was in the German Air Force, died near Odessa in the Crimea. We heard from a surviving comrade that his plane had been shot down and he was taken prisoner by the Russians. The memory of the day my grandmother came to give us the news of Mother's second brother's death was still with me. I can still see her and my grandmother huddling on the stairs holding each other, their heartrending sobs echoing through the hallway. Struck by the vehemence of their anguish, I remained mute. As if their grief were visible, I saw them as swathed within the cocoon of a dark cloud, which discharged itself with an endless flood of tears.

I didn't know about the nature of death then; I only knew that my two uncles would never come home again and that my two cousins would be left fatherless. Unformed thoughts swirling through my head reminded me that my father was also a soldier somewhere. Would I become fatherless too?

As was the custom after a death in the family, my grandmother and mother were dressed in black clothes only, which only served to magnify the abysmal sadness inherent in the scene. Almost everyone wore black during those years, because hardly a family escaped without the loss of loved ones. Those who didn't have any black clothing wore black armbands. It was a black and bleak time.

Ironically, Mother's other two brothers, who were US citizens, served in the American army. Of course we had no news of them, giving my grandparents and my mother more to worry about.

However, in contrast to the deadly harassment of the last few days, we didn't hear of any civilians being mistreated by the conquering US army. But then, our only source of news was the local grapevine, which couldn't tell us much about other parts of our region, not to mention what was going on in the rest of the country.

Nevertheless we were very relieved that it was the Americans, and not the Russians, who reached us first, and we finally allowed ourselves to breathe a little easier. I secretly wondered what Americans were like. Were they so different from us? Surely, they looked just like us and that was a very comforting thought. Since I had two American uncles, not to mention an American fairy godmother, whose loving gift of a golden heart necklace never left my neck, I was prepared to like them. They had to be good people. That's why I couldn't imagine why they bombed us so mercilessly.

After thinking about it some more, it occurred to me that American pilots had to do what they were told, whether they agreed with it or not. They had to follow orders, just like our soldiers. I understood that that's how things worked in a war. Besides, how could they see from high up in the sky all the blood and gore their actions produced on the ground? How could they possibly have known how bad it really was for all the women and children who were on the receiving end with no way to defend themselves?

With my limited knowledge of the world at large, I came to the conclusion that even good people sometimes had to do things, which went against everything they had been taught. That's the only way I could explain it to myself.

At least now that hostilities had ended in our area, there was no more need to seek shelter from bombs, fighter planes, or splinter bombs.

Hiding in basements, caves, and ditches wasn't my idea of a nice childhood. I sorely missed doing the normal things children do, like playing with friends and even going to school. When was the last time I laughed? When was the last time I saw my mother laugh? I couldn't remember. All in all, this was definitely a change for the better. For the first time in a long time hope appeared on the horizon.

But it was certainly the end of the Germany we had known. Our future, which was now determined by the victor, was very uncertain, and our lives were entirely in their hands. For the completely demoralized survivors this was a time filled with anxiety, bitterness, and an abysmal hopelessness. The entire country was in ruins, with millions dead or injured, and the surviving population was completely prostrate with grief and despair. Millions were starving and homeless, millions of children were orphaned, millions of women were widowed, and millions more were left physically and emotionally scarred for life. The defeat was complete!

The past years had been so horrible, the defeat so utterly devastating, that a better future seemed inconceivable. A normal life seemed like a myth invented by dreamers of impossible dreams. But our primeval instinct to live doesn't die, even under the most dire circumstances. As long as there is life, there is always hope.

*   *   *

Chapter 12

Coincidence or Heavenly Intervention?

When the 347th US Infantry Regiment began its occupation of Plauen and its surroundings on April 16, 1945, the war had ended in our part of Germany. It was finally over. Thank God!

All of us now lived crowded together in our small country cottage because we were all homeless and there was no other place to go. Our perception of the future was a large, nebulous void, but then the past had taught us to live one day at a time. We were incredibly relieved that the war was finally over, but also full of fear and trepidation about how our occupiers would deal with us. Our first introduction to life under occupation was flyers disseminating new laws instituted by the American military authorities.

Some of them were:

A curfew from 6 p.m. to 8 a.m.

Travel restrictions outside our place of residence.

Hand wagons, bicycles, and baby carriages were banned (later rescinded).

All assets were frozen, and all valuables including foreign currencies had to be handed over.

Gatherings of groups of more than three or four people were forbidden.

All men between the ages of 14-65 and all childless women ages 14-35 were required to sign up for rubble removal, or they would not receive ration cards.

A new mayor was sworn in to reestablish city government and to work with the American authorities, with English as the official language. None of these things affected us to any extent, and most of them were rescinded anyway after the official end of the war on May 8.

All things considered, we were happy with this turn of events and we said: "Thank God it's the Americans and not the Russians!"

Grandfather immediately got busy looking for a suitable piece of wood, and when he found one I set to work transforming it into a likeness of the American flag. Wielding a brush with enthusiasm, I was happy to contribute my artistic talent in creating this masterpiece. It was a very nice-looking flag, but painting all its white stars on a blue background with red and white stripes under Grandfather's direction wasn't easy. I worked very hard to get all the stripes straight and all the stars in the right place. It turned out very well in my opinion, and I was proud of my achievement. This piece of artwork, about 18 inches by 24 inches, was nailed on our front gate. Grandfather had put the garden property in Uncle Rudy's name before the war, and Rudy was an American citizen who lived in New Jersey. The flag was to apprise the incoming victorious army that this was American property and to be recognized as such.

It wasn't long before columns of armored cars, tanks and jeeps started rolling by. We children sat by the garden gate under the American flag with baskets of flowers and threw small bouquets at the passing army. It didn't take us long to find out that this was a good idea. Often the smiling GIs threw back packs of chewing gum, a novelty for us, or if we were real lucky, a Hershey bar. That was the first time I tasted chocolate. This change in our lives was definitely to our liking. Of course there were those who drove by and looked at us darkly with scowls on their faces. But scowls didn't kill like their bombs did, so we ignored their scowls and showered them with flowers anyway. In the following days and weeks, many jeeps stopped to

Welcoming American troops with flowers (sketch by Renate Stoever)

inquire about the meaning of the American flag at the gate. Grandfather was called to explain. He spoke some English, because he and my grandmother had been in New York in 1939 to visit their sons and to see the World's Fair.

I guess word got around on the army post of this curious state of affairs. An American flag in the middle of war-torn Germany? What was it doing there? Because of this we had quite a few visitors every day and Grandfather always had a lot of explaining to do. Friendly GIs usually had a few goodies for us children, so as far as we were concerned, this was a big improvement in life. No more air raids, no more bombs, no more running for shelter. It was May, the sun shone, the sky was blue, the meadows were full of flowers, and the trees were clothed in delicate greens once again. Birds sang joyfully in celebration of the miracle of spring and the splendor of a reawakened earth. With it came hope, for we too felt as if we had been reawakened to life after a dark and horrible night. The ravaged city seemed far away, a nightmare we didn't want to remember.

The GIs entering Plauen were shocked by the terrible destruction they saw. One of them who stopped at our gate to inquire about the American flag asked me in broken German: "Do you hate us for what we did to your city?"

"I don't hate you. It was war."

But then, I was a very old nine-year-old, forged and hardened in the crucible of war.

This was also when we met our first African American. His name was Charlie. At first we children were afraid of him and we cautiously kept our distance. He certainly looked different from anybody we had ever seen. But we soon realized that aside from his rich brown suntan and his curly black hair, he was the same as us. We grew to like him, because he made us laugh and he played with us. It had been so long since we had laughed that it felt like rain falling on a parched landscape. We were always happy to see him, and he was a welcome guest in our garden. Charlie was definitely our favorite visitor! Never mind that he tried to get my mother and my aunt to go to bed with him. This didn't bother us in the least. We didn't know what that meant anyhow. Charlie got nowhere, needless to say. Not even the nylon stockings he offered them as a gift could change their minds. I saw them standing next to the house talking. Charlie held the precious nylons out to them, but my mother and aunt frowned and shook their heads. I thought it very nice of Charlie and couldn't understand why my mother and aunt refused his wonderful gifts. When I asked my mother about it later, all I got were some very evasive answers. Very unsatisfactory! Adults were really hard to figure out.

Some of the young GIs who came to visit tried to teach us children a little English. The most important words we learned were: *OK*, *hello*, *thank you*, *please*, and *candy*." Others helped my grandfather water the young vegetable plants. They proudly showed us photos of their wives and of the children they hadn't seen in a long time. In a way our garden became a little piece of America for them. These young men were homesick and missed their families, so we were glad to serve as substitutes. Without exception they were fine young men. Under a weeping willow tree in a corner of the garden, Grandfather had placed a plaque in memory of his two sons, who had been killed in Russia. The young GIs would stop before it and respectfully remove their helmets. Their thoughts might have been: "There but for the grace of God go I." Having seen combat and death, they were very aware of the fragility of life and their own mortality.

Then one day, about a month into the occupation, three officers came to see us. It seemed more like an official visit and we were rather uneasy. Grandfather invited them to sit under the old apple tree by the gate. As usual, they questioned us about the American flag at the gate, but this was more like an interrogation, and not a friendly one at that. Grandfather explained again. The atmosphere was thick with tension. We felt like bugs squirming under a microscope, and we were extremely uncomfortable. In spite of Grandfather's explanations, the officers sat there with dour expressions and with frowns creasing their foreheads. They obviously didn't believe anything Grandfather said. Their faces told us that they had already convicted us of using the American flag under false pretenses. Possibly a grave offense! I could see my normally unflappable grandfather getting nervous, which made me nervous too. Then, in desperation, Grandfather brought out the box full of photos from his visit to the United States in 1939. The officers looked at them with mild interest. Only the photos of a baseball game at Yankee

Stadium elicited enthusiastic attention. Of course Grandfather also showed them photos of our two American uncles, Rudy and Carl. All of a sudden one of the officers took a closer look at one of the photos, pointed at my Uncle Rudy, and said: "I KNOW THAT MAN!"

There was momentary silence as we looked at each other in complete astonishment. How could that be? Of the five hundred thousand troops stationed in our area, a man who knew our Uncle Rudy just happened to be the one to stop by to interrogate us. He turned out to be a friend of our uncle's. Was it a coincidence? Or was it heavenly intervention?

It was nothing short of a miracle and one of life's strange occurrences that leave us mystified and in awe. Were our lives charted and preordained by a powerful force that directs the course of events? Or does that same force intervene at certain times to channel our lives in a different direction? If it wasn't coincidence, the intervention in this instance was benevolent and very much in our favor. Since I always had a lot of whys, it gave me a lot to think about. I finally decided that our guardian angels had arranged it, to see us through a potentially dangerous situation. As far as I was concerned, there was no other explanation.

The officer was as surprised as we were, and he too thought that to come upon the family of a friend under these circumstances was one in several billion. He explained the situation to his two companions, who finally let go of their frowns and smiled. As far as they were concerned, the mystery of the American flag was solved, and there was a satisfactory ending to their interrogation.

From then on, Uncle Rudy's friend came as often as he could, and things were much more relaxed. There was no more mistrust between victor and vanquished, and since we were not allowed to send or receive mail, he wrote to Uncle Rudy for us, to let him know that he met us, and that we had survived the war.

Shortly after this incident, Mother, my sister Margit, and I moved to the nearby village of Kauschwitz. A friend of my mother's who owned a house there cleaned out her dining room for us. So the precious bed, which we had saved out of the rubble of our apartment in Plauen was taken from the barn and carted there. We had to move, because the garden cottage was just not big enough for so many people for an extended period of time. Nevertheless we still walked the five miles to the garden every day to help with the planting, weeding, and watering.

My mother also had to think of where I would go to school in the fall. Because of the incessant bombings, I had already missed most of the third grade. Not that I minded that aspect of the war. School wasn't exactly one of my favorite activities.

Toward the end of June, Uncle Rudy's friend came, looking very troubled and depressed. He informed us that all American troops had been ordered to leave by June 30th and that they would be replaced by Russian troops. We were in shock! Why? I don't remember whether or not he explained. I only know that he was extremely upset. The war with Germany over, he had thought that they could go back home to their families, but instead he and his unit were ordered to the Pacific to fight another war. Our mouths hung open. This was very bad news for us too.

The Russians! The rumors we had heard about the advancing Russian troops were enough to scare anybody to death, and we feared the worst. So the day before their departure all our American friends came for the last time to say their sad good-byes. Even the heavens were crying that day, for it was raining. Charlie, our favorite GI, came too. He came on a bicycle, of all things. When he left, he took one of our old umbrellas with him. I still see him pedaling down the road, the big black umbrella held high in one hand, the other on the handle bar. At the time it didn't occur to me to wonder why Charlie came alone and on a bike, or why none of the others had given him a ride in their jeeps. I didn't know then that African American GIs were segregated in their own units, and there was little or no fraternization between them and the other units.

We were very sad to see them go to the uncertainty and danger of another war on the other side of the world, because we had become friends. We children would certainly miss Charlie.

In the next few days we saw column after column of American soldiers, tanks, trucks, and jeeps moving out. They were replaced by column after column of Russian soldiers in filthy, ragged uniforms and horse-drawn wagons. The difference between these two armies was very striking, to say the least. We watched this exchange with great misgivings and apprehensions.

Why did this incomprehensible switch take place? Why would the Americans give up territory they had conquered? Why would they just hand it over to the Russians? It just didn't make sense. We were completely at a loss to explain this frightening new development. We didn't know about Yalta yet, where Stalin, Churchill, and Roosevelt met to split up our world between them, condemning millions of people to miserable lives behind the "Iron Curtain."

Of course Grandfather had to take the American flag off the gate. We felt bereft without it, but no Russian flag took its place. We now looked toward a future that we knew would be bleak and dangerous. Freedom was out of reach.

* * *

Chapter 13

Russian Occupation

Summer 1945

Sadly, the American troops had withdrawn. What we had instead was a Russian occupation, a very repressive German Communist government, a completely demolished city, a curfew, and even less to eat than during the war. We were told that we were liberated from Nazi tyranny, but in truth we were liberated from all we owned, from freedom of movement, and we still had no freedom of speech. Luckily we had our lives, and that was the important thing.

Fortunately for us, the Russian troops didn't reach us until after the war was over. As occupational powers, the army's directives were different than during wartime. So we thanked our lucky stars that we were spared the horrible fate of those Germans farther east, who fell victim to Russian brutality while the war was still in progress. But as with any conquering army, the new peacetime regulations weren't always followed by the Russians, and we had to be extremely careful of our speech and all our actions. It was like living at the edge of an abyss, where one misstep could lead to your demise. So life went on with different types of demands on our survival skills.

The major form of employment was the removal of rubble and digging out the thousands of rotting corpses under the ruins. This work had to be done by women, since most men who survived the war were still in POW camps. These women even had a name: "Rubble Women." It was terrible and heartbreaking work that paid next to nothing, but somebody had to do it. These women's often-overlooked contribution to the rebuilding of our country was enormous, and a great testament to their strength of character. They were the unsung heroes of the postwar period.

Living in my mother's friend's house in Kauschwitz wasn't bad, aside from the cramped quarters of Lanie's dining room, which she had cleaned out to make room for us. But we were homeless and grateful for her generosity in giving us shelter, even though it greatly disrupted her household. Lanie and her family lived upstairs and her in-laws lived on the ground floor. The house was in the middle of a large garden, surrounded by a fence that was entered through a wide front gate. A nice-size swimming pool amid a rock garden looked very inviting, but unfortunately the only time the pool had water in it was when it rained. The rest of the time it was completely empty, which I found rather disappointing because I loved the water.

Every day we walked the five miles to our garden cottage in Joessnitz to help with the work. Weeding and watering was my job. So was taking care of the few rabbits my grandparents kept in a small pen. That was one chore I didn't mind, because the babies that inevitably came were so adorable. To my dismay some of the rabbits became our dinner on rare special occasions. But suddenly one night all the rabbits were stolen. Obviously somebody found out about our rabbits and made off with them in the middle of the night. Finding the empty stalls in the morning was quite a shock. After all the effort of raising them as our emergency food, they were taken to become somebody else's dinner. Who could have done this, we asked? Oma thought that it must have been some Russians who felt like having a nice rabbit stew. But then, Oma blamed everything on the Russians. There was no use speculating, for it could have been anybody. Everybody was starving and searching for food, so it shouldn't have surprised us as much as it did.

One of my less desirable jobs was to go with my grandfather to Plauen's former airport, which now was the Russian army post. Since the Russians had many more horses than trucks, there was a lot of horse manure piling up all over the place and the army post smelled accordingly. Its ripe odors traveled on the breeze and intensified as we came closer. So I guess they were glad to get rid of some of their malodorous heaps, for they generously allowed us to take all we wanted to use as fertilizer in our garden.

Going there with our hand wagon was always an unsettling affair, for our "liberators" could be very unpredictable. Walking among them, I hid my fear by looking as nonchalant as possible, even though I was quaking in my shoes. I felt like we were walking on thin ice that could crack at any moment.

While Opa was busy loading our wagon with his pitchfork, I looked around surreptitiously. The army post was really quite messy, and some of the soldiers' uniforms were so dirty and greasy that they looked like patent leather. I don't think that they had ever seen soap and water. They were a perfect habitat for all kinds of creepy, crawly things that bit and sucked blood. But the Russians must have been used to them, because I didn't see any of them scratching themselves. I was always glad when Opa was finally finished loading the wagon, so we could leave. I couldn't get away from there fast enough to escape the smell, and the possible threat our "liberators" posed.

Going home with the hand wagon full of manure was a very unpleasant trip. My grandfather pulled in the front and I pushed in the back. The fresh, wet manure was quite heavy, so I had to push as hard as I could. Of course some of the manure would run out the back of the wagon and splash all over my legs, the front of my dress, and onto my only pair of shoes. So by the time we got back to the garden I was a mess. I smelled ripe and looked like I had fallen into a cesspool. The excited, buzzing flies following me around told me that they found me very attractive. The same couldn't be said for Oma. When she saw me, she told me to wash and change my clothes immediately, and for once I was only too happy to obey without giving her an argument. But unlike me, the vegetable plants were very happy to get all that smelly stuff, and rewarded us with nice produce later on, which helped us survive this thing called "Peace."

Just as the American GIs had stopped at our garden gate, it was now the Russians, although there was no Russian flag at the gate to welcome them. They were always looking for women and vodka! Those were the days when my mother and my aunt made a mad dash for the barn in the back of the garden whenever there were Russian soldiers in the vicinity. They spent a lot of time there under the hay because rapes, beatings, and killings were commonplace. They only came out of the barn to rejoin us when it was safe to do so. I didn't really know what a rape was, but I did know that it was something awful the soldiers did to women. So I always prayed that Mother and Aunt Else would go undetected.

The Russian soldiers who came would look pointedly at me, my sister Margit, and my cousin Inge, and say in broken German: "Where Mother?"

"Mother dead!" my grandmother would say with furrowed brow, shaking her head sadly. The tension was thick enough to cut with a knife. Inge and I would put on our best performance of looking properly orphaned and grief-stricken. Sometimes we even managed to squeeze out a few tears, which wasn't difficult, since we were scared to death. We must have been quite convincing, because after looking around suspiciously and a short conference in their harsh-sounding language, they usually left. It didn't take us long to perfect our poor orphan routine, and to learn how to behave around unwelcome, potentially dangerous, visitors. It was a dangerous time to be a female over twelve. Luckily we were so skinny and undernourished that we looked even younger than we were.

One day two older officers and a young lieutenant came, and they seemed to like visiting us, or maybe they just wanted to get away from their smelly army post for a while. Of course it was also possible that they had orders to check us out. They came often, and we learned through their broken German and sign language that they missed their families back home terribly, so once again we became some sort of family substitutes. Only this time it was for the Russians instead of the Americans. It was rather touching and we didn't mind. I could sense their misery at being far away from their families for so long. They were not bad people. They were just like us and just as poor, even though they were with the conquering army. So they would sit on our old horsehair couch with us kids and try to communicate while my grandparents kept a sharp eye on us. My mother and aunt, taking no chances, were under the hay in the barn as usual.

Gregor, the blond and blue-eyed young lieutenant, kept telling me in his broken German that I reminded him of his little sister back home, whom he missed a lot. He told me that since I was an orphan, he wanted to take me back to Russia with him. In order to impress me, he said that Papa Stalin would certainly give me a large medal upon my arrival. I wasn't impressed! Papa Stalin wasn't my idea of a benevolent father I was anxious to meet.

That kind of talk didn't go over too well with my grandmother either. Out of the corner of my eye I could see her roll her eyes and make a face, but I certainly didn't worry about it. There was no way I would go to Russia! Just in case he was serious, my solution to this worst-case scenario was that I might have to die a sudden death and join my mother and aunt under the hay. I had it all figured out.

Once in a while they would slip us kids a mark or two. They really had nothing else to give. They were almost as poor as we were; they were nothing like the rich American soldiers—no chewing gum, no Hershey bars. Very disappointing! Mother Russia certainly didn't spoil her sons in uniform.

Just as Americans always chewed gum, the Russians always chewed sunflower seeds. To augment their diet of vodka and sunflower seeds, they would climb over our fence and help themselves to some of the fruit ripening on our trees. They were hungry too.

One time Opa offered our visitors some apples, but they wouldn't accept them until Opa cut one of the apples in half and bit into it. They obviously had fears of their own, and didn't trust us not to poison them. I thought that very strange and also quite sad.

The last time I saw Gregor was in late summer. I was on my way to the garden, walking along the main road leading out of Plauen. There was Gregor, marching a platoon of about fifty soldiers on the opposite side of the road. I called and waved to him. Gregor ordered his troops to stop, and crossed the road to talk to me. He asked me how I was. I remember telling him that I was hungry, which was no lie; I was always hungry! So he gave me two marks, which didn't help my empty stomach, but it was a very kind gesture. I never saw him again after that, but I always remembered his kindness to a little girl. I have often wondered what happened to him, and how his life turned out. Of course not all the Russians were like Gregor and his friends. We children learned to always be on the alert, and to steer clear of the soldiers who prowled the woods around Plauen.

One night three drunken soldiers came to our garden cottage, banging on the door, demanding women and vodka. So Grandfather opened the small window near the door just a slit and told them: "Nyet women, nyet vodka." That's when one of them pushed a gun through the narrow opening and started shooting. The shots took large chunks of plaster out of the wall, barely missing my elderly Aunt Frieda on the couch. My grandfather, who stood pressed against the wall at the side of the window, hit the soldier's hand with a pitchfork. The soldier howled in pain, dropped the gun inside the house and made a fast retreat with the others. This had the potential of a disaster for our whole family, but once again, we were lucky. The next day my grandfather went to the commandant with the story and handed over the gun. That was the end of that, thank God! We felt that the Russians should have had the 8 p.m. curfew they imposed on us, so that they would stay on their posts at night and leave us alone.

As time passed and things settled down, my mother and aunt came out of hiding to take part in our daily lives—with caution, of course. But then, caution was demanded of all of us. Peace turned out to be a different kind of struggle, with different kinds of fears.

* * *

Chapter 14

Putzi the Spitz

By August 1945 we were slowly adjusting to the shock of being occupied by Russian troops. The war might have been over for the Allies, but it wasn't over for us by any means. Coping with life in our disintegrated world and Russian occupation posed immense problems for us. I was nine years old going on forty, and certainly old enough to understand our situation.

Almost all German men were either dead, missing, or in POW camps, which left the women, children, and old people to shift for themselves as best they could under very difficult circumstances. My father was among the missing, and we had no idea what had become of him. The last we heard was that he was somewhere on the Eastern Front, and without news of his fate we were terribly worried.

One day toward the end of summer my mother heard of a POW camp that could be reached by train, a few of which were finally running again. She decided it was worth a try to go there to look for my father. Anna, a friend of hers whose husband was also missing, thought it a good idea too, and decided to come along. Of course she insisted on bringing her dog, because she never went anywhere without him.

So my mother and I, and Anna and her dog Putzi, a very cute, pure-white Spitz, boarded a train, which would bring us to a town near the camp. We had just settled into our compartment when the door opened and a high-ranking Russian officer came in. Needless to say, that threw us into a silent panic. We immediately feared the worst, like being dragged off to some detention camp for some transgression or other. Who knew, maybe we weren't even supposed to be on the train? Our lives had become a journey on quicksand, where one step in the wrong direction could take you away forever. We were very afraid of our occupiers, even though some of them may have been quite decent. But you never knew which kind you were dealing with, so caution was always called for.

In this instance, as it turned out, the officer was merely a fellow traveler who shared our compartment, so our fear subsided somewhat. The officer looked like he was in his late forties and a bit on the stout side. We were of course quite intimidated by all the important-looking medals on his chest and the dour look on his face, which told us that we were in the presence of an esteemed personage. As the train pulled out, we sat with downcast eyes in frozen silence. Even I was quiet, which was unusual for me. I shrank a little further into my seat by the window, trying to make myself less conspicuous, for fear of doing or saying something that would get us into trouble. I was on my best behavior.

The only one not intimidated by the presence of the officer was the dog. He was scampering about, sniffing everything the way dogs do, and wagging his tail at the Russian to get his attention. Putzi must have liked what he smelled. Anna tried her best to get him away from the officer and to sit and stay, but it was useless. He refused to settle down and blithely ignored Anna's commands.

The Russian, who was probably a bit bored by this silent train ride, started to take notice of the dog and began to play with him. Needing no encouragement, Putzi jumped up on his lap and licked his face, letting him know that at least he liked him, even if none of us did. The two quickly became the best of friends. I watched this with some interest, wondering what this normally rather reserved dog was up to. He had certainly never fussed over me like that. On the contrary, he always ignored my friendly overtures with royal disdain.

This went on for a while when suddenly a weird noise disrupted the duo's playful antics. An absolutely horrible smell spread through the entire compartment. One look told me that the dog had made very explosive diarrhea all over the Russian officer. The poor man sat there in shock, holding out his hands, which were dripping with a stinking brown sauce. He looked with horror at what had been his clean pressed uniform and at his medal-covered chest, all of which was now covered with horrible, evil-smelling dog do! He was a mess, and a very smelly one at that. His uniform was certainly ruined, and so were some of his medals! The uniform could be replaced, but the medals were a different matter. Replacing them, or cleaning and deodorizing them, would be a big problem.

The stench was so terrible, I gagged and felt like throwing up. Putzi sure had exploded a very powerful stink bomb. The culprit had of course scampered off the officer's lap and hid whining under the seat.

I was secretly pleased with this turn of events and had a very hard time hiding my feelings. Luckily I was sitting next to the window. I turned my head toward it, trying to suppress the laughter bubbling up in me. Tears ran down my cheeks while Mother and Anna apologized profusely for the dog's misdeed. Their efforts to get him to leave his safe place under the seat were unsuccessful. Fearing retribution, Putzi stayed where he was. Lucky for him, they didn't send dogs to Siberia. When I had myself somewhat under control, I saw the worried glances my mother exchanged with her friend, and I knew that they wondered whether this incident would have adverse repercussions for us. So did I.

Red in the face with rage, looking positively apoplectic, the officer shouted quite a few things in Russian, which I'm sure were not complimentary. It was a good thing we didn't understand Russian. Petrified, we sat in stony silence as he gave vent to his fury in angry tirades, which reverberated in our compartment. He yelled so loudly that I wondered if everybody on the train could hear him. Still grumbling and venting his spleen, he got off at the next stop, taking the brown sauce clinging to his uniform and the horrible stink with him. I'm sure that everybody who encountered him held their noses and gave him a wide berth.

Considering ourselves extremely lucky to be spared any more serious consequences than his vociferous rants, and heaving big sighs of relief, we finally allowed ourselves to relax. I was now finally able to release the laughter that I had stifled for so long. I laughed till my sides hurt. I told Putzi not to worry, these things happen to the best of dogs. As if he understood, the dog finally dared to leave his place of safety. He was none too clean or sweet-smelling either, and he certainly wasn't all white anymore. Hugging or petting him was out of the question.

After another stop, we reached our destination. Stinky Putzi in tow, we walked across some fields to the POW camp. Surrounded by a high barbwire fence, the camp was situated in an open meadow, without housing or shelter of any sort. I hated to think about what happened to those poor men when it rained and the meadow turned to mud. Where would they find shelter? Fall was not far away. Would they still be there in the winter and freeze to death? The German POWs sat on the ground in filthy, ragged uniforms; some wore dirty bandages and looked very ill. Their shaven heads emphasized their emaciated look; their eyes expressed an abysmal hopelessness and resignation. They were a sorry sight! What would happen to these men? How long would they be kept there? Were the healthier ones destined to be shipped to Siberia as forced labor? Most of them would definitely not survive. Their fate was almost certain death. I felt very sorry for these poor wretches, who had given their all for their country. Was this their reward?

We managed to get some of the men to come near the fence. There were quite a few other women like my mother and Anna holding out photos of their missing husbands, fathers, sons, and brothers, asking if anyone had seen them or knew anything about them. The POWs shook their heads sadly when we showed them my father's photo. No one had seen my father or knew anything about him. Anna's search for her husband was also without results.

Then some Russian soldiers yelling and gesturing with rifles chased us away. We needed no translation. Their meaning was clear. I was glad to leave this place with its sorry-looking prisoners, glad that my father was not among them! Yet he might be in a camp just like this one, or maybe he was already dead. The thought did nothing to lift my spirits, so I banished it to the pit where all my unwelcome thoughts were kept. As long as there was no negative news, there was always the hope that he was alive and would come back to us.

The trip home was uneventful. No Russian officer joined us to play with the now white-brown and still very smelly Putzi. He had been very subdued and well behaved since the incident with the Russian officer earlier in the day.

My mother was deeply disappointed that the trip had been in vain, so we were very subdued too. She was extremely worried, especially after what had happened to the husband of another friend of hers. He had been released from a Russian POW camp and managed to make it home, but collapsed and died at the door in front his wife and children.

I remembered playing with their two girls when they came to visit with their mother. My heart went out to them, and I couldn't imagine how they must have felt.

This terrible news increased our worry about my father's fate. But we were not alone. There were millions of women and children all over Germany anxiously worrying and waiting. Millions of mother's hearts were heavy, praying for their sons to come home. For some, their prayers would be heard, but for most they would be in vain. In my mind I saw all of Germany awash in tears.

Our trip to find Father had come to nothing aside from a certain white Spitz accidentally telling a Russian officer how welcome our occupiers were. I definitely will never forget a very mischievous little Spitz called Putzi!

* * *

Chapter 15

A Valuable Lesson

One day in late August 1945 we heard through the grapevine that a stationery store in Plauen had reopened in its basement. September and the beginning of school wasn't far away, and I had neither pencils, paper, nor books.

Since it was a beautiful, sunny day, I decided that it would be a good time to go into Plauen to see if I would be able to get some pencils and paper. I hadn't been in Plauen since that last frightful trip in April, when Mother and I went there to salvage some of our belongings. Busy with laundry, which was an all-day chore, she let me go alone because she trusted me enough to avoid dangerous situations. Of course she told me to be careful, but it didn't occur to either of us that situations might arise that I was too young and too inexperienced to handle. After all, the war was over, and our new Communist government and our Russian occupiers supposedly had everything under control.

I knew that it would be a long walk to the store in the center of Plauen, but I didn't mind, because we had become used to walking long distances. Happily wandering along the country road bordered by trees, fields, and meadows, I felt very grown up and self-confident. Full of myself, nothing could shake my optimism to somehow get the materials I needed for school. After passing through a short stretch of pines, I arrived at Plauen's outskirts. This was an area with old villas that used to belong to the city's more prosperous citizens, and that had remained relatively unscathed.

Walking along Bahnhof Strasse, Plauen's main traffic artery, evidence of the bombings and the destruction increased the farther I went. Nothing much had changed since I was there last, except that Bahnhof Strasse and the streetcar tracks had been cleared of rubble and most of the bomb craters were filled in. So it looked a little better than it did on my last visit in April. The street was visible and clearly delineated now, but I saw very few people. Plauen seemed to have become a ghost town of sorts. Ruins still flanked both sides of the street, interspersed with areas where only detritus remained of the buildings once standing there. Weeds, finding conditions favorable, were sprouting among the rubble. Here and there chimneys and some facades were left standing, like monuments commemorating a cataclysmic event. They were often the only verticals in a lunar landscape, which had a macabre feeling in its barren ugliness. I registered it without emotion like I did everything else, and automatically tucked it away in the storage vault of my memory, adding it to the mélange of things already there.

At one point I stopped to rest, because my feet hurt in shoes that were much too small for me. At age nine I had long since outgrown them, just as I had outgrown the short skirt I wore. The skirt, which was red with little white hearts, had been my favorite, and was now my only one. Sadly, I realized that its days were numbered, for it didn't grow like I did. Unfortunately there was nothing to replace the skirt or the shoes, which were even harder to replace than the skirt. Mother would have to ask around to see if any of her friends had some hand-me-downs in my size. Hopefully Mother would find some shoes for me soon, because my feet weren't getting any smaller. Winter wasn't far away and the thought of going barefoot in ice and snow wasn't very comforting.

I sat down on a chunk of broken concrete, took my shoes off, and shook out the stones that had lodged in them. I stretched my legs, wiggled my toes to relieve the cramps, and inspected the blisters that were beginning to form on my feet. Directly across the street I noticed a big truck parked in front of what had been a large building. I wondered if it was the building I had heard about, where over two hundred people had died during the horrific bombing on April 10th. The basement entrance had been freed of rubble, and I saw several men going in and out. I idly wondered what they were doing. Then I saw them carry out people-sized bundles, and I realized that they were still bringing out bodies, even though four months had passed since the end of the war. Some of the bundles were small, and I thought that they might be bodies of children like me. I started to count, but I gave up after a while, because I lost count. I assumed that they were taken to a cemetery for proper burial. Once again I thanked our lucky stars that we hadn't been in the city that horrible night. Experiencing it from seven miles away was bad enough. I watched for a while, so used to death and destruction that I wasn't particularly disturbed by what I saw. As usual, my survival instinct told me to shut it out and prevent my emotions from becoming involved.

After I had rested a bit, I put my painful shoes back on and, ignoring my aching feet, I went on my way. The store I was looking for was several long blocks down the hill from where we used to live. I was hoping that the grapevine was right, and that I would be able to buy some pencils and paper. However, when I finally arrived, all that was left of the store was another fire-gutted, partially standing building. The store was obviously gone, and I saw no opening that led to a basement store open for business. The "grapevine" was wrong, or maybe I had the wrong store. Disappointed, I started the long trek home.

Then I remembered the other store, near my former school, where the people knew me and always had some paper and pencils for me. It was only two short blocks from Bahnhof Strasse, so I wouldn't lose too much time looking for it. I decided to see if by some miracle it still existed. Maybe I wouldn't go home empty-handed after all. The thought that I would return with nothing but badly blistered feet to show for my efforts wasn't very appealing.

Unfortunately the area where the store had been didn't look any different from the rest of Plauen. Burnt-out, gutted buildings and heaps of rubble behind fire-blackened facades dominated this completely deserted area. Since it was a side street there had been no rubble removal yet, so I had to clamber over broken bricks and debris to reach my objective. When I found the building where the store had been, it too was only one of the many still-standing facades, its innards filled with stinking rubble. I was very disappointed of course, but I should have known, if only by the appearance of what had once been a street.

A man in ragged clothes stood in what had been the store's entrance. His ragged appearance wasn't unusual, because people had lost most of their clothes along with all their other possessions during the bombings. His presence dispelled the loneliness of this empty wasteland, and I took comfort in that. I was glad to see another human being. So I wasn't the least apprehensive or suspicious when he asked me: "What are you doing here all by yourself, little one? What are you looking for?"

In my childish naïveté I told him: "There used to be a stationery store in this building, and you are standing in what used to be the door. I was hoping that the store might still be here. School is starting soon, and I don't have any pencils or paper. I knew the people who owned the store. They were very nice, and always gave me what I needed, even when paper and pencils were scarce."

"That's really a shame, but as you can see, the store is gone, like everything else." he said, shaking his head sympathetically. "I know the people too; they are good friends of mine."

"What happened to the people?" I asked. "I hope that they're OK."

"Oh, they now live on Plauen's outskirts. They're fine. You needn't worry about them," he replied. "I'm sorry, I wish I could help you find school supplies, but I really don't know where you could find them. Unfortunately I can't give you any advice. Keep looking. Maybe you'll find them elsewhere."

Dejected and disappointed, I turned to go when the man suddenly retreated farther back into the building's rubble and beckoned me to come and join him there. He wanted to show me something, he said. I didn't budge from where I stood, for I couldn't imagine what there was to see in all that rubble except more of the same. Cold fingers of fear ran up and down my spine with the sudden awareness that I was all alone with this strange man in this desolate neighborhood. My sixth sense told me to beware, and alarm bells started ringing in my head. Thank God they did, because just then, he started to expose himself, still beckoning to me to come closer.

Now frightened, I turned and ran all the way back to Bahnhof Strasse as fast as my painful feet would carry me. Stumbling over rubble and falling down several times, I picked myself up and kept running. After covering several blocks, I alternated running with walking, always looking behind me, still afraid that he might be following me. I didn't relax until I reached the city's outskirts and the comforting familiarity of the meadows and fields.

I knew that I had just escaped a terrible fate, and felt angry at myself for being so trusting. There was really no excuse for what I felt to be my incredible stupidity. It was embarrassing, to say the least. All I came home with were blistered feet and severely damaged self-confidence. The sobering knowledge that I wasn't as grown up as I thought, and that I still had a lot to learn about the world and its people, gave me pause to rethink the picture I had of myself. Of course I never told my mother about it, because she probably wouldn't have let me out of her sight anymore, and that would have ruined my cherished independence.

In the past Plauen had been very safe because all criminal elements were under lock and key. There was no looting after the bombings, when anybody could have just walked into our wide-open apartment and helped themselves to whatever struck their fancy. What neither Mother nor I realized was that after the war all the criminals were released from jail, free to follow whatever perversions put them there in the first place.

So I learned an important lesson that day, and I resolved to be more careful and less trusting in the future. This lapse in caution might have cost me my life. I could have been just another case of a missing child found dead and mutilated in the ruins.

* * *

Chapter 16

The Psychic

The Russian occupational forces and East Germany's Communist government were now firmly established. All the German Communists and their sympathizers who went underground during the Hitler years now came out into the open and ran our lives in conjunction with the Russian occupational forces. Wilhelm Piek, a dyed in the wool Communist, became the first president of the new state, called the Deutsche Demokratische Republik or the DDR.

Most of our men were either dead, missing, or in POW camps. Women, desperate in their search for information about their husbands, left no stone unturned in their quest. My mother even went to see a psychic, who read the future in cards and who was said to be able to talk to spirits. I wasn't exactly sure what a psychic was. I thought it was someone like an ancient crone who had warts on her nose and sat in a spooky dark room with a black cat and an owl, dealing with spirits, ghosts, and other scary things. Maybe she could also call on them to do her bidding. This intrigued and worried me at the same time.

My fertile imagination conjured up a picture of my mother sitting in a darkened room with moaning ghosts and spirits swirling around her like swaths of mist, their voices whispering unintelligible things in the darkness. This made me quite apprehensive. Who knew what kind of spirits they were? Maybe some of them were mean and nasty, if not downright evil. I imagined their skeletal, phantom fingers touching my mother, trying to pull her into their nefarious realm. What if some of them followed her home to bedevil us? As usual, my mind was busy contemplating all kinds of possible and impossible scenarios. So I was very relieved when she came home from the psychic unharmed.

Of course I had a lot of questions for her. Mother wasn't only discouraged, but also quite annoyed with herself. She was very disgruntled and kept muttering: "She probably tells that to all the women who want to know what happened to their husbands! What a fraud!"

"What did she tell you? What did she say?" I asked.

"She said that your father is in a POW camp in Poland, and he will be home in about a week!"

That really did seem rather fantastic and unbelievable. My mother was absolutely disgusted with this ridiculous prediction, and felt that this trip to the psychic had been a complete waste of time. She was in a very depressed and miserable mood, which as far as I could see seemed to be the major result of her encounter with spirits.

"What else did she say?" I pressed her, wanting to know every little detail.

To stop me from pestering her further, she finally told me with great reluctance: "She also said that we wouldn't have to worry about you in the future, but that your sister Margit would give us a lot of grief!" That particularly upset her, for my sister with her blond curls and her elfin face was the sweetest and most gentle child imaginable. She was a mother's dream! So we spoke no more about it, even though I would have liked to know if she saw any ghosts or spirits, and what they looked like.

Lo and behold, about a week later a stranger clad in rags appeared at our garden property in Joessnitz. He told us that he had just been released from a POW camp in Poland, where he met and befriended my father. He was also from Plauen and a longtime Communist. Most likely he was a minor party member, but even that was very advantageous under the circumstances. His Communist background, insignificant as it may have been, probably gave him some extra clout in the camp. Since he liked my father, he helped him hide in the camp kitchen whenever the Russians came looking for prisoners to be shipped to some gulag as slave labor. Thanks to this man's help, my father probably escaped a trip to Siberia, which would have been a certain death sentence. He told us that he used his influence as a Communist to obtain my father's release, and said that my father should be home in a few days. We were all deliriously happy and excited at this news, and we were very grateful to this stranger for what he had done for our father. Yet, we were almost afraid to believe it.

Nevertheless, in anticipation of my father's return, my mother immediately put me to work darning old socks. Despite my inexperience, I did my best to fill in the holes in the old socks. I darned with more enthusiasm than skill. This was a labor of love, for I had not seen my father in over two years, and I shared my mother's worries about his fate.

Then about a week later, a strange apparition, looking more like a scarecrow than a person, stood at our gate. I went there hesitantly, afraid to open it. I didn't know that it was my own father until the apparition spoke in my father's voice: "Renate! Don't you know me?"

I had the gate open in a second, shouting and screaming with joy. I almost knocked him over in my excitement, because he was so weak and exhausted. He was in filthy rags, his shaven skull emphasizing his gauntness. His eyes, sunken deep in their sockets, seemed far too large in his emaciated face. He was down to ninety pounds. He smelled terrible and looked like a walking, talking skeleton. But what did I care if he smelled bad, and that his filthy rags probably harbored several generations of fleas? He was my father and I was overjoyed to have him back with us again. I loved him, fleas or not. Then my mother and Margit came running, and there were a lot of happy tears and hugs. Our prayers had been answered and our happy excitement knew no bounds. My mother was incredibly happy and relieved now that he was actually home again. What joy to have him back, all ninety pounds of him. Margit and I had a father again, but I felt very sorry for all the children who prayed and waited in vain for their father's return. I thought of how very lucky we were.

Mother immediately gave him something to eat and drink. It wasn't much, even though we had saved as much food as we could since the stranger's appearance. After Father had rested a little and washed, he put on some of his clothes, which Mother had rescued from our apartment in Plauen. Of course they were much too large for his shrunken frame. They just hung on him, and looked like he had borrowed them from a much larger person.

Mother had to keep admonishing me to let him rest, because in my childish exuberance and my happiness, I plied him with affection and endless questions. Of course I was also anxious to show him the great job I thought I had done darning his socks. I was all over him like a happy puppy. So, with great effort, I toned down my enthusiasm, because my father's poor condition was obvious even to me.

I couldn't help thinking of the psychic and what she had told my mother. She was right after all, incredible as it was. I wondered how she could have known. Did some spirit tell her, or was it just a lucky guess? I wondered if the things she told my mother about my sister and me would also come true. As a matter of fact, they certainly did! I have seen many magical things happen in my life, and this was just another one of them.

Since the psychic's predictions came true to such an amazing extent, my opinion of psychics changed considerably for the better. It also gave me a lot to think about! Inquisitive as always, there were a lot of things I wanted to know: Who or what were spirits? Where did they come from? What did they look like? Did they look scary? Were some of them evil? How did psychics communicate with them? Did they speak like we did? Why couldn't everybody talk to them? It was a shame that Mother hadn't taken me along on that interesting visit to the psychic. Who knew what else the spirits said to my mother that she didn't tell me about?

My father's safe return was properly celebrated in our garden cottage the following week. Our whole family had scraped together as many potatoes as they could, and my grandmother used them to make a big pot of dumplings. My father was so starved that he ate thirteen of them, and it was nothing short of a miracle that they didn't kill him. But he survived the thirteen dumplings, and he probably would have eaten even more had my grandmother not stopped him, because we heard that people could die from overeating after long periods of starvation.

He didn't have much time to recover, however, for the city of Plauen soon put him to work to help free the main roads of rubble and fill in the deep bomb craters. There were also many bodies still buried under the rubble that had to be dug out, identified if possible, and properly buried. Not a great job for someone in poor physical condition. But ration cards came with the job. You had to work if you wanted to eat in the worker's paradise.

That's when the Swiss cheese we had saved for Father's return would have helped to put some flesh on his bones and to get some of his strength back a little quicker. But it was gone. Shortly after the Communist takeover, to our shock and dismay a bunch of sour-faced Communists officials came to search our cottage. They weren't nice at all! They just barked at us, ordered us around, and asked a lot of questions. Grandfather dealt with them as best he could while the rest of us stood in shocked silence, thoroughly intimidated by this display of authority.

Unfortunately they found our little cache of food in the root cellar and confiscated all of it. Of course the cheese was the main item. Close to tears, we could only stand there and watch them take it away, and we considered ourselves lucky that they didn't take any of us too.

Our plan to save the cheese for Father certainly went awry. We were also very sorry that we hadn't eaten it ourselves. At least we could have enjoyed it, and been a little less hungry. Moral of the story in a "liberated" Germany under Soviet occupation: "Eat what you can, when you can!"

Sadly I wondered who was enjoying our Swiss cheese now. Its memory was slow to fade, and my mouth watered just thinking of its golden goodness. Probably the sour-faced men who had taken it away were now filling their stomachs with it, just when my father was in dire need of it. It just wasn't fair!

Thank God we had a little produce and fruit from the garden to give to my father. That was a big help in getting him back on his feet. The rations of food allotted to us by our "liberators" were ridiculously meager. Aside from that, most of the things listed on the ration cards weren't even available. Bread, if you could get it, was sold wet, so that it weighed more. Of course it weighed much less after it dried, so we didn't really get our allotted amount. A fine trick that I thought absolutely obnoxious. Did they really think we were so stupid that we wouldn't notice? A few times, when hunger became unbearable, I cut a tiny thin slice from the loaf of bread we kept in a closet. I felt very guilty doing it, because I knew that it came off Margit's and my parent's small rations, and that they were as hungry as I was. So, with gritted teeth and great determination, I avoided going near the closet and its temptation as much as possible. My little golden heart had to serve as a substitute, and I chewed on it with abandon.

My thoughts traveled in some rather unsettling directions. Were the victors now trying to kill the survivors of the war through starvation? It certainly looked like it!

I was permanently hungry. We were all on an involuntary starvation diet!

* * *

Chapter 17

A Hard Winter

When September came, I entered the fourth grade in the Kauschwitz village school. It was a one-room schoolhouse where several grades were taught in the same room. After the many different schools I had been to in Plauen, this was an entirely new experience for me. Our teacher was a nice young woman whom I liked much better than the very strict teachers I had in Plauen. She kept this diverse class in line with discipline tempered with a pleasant personality and kindness. Even though I had missed most of the third grade, I was able to do the work and had no problem catching up.

School started at 8 a.m. and since it was an hour's walk, I had to leave home before seven. Walking across the fields, which had already been harvested, or on a narrow sunken path between the fields, was very enjoyable, provided it wasn't raining. When the weather was good and the sun tinted everything in its golden glow, the dew on the grass glittered like millions of tiny diamonds. It was like walking through a wonderland. Everything in the crystal clear air appeared in sharp detail, multiplying my pleasure with the world around me. Taking the longer path was also interesting. It ran through a deep gully between the fields and was bordered on both sides by thick bushes. Their overhanging branches formed a tunnel that made me feel safe and protected. When breezes swayed the branches, my feet traversed lacy, ever-changing patterns created by the sun in this shadowed hollow. There was beauty everywhere, and I absorbed its life-giving elixir.

I often stopped to examine an interesting weed or an oddly shaped stone, or to watch the antics of a bird. There was the smell of the earth and wild grasses, flocks of birds flying south in formation, and small animals running for cover on silent feet. These mornings were wonderfully peaceful. After years of terror, when our lives were in the balance every single day, it was a healing balm for my wounded soul.

September passed in relative peace, but one day in October I came home from school to find the whole house in turmoil. The gates were wide open and the yard was crowded with Russian vehicles, soldiers, and officers shouting orders in that strange Russian tongue to which our ears were not yet fully accustomed. All I could make out was "*Dawai, dawai*!"—which I knew meant "Move it, and be quick about it."

Lanie, who owned the house, was stunned by the sudden turn of events. She just stood there crying and wringing her hands. Mother immediately pulled me aside and told me that the Russians had requisitioned the house and that we had to be out by nightfall. Where we would go was not their concern.

After some negotiations, Lanie and her family were allowed to stay upstairs in one room, but we had to see where we could find shelter. They certainly didn't give us much time to do so.

"Where will we go?" I asked my visibly upset mother. I already saw us sleeping under some bushes in the woods, beseeching heaven to stop the rain and the snow.

"I don't know," she said, "but I'll go see if I can find us a room somewhere. You stay here with Margit and start packing. And stay away from the Russians!" she added.

Since I could hear them yelling in the courtyard and clomping noisily in and out of the house, the warning was quite unnecessary.

Father was still at work in Plauen, so my poor mother had to run around and beg people in the neighborhood to take us in, while I waited with bated breath for her to return with good news. When she finally came back, she told me that she had managed to talk a widow into letting us a room on the second floor of her small house.

In the meantime my father came home from his rubble removal job in Plauen, and we all pitched in to quickly finish packing our few belongings. We didn't have much, so it didn't take long to cart everything to our new lodgings, including the precious double bed in which all four of us slept. The room we were lucky enough to get was very small, so with the widow's permission we set up our bed in her attic amid all her odds and ends. It was a frigid, rather dismal, place to sleep, but we were not in a position to be choosy. Luckily our small room on the second floor had a stove, an old couch, a table, and an armoire, for aside from our bed, we had no furniture of our own.

During the next few days everybody was required to report for inoculations against cholera, typhus, and typhoid fever, which had become big health hazards. There was a long line of about a hundred sad-looking people waiting their turn. The injections were very painful, because they used the same needle for everyone and it had become quite blunted by the time it was our turn. Margit and the younger children screamed and cried when the blunted needles were shoved into their arms and scrawny chests. I would have liked to do the same, but felt that at age nine I was too old to cry. So I defiantly bit my lip and managed to present a brave front when it was my turn. We had a very bad night, with fever and chills from all the shots, but aside from sore arms and chests, we felt better the next day.

Soon autumn came in earnest and the air had a new sharpness to it. When I left for school in the morning, the grass looked yellow and withered. Frost silvered it and delicate spiderwebs on the stubble fields glistened like jeweled treasures in the early morning sun. At times a fine mist lay in thick swaths over the fields, softening the contours of a world that had become very still, as if holding its breath while waiting for the snow and ice of winter to come. Only the mist moved, its fingers caressing the bare bushes as if to comfort them in their nakedness. The leaves on the bushes along the path in the gully were mostly gone too, their last few brown leaves rattling in sudden gusts of wind. Bare branches reached out and moved with the wind in their last dance before winter would turn them stiff and frozen.

Those were the days when my mother, like untold others, was gone until late at night hunting for food, while Father was at work in Plauen. It was so commonplace that a new word describing this activity was coined. It was called "hamstering," after the little furry hamsters that gather food to bring home to their nests.

Sometimes Mother was able to take a train to do her hamstering, but usually she had to walk many miles in all kinds of weather to the surrounding villages to beg, buy, or barter for a little food from the farmers. For barter she used aprons she had made from a silk parachute

Opa found in a field toward the end of the war. It was so large and heavy that we had to retrieve it with our wagon. I remember its huge size as it lay spread out on the grass in our garden. Inspecting the parachute more closely, I noticed that the silky threads were intricately woven into a checkered pattern producing a dense basket weave, and I couldn't stop marveling at the texture of its fabric. The parachute was cut up right then and there into smaller, more manageable, pieces, and stored in our barn for future use. In those chaotic, uncertain times, you never knew when or how things like that would come in handy.

Of course I wondered what had happened to the pilot was who had used it to eject from his airplane. What was his nationality? Was he American or British? There was no way to tell for sure, but we thought that he was probably an American. Since we didn't find a body, it was safe to assume that he was still alive somewhere.

Later on, the parachute's nondescript beige color was transformed with red or turquoise dye into usable fabric from which Mother could sew all kinds of things. Since Mother's sewing machine had been gobbled up by the bombs, everything had to be sewn by hand, so she sewed aprons, which were quick and easy to make. These proved to be desirable items, because nothing of the sort could be had anywhere. So the parachute that a former enemy had left in the fields helped feed us when we were near starvation. My poor mother went above and beyond her physical abilities in her efforts to bring home food. She usually came home late at night, gray-faced and completely exhausted, carrying some potatoes or grain on her back. She often came home with nothing, so we had to go hungry. The grain Mother brought home at times could be taken to a baker and exchanged for bread. We considered ourselves lucky to have a slice of dry bread with nothing on it. Our ration cards, which people called "Death Cards," were practically useless, for none of the things on the cards were available. Any kind of fat—dairy or meat—were only figments of the imagination.

But food wasn't the only thing that was scarce. Fuel for the stove was another thing that was virtually unobtainable. All the coal mined in our region went to Russia. What did they care if we froze to death? So while Mother was away, Margit and I were busy scouring the surrounding forest for firewood, which was an almost impossible job, because the woods were already picked clean of every scrap of wood. Even the tree branches had been broken off to the height of a tall man, far too high for us to reach. Consequently we weren't very successful, but even the few sticks we brought home helped.

Mother had put me in charge of Margit after school, a vexing chore if there ever was one. We fought constantly, because Margit resented my babysitting and challenged me at every turn; or maybe I just wasn't a very good boss. As far as I was concerned, it was a thankless task, but I knew that both our parents did everything humanly possible for our survival, so I did my best to help.

November came and my father was still on rubble-clearing duty in Plauen, when one day he came home looking very sick. He had been throwing up, because while digging in the ruins he pulled at something green sticking out of the rubble. It was someone's decayed arm, which came off in his hands. Of course he had to unearth the rest of the gruesome remains piece by putrefied piece. In that same rubble he had also found an almost undamaged tin with crayons, which he brought home for me, since he knew that I liked to draw. These were the first crayons I ever had, yet I could never look at them without thinking of his other grisly find, and since I had no paper to draw on, they weren't very useful.

Later father was transferred to work for the Russians at the railroad depot, which was a very busy place. Whole factories were being dismantled and shipped to Russia, requiring a large work force. One day while working there, one of the wagons slated to go to Russia caught fire. Of course the Russians didn't want the half-burned and charred sacks of peas and cubes of what looked like dried pressed grass. (To this day I don't know what it was.) So the German workers were allowed to take these treasures.

My father's share of the charred dried peas and pressed grass cubes saved us from starving to death that winter. It was charred peas and "grass" boiled in water, day after day after day. Sometimes, if we were lucky, there was a potato in this watery soup. It tasted awful and the bitter, burnt taste lingered in my mouth for hours. It wasn't very filling either, but it was better than nothing. We were lucky to have this ghastly stew, so none of us complained. It wouldn't have helped anyway. As they say: "When the devil is hungry enough, he'll eat flies." And God were we hungry! So we ate anything to stay alive. To this day I'm not crazy about peas. They always remind me of those awful times.

As fall passed into winter, getting to school in the morning became increasingly difficult. It was still dark and bitter cold when I left at daybreak, with the blue-shadowed snow my only source of light. On clear mornings the stars still glittered in the sky like precious gems, paling when a rising sun tinged the snowy land in a rosy glow. Only the sound of tinkling ice when sudden winds swept over the fields broke the silence of my solitary walk to school.

After one particularly heavy snowfall, I was unable to use the path in the gully, because its eight-foot depth was filled to the top with snowdrifts. So I had to follow its course along the top, but even there the snow was up to my knees, and I left deep furrows as I went along. Whenever I brushed against one of the bushes, snow would fall off the branches with a soft plop, showering me with its soft, cold whiteness. Had I slipped and fallen into the gully, they wouldn't have found me till spring. I was so covered with snow and ice by the time I reached school that the teacher removed my wet clothes and my one and only pair of shoes, wrapped me in a blanket, and sat me next to the potbellied stove. Of course my shoes and clothes never fully dried out, so when it was time to go home, I had to put the same wet clothes back on. Strangely enough, I can't remember ever catching a cold, even though we almost froze to death in the widow's attic.

This was also a very anxiety-ridden winter. Germany's reeducation began in earnest, and privacy had become as important as a roof over our heads. The danger came from an accidentally overheard, politically incorrect, conversation that could be reported to the authorities. Neighbor informed on neighbor, either to settle an old score or for the gain it would bring. You couldn't trust anyone, not even your best friend, because the secret police had informants everywhere looking for people with undesirable political inclinations. Unfortunates, who were denounced or accidentally betrayed by a carelessly uttered word, disappeared without a trace, never to be seen again. You never knew who would be next. Russia was always in need of more slave labor for its gulags.

To add to our woes, a proposed law demanded the removal of children from parents who were deemed politically unfit. That really worried me. The thought of being taken from parents who loved me and given to someone chosen by the state kept me awake at night. It became very dangerous to voice your thoughts and opinions or to say anything even remotely critical of the new Communist government. These were a new kind of fears we had to deal with. We were effectively frightened into submission.

There was one incident that gave me many sleepless nights for a month. I was outside with some neighborhood children when someone mentioned the death of a high-ranking Communist official. I laughed and said: "So what! No great loss! Good riddance!" The others looked at me like I was crazy. Then, out of the corner of my eye, I noticed a man watching us and I wondered if he had heard me. Would he denounce me and my parents to the authorities? After that I was scared to death that the government would come and take me from my parents, or punish them for not educating me the politically correct way. When nothing happened after a month or so I relaxed, but I promised myself to keep my big mouth under control.

* * *

Chapter 18

The Fruit Police

Spring 1946

Life under the Communist system was full of unpleasant surprises. We barely survived that first winter after the war, mainly because food and shelter were very difficult to find. Living in the widow's one family house was by no means ideal, because aside from the cramped quarters, the widow wasn't too happy with our presence. But it was a roof over our heads, and we had no other choice. Both my maternal and paternal grandparents who had lost their homes in the bombings had to spend the winter in rented rooms on the outskirts of Plauen, just like us.

But everything passes, both the good and the bad. So this terrible winter passed too and gave way to spring. We had survived when many others hadn't. Near starvation had reduced us to skin and bones, but we were still alive, and when spring finally came, we were able to go out to our garden property in Joessnitz again. Unfortunately our small summer house was just that, a two room unheated cottage to be used only in the summer. But now, with the arrival of spring and warmer temperatures my grandparents moved back into our garden cottage again, and they began to ready the ground for seeding and planting.

Even though we still lived in Kauschwitz, Mother, Margit and I joined them there daily to help. Father, who was at work in Plauen during the week, joined us on weekends to give Opa a hand with some of the heavier work. It was essential that we combined our efforts to grow food, because the produce the garden would yield was very important for our survival. We planted everything from lettuce to potatoes to cabbage to beans. Whatever was available was planted. The five-mile walk from Kauschwitz to Joessnitz was a pleasure after the depressing winter when it seemed that even nature had conspired to punish us. The terrible feeling of hopelessness that beset us all winter, melted away with the last of the snow.

Our world came back to life now with an unimaginable splendor as if to reassure us that life was still worth living. The clear blue skies and the warmth of the sun revived our spirits. The breeze wafting through the tall dark pine forest and the flower-laden meadows seemed to whisper a joyous welcome as we passed through them on our way to the garden. The birds had returned from their winter homes in the south and were busily flitting from tree to tree, building nests and endlessly calling to each other. Insects were humming as they visited blossom after blossom. The scent of the reawakened earth delighted our senses and revived our spirits, giving birth to hope for a better future.

Even my hour long walk to school was a pleasure again, as bright greens appeared everywhere after gentle spring rains. I observed the daily changes with delight, as the bushes along the gully sprouted delicate green leaves and tiny buds promised white flowers. A little later on, the gully was roofed over with branches full of myriad small white blooms that became an enchantingly beautiful hollow. At the end of their short life, light breezes shook them loose, filling the air with dancing white blossoms. Some of them clung to my clothes and my hair before settling softly on the ground, covering it with a soft white blanket. It was pure joy.

The only things disturbing our peace were the occasional flashbacks to the previous spring. Even though it was a year later, a sense of approaching danger was still so ingrained in our psyche that we often stopped what we were doing to listen for approaching bombers. Then we would suddenly realize that all this was in the past. There was nothing to fear from the sky anymore. There was no longer a need to be constantly on guard and poised for flight at the sound of approaching planes.

This new unaccustomed sense of tranquility made this spring all the more precious! A profusion of wildflowers turned the meadows into colorful carpets. Over thirty fruit trees in our garden were in full bloom. The garden had become an enchanted realm where fairies reigned and observed us poor mortals with detached amusement.

Of course I knew all about fairies. They were delicate beautiful creatures with long silvery hair and gossamer wings whose diaphanous garments flowed behind them like vaporous mists. Blossoms scattered over their hair and veils enhanced their ephemeral beauty. If I squinted, I could almost see them drifting between the trees as they shook some blossoms loose, which gracefully floated to the ground, dotting it with soft whites and pinks. So I walked around squinting, because I didn't want to miss seeing the fairies.

Unfortunately this enchantment was broken one day by two men at our gate demanding entry. They were very officious looking men, representing our Communist government. They came to look at the blossoming trees, but they were not interested in their beauty. To our dismay, their objective was to look at the blossoms and estimate the amount of fruit the trees would produce, so they could calculate how much fruit we would have to deliver to the state. We watched them with misgivings, but could only stand in submissive silence as they walked from tree to tree with their notebooks, jotting down each tree's estimated crop.

Mother's face was a mask and Oma looked worried while Opa fielded their curt questions:

"These are apple trees?" one of them asked. "Yes".

"What are these?" "Plum trees," Opa responded with a stony face, as he was forced to show them around the entire property. Oma, Mother and I trailed behind like part of a funeral procession.

Thoroughly intimidated, we spoke to each other with our eyes, which spoke volumes. Mother's eyes warned me to be quiet, just in case I would voice one of my readily available opinions and worsen an already tense situation. She need not have worried. The men's demeanor displayed such an air of menacing authority that I knew to keep silent.

The fairies, who didn't seem to like the men any more than we did, had disappeared at their approach, but I was secretly hoping that some of the them had stayed to watch over the raspberry bushes at the far end of our property. There were also gooseberry and cranberry bushes that the Government men had overlooked. Maybe they didn't think them worth their while or maybe they didn't know what they were. I was certainly glad of that.

When the men were done with the trees, they turned their attention to our cottage looking for anything of value they could confiscate, but all they could take with them was a big disappointment. We had nothing but the bare essentials. We all heaved a big sigh of relief when they left, taking their sour faces with them. Our tension eased and we were now able to vent our indignation and resentment over this state of affairs.

Oma was the first to air her grievances: "Thank God they're gone! What else will they take from us? What next?"

"What a bunch of sour balls. Did they have to be so disagreeable?" I chimed in. "I hope they don't ever come back. They give me the creeps."

Mother grumbled: "The way they behave can really scare you. They treat us like dirt. I'm not anxious to see them again either. Whenever they show up, you better beware. They are always bad news."

Opa shook his head and tried to calm us down: "There is nothing we can do, so there's no use getting all worked up about it. We've been through worse. We'll manage. Be glad and thank your lucky stars that was all they wanted."

Of course we were concerned about the amount of fruit we were supposed to deliver. Oma shook her head: "I don't like this. You know what worries me? What if there isn't anything left over for us after we deliver their stipulated amount?"

"We'll cross that bridge when we get to it," was Opa's calming reply. "We'll do the best we can."

"Ja," I said, "but what if some pest makes all the fruit wormy or the birds eat half of it? What if we have frost? What do we do then?" At this, Oma looked more worried than ever and Mother gave me what I called "the look". She usually gave it to me whenever my mouth ran away without my brain.

"No more what ifs," Opa said. "There's no use speculating. We'll be fine. Why don't you get busy and go do some weeding over by the gooseberry bushes." That was the signal for me to keep quiet, and off I went with my little hoe to do as I was told.

Unfortunately a few days later we did have frost and half the blossoms withered and fell to the ground, covering it like fresh fallen snow. Nevertheless we were still required to deliver their calculated amount, which would leave us with next to nothing for ourselves.

Adding insult to injury, we were also expected to do all the harvesting and then cart the fruit to Plauen. There was nothing we could do except comply. We were lucky they left us the produce, and we had to be content with that. It was more than most others had. So we kept weeding, watering, fertilizing and pampering the fledgling plants from morning to night. It kept us very busy and too tired to dwell on our problems.

As it turned out, our fears concerning the fruit were justified. Once Opa had made the required delivery, for which he received a few marks, we had no choice but to be happy with what little was left. That was another thing that took some getting used to. What you thought was yours, wasn't really yours anymore. It belonged to everybody and they could come and take it any time they wanted.

Now that the situation had settled down somewhat, Russian soldiers were not quite the problem they were shortly after our "liberation". But we still had to be wary and carefully avoided crossing their paths as much as possible. There was no sense in tempting fate.

We now had to contend with two forces wielding heavy-handed power over us. One was the Communist government, which was comprised of German Communists, the other was the Russian occupational force. We had to walk a fine line between the two at all times. They were our masters and could do whatever they wished. We were the vanquished, without rights. Occupational law superseded the laws of the newly created German Communist government that governed under the tutelage and control of Moscow.

We learned to be careful about expressing any of our thoughts and opinions, lest we wind up behind bars or in some gulag. It happened to more than one naive soul who mistakenly thought that we were free.

Life was a continuous learning experience and you had to be able to shift quickly with the prevailing winds. The saying that the strong oak breaks in a storm but the willow bends and survives, was very true. So we bent in the storms, yet managed to avoid sacrificing our values and opinions. Thoughts were still free!

* * *

Chapter 19

Operation Rubble

Summer 1946

As summer approached, my parents decided to move back to Plauen. They didn't want to spend another winter in Kauschwitz under the widow's supervision. Not only that, but thanks in part to me, we had worn out our welcome with the widow, who wasn't too happy to have us there in the first place. Since her house had only one bathroom on the ground floor, we had a pail for emergencies in our attic "bedroom." It was my daily chore to make the bed and to take the pail downstairs to empty it into the toilet. It was a job I loathed, so one fine spring day when Mother was out food-hunting, I had a terrific brainstorm. I decided to simply empty the pail from the small attic window. It was rather high up, but climbing on an old chair, I managed. It was easier than lugging the pail all the way to the ground floor. Besides, I reasoned, who would know? My mission accomplished, it only took a minute for the widow to come storming up the stairs yelling and screaming, telling me in no uncertain terms that I had just committed an unspeakable crime that deserved severe punishment. She was so enraged that some of her rants were an unintelligible stream of invectives.

I found out to my horror that the attic window was directly above her kitchen window, and to make matters worse, she had just been leaning out the wide-open window admiring her flower garden when I emptied the pail. Considering this unhappy circumstance, I couldn't really blame her for being furious, so I took my well-deserved lumps with proper remorse and promised to never do it again. I also knew that I could expect more recriminations from my parents when they came home. Of course my parents were informed of my transgression the minute they walked in the door, and I received more reprimands, coupled with their disappointment in me. As a result, my laziness was punished with extra chores. To say that it hadn't been a very good day for me was an understatement. My parents managed to smooth things over with our landlady, but our already tenuous relationship remained strained. Angry looks from the widow were mine for the rest of our stay. She never forgave me. But that wasn't the only reason for my parents' decision to move. We were very cramped and we had no privacy.

However, before we could make the move back to Plauen and the freedom of our own home, we had to clean up the debris at my paternal grandparent's four-story apartment house. It had received heavy damage during the last bombing, and only the front half of the building was still standing. What had been the back wall, the bathrooms, and the stair landings was now a heap of rubble so high that it reached past the second floor. The entire back of the house was completely open. I thought that it looked like a dollhouse for a family of very messy giants, and now it was our job to clean up after them.

The big rubble removal operation began sometime in June, and it was a family affair. Everybody pitched in, including us children. Because of the length of time that had passed since the bombings, everything within the huge pile of rubble had hardened into a solid mass, so a pickax was needed to separate it into smaller pieces. Disposal was easy, because all that was left of the buildings next to ours were mountains of debris. The extra detritus we piled on certainly didn't make any difference. Bricks, which were dug out of the debris by the adults, were carefully sorted and put aside. It was my job to hack the cement off the bricks with a hammer and stack them neatly in the back of the property. It was very boring and difficult work for small hands like mine, but even little Margit did her best to hack at the cement clinging to the bricks, so I tried not to complain too much.

Nevertheless, whenever my hands started to hurt too much, I escaped up the pile of rubble to the upper floors of the house. Since all the landings were missing, the only way to reach the next floor was to hang on the banister and swing over thin air to the next flight of stairs. Of course I thought that absolutely great fun. Dangling from the third-floor banister and swinging from it was an exciting feat of daring. It made me feel like a trapeze artist working without a net. The element of danger made it even more of a thrill and all the more fun. With the usual confidence of the young, the possibility of getting hurt never entered my mind.

I found a lot of things to interest me in the upper reaches of the house, which I reconnoitered thoroughly. There were all those dangling wires, the exposed plumbing, and the pretty patterns in the torn linoleum. Whatever furniture had been there was now part of the huge heap of rubble attached to the house like an ugly growth. I tried to imagine what those apartments had been like before everything was destroyed and wondered where the people who used to live there were now.

When the adults became aware of my activities, they yelled: "What are you doing up there? Get down this minute! Do you want to break your neck? Don't you know that what you are doing is dangerous? What if a floor collapses or you fall!"

At first I pretended not to hear them, but not for long, because my father was getting angry: "Come down immediately and make yourself useful! Here is your hammer; clean the bricks and stack them!" I came down reluctantly to continue with my boring brick-cleaning job, which wasn't exactly my idea of fun!

My other way of escaping this tedious chore was to climb over heaps of debris to what was left of an embroidery factory in the center of the block. The walls and the roof were blown away, but the heavy, fifteen-yard-long embroidery machines bolted to a cement floor were still there. Rusty, bent needles projecting at four-inch intervals were poised to continue embroidering the remnants of ragged fabric, which used to span their entire length. Even all the many spools of colored silk thread were still on the machines. I removed some of them, naively hoping that they could still be used, but they were completely ruined and couldn't be unraveled. After all, it had rained and snowed on them for a year and a half. Stacks of half-burnt fabric sat around in big clumps. Of course everything was rusty or charred and smelled awful, but nevertheless extremely fascinating for a curious ten-year-old. Unfortunately I was soon missed, and called back to work at what I called our "brick factory," where the stack of cleaned bricks had acquired a respectable size by now.

When I became more of a nuisance than a help, I was shipped off to our garden, where my grandparents always had plenty of work for me. They sent me off to the surrounding fields with a basket and a small hoe to dig the fields for potatoes the farmers had missed. Always hungry, I dug with great fervor, and always managed to come back with a basket full of potatoes. They were usually small or damaged, but they were good enough to fill our perpetually empty stomachs. It was backbreaking work, especially on days when the hot sun baked the dusty fields, and turned the earth as hard as cement. Of course I wasn't the only one out there digging. I had plenty of company, because everybody was hungry, and many other people were doing the same thing. I was so tired after a day in the fields that I was glad to go to bed at night. When the grain was harvested I was in the fields again, looking for any wheat the farmers had missed. This was not quite as successful as the potato hunt, but I never came back empty-handed, and every little bit helped feed us. Sometimes my cousin Inge was there too. She was four years older and her presence even made the hard work fun. I could always depend on her to think of many interesting things to do, which usually weren't appreciated by the adults.

One night Inge and I climbed out the window in the middle of the night and went to a nearby wheat field to augment our meager find of the day. The grain stood tall and tempting, rippling like silver ocean waves in the moonlight. We used scissors to snip off wheat all along one edge of the field, not daring to set foot inside and trample the precious grain. Of course we felt guilty, because we knew that this was stealing. But if it meant a few extra slices of bread, it was worth the risk. Not sure if the field was guarded or not, we expected the farmer's wrath to come down on us any minute. So we ran back home with our ill-gotten gains as if pursued by a pack of bloodhounds. We tiptoed back into the house and crawled into our bed, congratulating ourselves on our successful excursion.

Luckily our grandparents slept through it all, or at least that's what we thought. The tongue-lashing we got in the morning, including a sermon on honesty delivered by Opa, told us otherwise: "What on earth were you thinking to sneak out of the house in the middle of the night? Can't we even trust you to stay in your beds at night? Stealing grain! You know that stealing is wrong. You could have gotten yourself into a lot of trouble." There he paused to let it sink in: "You never ever touch anything that isn't yours. Don't ever let us catch you doing anything like this again."

Oma shook her head: "What a foolhardy thing to do. There's no telling what could have happened out there by yourselves in the middle of the night. What you kids don't think of."

And so it went. Inge and I let their well-deserved ire pass over us with hanging heads and downcast eyes. We were properly chastened and on our best behavior that day, but not much longer.

Oma sure had her hands full with us. After she combed and braided our long hair in the morning, we watched her fix our breakfast with hungry eyes. Since food was in such short supply, all she could make for us was a flour drink, which consisted of water with some flour sprinkled into it. When she was about to add a pinch of salt, we yelled in unison: "No salt! No salt! We want sugar!" After our objections, Oma relented and added a little sugar, omitting the salt. But we found out that it didn't taste good at all! As a matter of fact, it tasted awful! But she made us drink it in order to teach us a lesson. We learned that even on sweet dishes some salt is needed to give the proper taste. Since this wasn't much of a breakfast, we tried to find other ways to fill our stomachs.

As the apples and pears started to ripen, Inge and I could scarcely contain ourselves. Even though Grandfather told us not to touch them before they were ripe, we were up in the trees the minute he was out of sight. We stuffed ourselves to our hearts content with the green apples and pears, but not long afterwards we both started to feel terrible. Inge was holding her stomach and yammering: "I don't feel so good. My stomach feels awful. I think I have to throw up." I felt the same. Our stomachs felt like they were going to explode. So we ran behind the house to hide, and threw up against its wall in unison. The noise we made with our retching and moans and groans was enough to wake the dead, so Grandfather had no problem finding us. Of course Inge was scolded the most, because she was the older one and should have set a good example. That was a new and pleasant experience for me, because at home I was the older one, and always responsible for my younger sister's behavior. Being the younger one definitely had some advantages! When our grandparents had enough of us and our escapades, we were sent back to our parents. In my case, it was back to "Operation Rubble" and my brick-cleaning job.

While I was gone, my parents and my other grandparents had been hard at work fixing up our house in Plauen. Since they too had to spend the winter in a tiny rented room, they were as anxious as us to move back into the privacy of their own home, and did everything possible to make at least part of the house livable. It was no easy task for these two old people, but they did their best to do their share in this undertaking. The end result of living in their own home and with family would be worth all the effort.

The best thing that happened that summer was that we received mail from my uncles in New Jersey. We were beside ourselves with joy. Finally, after all this time, we were allowed to get mail and send mail abroad. Since the end of the war we had been living in a solitary confinement of a sort, which finally began to give way. The door to the outside world started to open, even if it was only a small crack. News about the rest of the world was still very sparse. Most of what we learned about the outside world was by word of mouth. All the newspapers were full of Communist propaganda designed to reeducate us. As far as we were concerned, they were only good for one thing, which was to serve as toilet paper. It was another one of my more important jobs to cut the newspapers into small squares for that particular purpose. This very interesting and educational toilet paper was left under a brick in our fancy, open-air bathroom. I thought the use we made of their newspaper was very appropriate.

Since all the bathrooms had been torn away, all that was left was a hole in the ground. To give us a semblance of a toilet, Father stacked bricks around the hole and placed a board with an opening on top. Piled-up bricks and rubble served as a shield to give us a little privacy. Our creativity in making do was endless. This arrangement wasn't very good when it rained, but as usual we managed. So the next thing to do was to replace the landing from the first to the second floor with hard-to-obtain, sizable boards. This enabled us to reach the second floor more easily, but it left the rest of the upper floors without landings for me to enjoy as my favorite playground.

After all that was done, the happy day arrived when my grandparents, my parents, my sister Margit, and I were finally able to cart our few belongings to Plauen. We moved into two rooms on the second floor of the less damaged side of the house. The four of us took the larger room, which had been my grandfather's design studio, while my grandparents moved into the smaller room, which used to be his office. It wasn't exactly palatial, but it was our own and we finally had some sorely missed privacy!

So what if the roof had big holes in it, the bathroom was a hole in the ground, and that there was neither heat, water, nor electricity. It was home sweet home, and all things considered, the best place we had since the end of the war.

* * *

Chapter 20

The "Red Star" School

Plauen, September 1946

We were finally able to move back to Plauen in late August, just in time for me to start the fifth grade. It was another change for me to another school with different teachers and different children, but I was getting used to that. Nothing in our lives was static or predictable.

Our severely bomb-damaged home had no water, so my mother sent me down the block with a pail to fetch water from a still-functioning fire hydrant. I had to make many such trips every day, because the water was heavier than I thought, and even carrying a half-full pail up our steep hill was very hard.

School, on the other hand, was easy. It seemed like a nice vacation, and I definitely preferred it to cleaning bricks, hauling water, or scouring the rubble for firewood. My school was in a damaged but viable building. Bombs had left hundreds of pockmarks inside, and out and everything in it was old and damaged. Every dilapidated desk in my class of about thirty had an inkwell because even pencils were scarce. Since everything, including ink, was in short supply, the inkwells were augmented with water. Consequently we wrote with watery, pale-blue ink that was barely visible on the poor-quality paper. We had no books either, which meant that we had to rely on notes taken with this nearly invisible ink. It was a good thing that I had good eyesight!

Of course we had to learn Russian, which had a totally different alphabet with different sounds, some of which I found very difficult to pronounce. Learning to write the new alphabet wasn't any easier. Our daily homework—to memorize the pronunciation, spelling, and writing of scores of Russian words—was a chore I did with great reluctance mixed with no small amount of resentment. I wasn't happy about this new subject, mainly because it was the language of our "liberators." It was also compulsory, which made me like it even less. Most of my classmates felt just like I did. Therefore we didn't make it easy for our Russian teacher, who was a pretty woman. We made quite a nuisance of ourselves and did everything we could to disrupt the class. We were a royal pain! My friends and I had to stay after school quite often to write essays, apologizing for our misbehavior and explaining the importance of learning Russian. And it was important, because even if you had an A in every other subject, but failed Russian, you had to repeat the whole grade. So I made sure I passed Russian, even if it wasn't by much.

We expressed our disgust over this state of affairs by telling each other Russian jokes, like this one:

Little Else comes to school and tells the teacher that her cat had a litter of kittens, so the teacher asks her: "I hope that they are all good Communists?"

"Yes, teacher," little Else replies, "they are all good Communists"

"That's good," said the teacher. "That's what we like to hear!"

Three weeks later the teacher asks Else about her kittens and wants to know if they are still good Communists. Else grins and says: "No teacher, they are not Communists anymore. You see, they were blind when they were born, but they can see now!"

There was another one we liked to tell: Russians were very fond of watches, which were a novelty to them. No German could walk around with a watch and expect to keep it. Some of the Russians wore as many watches as would fit up to their armpits. You could almost hear them ticking before you saw them. As it happened, a watch worn by one of the Russians was not working anymore, so he went to a watchmaker and complained: "No more tic-tic!" The watchmaker opened the watch and found a dead louse. He took it out with a pair of pincers and showed it to the Russian, who exclaimed in awe: "Ah, macheeniste, hee dead!" It was well known that the Russians had lice and fleas, so that joke was rather close to the truth.

We laughed at the stories we heard about the Russians who washed their potatoes in toilet bowls. When the toilet was accidentally flushed and the potatoes disappeared, they were astonished and extremely upset. Furious, they shot at the toilets, because they thought it was sabotage. When they realized the purpose of flushing, toilets were torn out of buildings and shipped to Russia. They didn't understand that plumbing and sewer pipes were needed to make them work. Jokes and tales like these made us feel better, and helped make life a little more bearable. Humor was about all we had left. Thank God they hadn't taken that too.

Then one day I heard through the grapevine that there was someone at the other end of town who gave private English lessons for one mark an hour. Out of pure belligerence and obstinacy I decided to use my one mark a week pocket money to learn English. It had to be done in secret, because this activity was frowned upon by our Communist government, which made it all the more fun. Not even the long walk through dismal, debris-strewn neighborhoods deterred me. I threw myself into learning English with an enthusiasm that would have astounded my Russian teacher if she had seen it. I relished my little revolt, which was to stand me in good stead later on. Not only that, it made my parents happy to see me put the money I had wheedled out of them to good use.

We had no toys of any kind, so providing my mother had no chores for me, I amused myself by reading after I had done my homework. Since all our libraries were gone, I read whatever I could get my hands on, with the exception of our Communist newspapers, of course. Luckily Mother had rescued a few of my father's books from our apartment. They were mostly about foreign countries and continents. I read about Asia, Africa, South America, and other exotic places. I traveled the world, even if it was only on the wings of my mind. Those books took me to wonderful places, far removed from a devastated Germany.

I traversed South American jungles, saw jaguars and anacondas, and was awed by man-eating fish called piranhas. I was fascinated by African tribes and their rituals. Spellbound by Africa's abundant wildlife, I ran with zebras, gazelles, and wildebeests to escape the hungry lions and leopards. Our kitchen became an African plain populated by elephants, hippos, and rhinos, or whatever I was reading about at the time. Ancient Egyptian pyramids and their history also intrigued me to no end and gave me a lot of food for thought. I saw myself jeweled and clothed in fine, diaphanous Egyptian cotton, wandering between the massive columns of a Thebes palace, holding my pet cheetah on a leash. I was rarely bored.

As luck would have it, my grandfather heard of someone who had two old sets of Karl May books for sale. Karl May was a very popular German author who wrote fascinating stories about foreign countries and cultures he had never seen. His best- known and best-loved books were stories about American Indians, which I would have loved to read, especially since I remembered all the Indian stories my grandfather used to tell us at bedtime. But unfortunately the nine volumes for sale were some of his lesser- known works. I was a little disappointed, but since I had already read my father's books over and over, I was glad to get something new to read.

I had to get them myself in another part of town, and it was a long walk up and down steep hills. The books were so heavy that I didn't think I would make it home with my arms still attached to my body. But I did, and they were definitely worth the effort. They were treasures, which kept me happy and content for a long time. Since we had no electricity, I read at night by the murky light of one of my mother's homemade candles. They were another of my mother's ingenious inventions. She had managed to get some beeswax from a friend of a friend who kept bees. The candle-making process was always quite a production. The beeswax was melted down and poured into an old coffee cup. A string was placed in the middle and the whole thing was allowed to cool. Voila! A candle! The light these candles gave us was dim and very smoky, but they were better than nothing after darkness settled in.

My books were so interesting that I didn't stop reading until my parents yelled at me that I would go blind in this dim light if I kept it up, and that it was time for bed anyway. After some delaying tactics, I closed my book with great reluctance and did as I was told. To tell the truth, my parents had a point, because my eyes did smart from the dim, sooty light of the cup candles. But I couldn't wait for the next day to continue my reading.

Thanks to my new reading material, I was able to I escape the ugly present to the point that I didn't hear a thing, even when my mother spoke to me or told me to do something or other. How could I, when my mind was somewhere in Egypt or India? Finally, after another episode when I didn't hear her tell me to get water, she threatened to burn the books. Since I knew that my mother never made idle threats, I did my best to listen from then on. I didn't want to lose my best friends. They told me that there was another world beyond all the misery we lived in, and I was determined to find it some day. In the meantime I had to be satisfied with what I read in my books and what I learned in school about history and geography. With my mind always occupied with interesting subjects, I didn't dwell on the world in which I lived.

But then one day when I was walking home from school, something happened that I remember to this day. I can still feel what I did then slicing through me like a knife. I can still see what I saw then in vivid detail.

My school was about a half-hour walk from our house, and the difference between my pleasant journey through fields and meadows to the village school in Kauschwitz and my trip to school in Plauen was like night and day. Here the terrible results of war were all around me. Instead of the clear, invigorating country air, the scent of flowers and growing things, I smelled decay, mold, and soot.

My walk to school took me over tons of rubble, since all the roads and sidewalks were completely gone and buried. Often not even a chimney or a wall stood in these gently rolling hills over what were the remains of once nice neighborhoods. It crossed my mind more than once that I might be walking over buried bodies. Were their souls, unhappy and confused, drifting among the rubble looking for their homes and lost loved- ones? Not a thought to brighten my day. When it was windy, dust devils danced over the rubble, swirling dust and debris around this completely devastated area. Their dust-laden veils intensified the impression of a strange, alternate universe devoid of anything that might point to a past civilization. I had to climb over and around large chunks of broken concrete and follow the tiny paths people had worn threading their way through this labyrinth. Here sadness hovered like a shadow, shed tears still hung in the air, and pain and terror still echoed.

That particular day the sky was a beautiful, clear blue with fluffy white clouds. The sun shone brightly with a cheerfulness I didn't feel. I wondered how it was that the sun had not changed as my world had. The sun was still the same and shed its brilliance over all this destruction around me with the same equanimity as it had when my world was whole. I was trying to understand why it hadn't also changed? Should it shine so brightly when my whole world had come asunder? Shouldn't it have dimmed and veiled its brilliant face in mourning for the wretched vista below?

I remember stopping, and even though everything had been like this for a year and a half, it was as if I suddenly awoke from a long coma and saw it for the first time. My guard down, the enormity of the destruction hit me on an emotional level. Up to this point I had not allowed it to register. I had shut it out and concentrated on sheer survival.

I stood there as if paralyzed. My eyes brimming with unshed tears as I took in the desolation in front of me, in back of me, to my left, and to my right. Wherever I looked, there was nothing but a nightmare of rubble, twisted steel girders, broken concrete, and bricks. Pain at seeing my world as it really was washed over me like a tidal wave, which threatened to hurl me into the abyss where our nightmares are kept. I knew instinctively that if I shed one tear I wouldn't be able to stop crying. So I quickly shut down again and with my guard back in place, I went on my way.

I went back to living blindfolded as I had before that searing incident when the world around me suddenly lit up in all its cruelty, pain, and ugliness in a grotesquely exposed reality. Those few seconds, when I really saw not only with my eyes, but also with my heart and soul, has stayed with me all my life. It made me look at the world sadly, because I saw and recognized the ugliness under the thin veneer of civilization. All we build and own can be taken from us in a flash, only leaving us with our lives if we are lucky. I also realized for the first time how much we are pawns of the powerful people who run our governments, how short and fragile our lives really are, and how little we matter in the scheme of things.

That's when I decided to go for religious instruction at a nearby church, hoping to find the solace I couldn't find elsewhere. The fact that it was frowned upon by the Communists was irrelevant as far as I was concerned. Aside from comfort, I was looking for answers. I had a lot of whys.

When I arrived, I found that all that was left of the church was the basement, where a small area had been cleared so it could be used as a classroom. Descending the broken steps to what had been the church basement was like entering an archeological dig in the Egyptian desert. But there were no treasures to be found, only more dust and debris. Sitting on the floor in the dirt with the other children, listening to the pastor talk about Jesus and his Apostles, I could see the sky through portions of the broken basement ceiling. I could see the broken brickwork, the bent girders, and twisted metal rods above me. Dust motes danced in shafts of light coming through large holes overhead. I felt like I was one of those dust motes, tiny and insignificant, helplessly drifting on the current of life, at the mercy of powers beyond my control. The basement's spooky atmosphere, the smell of dust, decay, and mold, did nothing to mend my broken spirit.

Somehow the answers I was looking for just weren't there. The treasure trove of knowledge and salvation didn't reveal itself to me. I was unable to connect our recent past or our present situation with Jesus and His Apostles. Where and how did Jesus fit into the chaos and misery our lives had become? From what I had seen, nobody seemed to pay any attention to His message of love and peace.

* * *

Chapter 21

The Pigeon

Plauen, October 1946

Life in Plauen was not easy and there were problems galore, but it was home. Our biggest worry of course was the missing back wall of my grandparent's four-story apartment house. However, to our great relief things were beginning to look up. The back wall was finally in the process of being rebuilt with the bricks we had dug out of the rubble during the summer. That helped prevent further collapse and more damage to the exposed apartments. Even though there was no shortage of work for masons in a destroyed city like Plauen, my grandfather managed to find two bricklayers to rebuild the wall before winter set in.

Rebuilding the wall took several weeks and I liked watching the men work. It was amazing to see how the new wall took form brick by hard-won brick. Looking at them, I wondered which were the ones I had cleaned. Even though I hadn't been a very enthusiastic brick cleaner, I now felt proud that I had contributed my efforts to the new wall. Sometimes, when I stuck around watching the men too long, they would jokingly ask: "Do you want to help? We could use some help. We'll show you how to lay bricks, or you can mix cement, if you like that better." At that, I would shake my head and run. I had no intention of becoming a bricklayer or a cement mixer.

When the wall was finally finished, it gave us a small extra room in addition to the two we already had. The largest room became the communal kitchen, while the other two served as bedrooms, one for the four of us and the other for my grandparents. Luckily we had windows of sorts for our three rooms. They were actually storm windows that had been stored in the basement, where a few of them survived the bombings. The fit wasn't exactly perfect, because everything in the house had shifted from the impact of the bombs, but they were better than nothing. Since we had no windows for the rest of the house, the wind whistled through the empty window openings, bringing with it the dust from the surrounding ruins and depositing it everywhere. Plywood, which could have covered the openings, wasn't available anywhere. Even cardboard was almost impossible to get. We lacked even the most basic materials to help us make the house a little more livable. As it was, we had to count ourselves lucky that we were able to get enough lumber to replace the second-floor landing so we could get to our apartment without risking breaking our necks swinging around the landing. And with the back wall restored, we didn't have to worry that the house would collapse with us in it.

One day, after I had done my homework and having escaped my mother's eagle eye and the chores she always had for me, I went exploring again to the third and fourth floor. A musty smell permeated everything on both floors. Mold was growing everywhere since the apartments had been open to the elements for over a year without a wall to protect them. Nevertheless I found that part of the house very interesting.

The apartments on the top floors were uninhabitable, of course. Nobody lived there anymore except the ghosts. From what I heard, ghosts were very interesting and elusive entities. They supposedly moaned and groaned a lot, but that didn't frighten me. Sometimes I thought I heard them at night, but it was probably just the wind chasing debris through the open apartments or maybe it was the rats. Rats had grown inordinately large and aggressive on their diet of corpses buried under the rubble, so we took great care to avoid them, because they also began attacking the living.

Considering the state of our house and the rest of the city, it stood to reason that there were not only a lot of rats, but a lot of ghosts as well. In fact the whole city was probably swarming with ghosts. My imagination saw them wafting through the ruins in vaporous swaths, confused and crying, thinking themselves in hell. So it wasn't unreasonable to assume that some of those poor souls were hiding on our upper floors.

I was looking for ghosts, and I was curious to find out if all the stories I heard about them were true. Unfortunately I didn't find any, even though I searched every nook and cranny. I finally decided that they probably only came out at night when nobody was around. That was really very disappointing! But then, I couldn't really blame them. The monstrous destruction of our city was less visible in the dark and therefore less depressing. Being a ghost must have been depressing enough, even though their disembodied state had some advantages. Their ability to go through walls and scare people out of their wits sounded like a lot of fun and very appealing. Just thinking about the mayhem I could cause as a ghost in my Russian class without the risk of punishment gave me giggling fits.

But there was no way I could have gone up to those apartments at night, not even for the ghosts. It would have been too difficult to sneak past my parents since all of us not only slept in the same room but also in the same bed. Aside from that, climbing up there in the dark with only a cup candle to light my way would have been too scary and too dangerous, even without the ghosts. On the other hand, I wasn't sure about what I would have done if I actually met one.

So I gave up my search for ghosts in favor of playing around on the banister. Since the landings on the third and fourth floors were still missing, I was having a really great time swinging from the banister with artistic abandon. The circus missed a splendid opportunity for an exciting new act. It was a good thing my mother didn't see me performing because that would have landed me in a lot of trouble. Most likely she would have given me extra chores to do, like darning socks or hauling water.

Then one day, as I swung myself around to the fourth floor, I saw a pigeon that was caught in the fancy scrollwork of the wrought iron banister. It was fluttering and squawking, desperately trying to free itself. But the more it struggled, the tighter it wedged itself in its trap. The scrolls held it fast. I watched it for a time, but its frantic efforts to free itself were in vain! I felt very sorry for it, but was afraid to help it for fear of hurting it further. Even talking softly to the bird didn't calm it down. Its fear only increased its frantic attempts to escape. I was completely at a loss as to how to help the poor thing, so I went to tell my mother about it. Since I had been told more than once not to play on the banisters, I risked her displeasure and possible punishment for my disobedience. But to my relief, I only got a mild rebuke with the admonition to stay away from the dangerous upper floors. She told me that Father would take care of my feathered friend when he came home from work. So I felt very virtuous as the pigeon's savior and I couldn't wait for my father to come and give the pigeon its freedom.

When my father came home and heard the story, he immediately climbed up to the fourth floor to see to the pigeon, but not to free it as I thought. It squawked piteously when he brought it down and gave it to my mother. To my dismay the family decided to have it for dinner and Mother became its executioner. It had been over two years since we had eaten meat, and we had all but forgotten what it tasted like. Now luck gave us a pigeon, and even though it was so little, it was better than nothing. The rations given to us by our Russian liberators allowed adults a daily maximum of 1200 calories, 1800 for men who did hard labor and 600 calories for a child, but that was only if you were able to find what was listed on the ration cards—a joke that we didn't find very funny.

So my poor little pigeon met its fate on Mother's stove. Not only was I unsuccessful as a ghost hunter, but I was also a definite failure at rescuing pigeons. I felt terrible! It was my fault that the luckless pigeon was destined to become dinner instead of winging its way to freedom. So much for my good intentions!

That evening, by the flickering light of our homemade candle, which barely lit the table, leaving the rest of the room in stygian darkness, all six of us were looking at the tiny pigeon on a plate in the middle of the table. Twelve hungry eyes were glued to its sorry remains. Without its feathers it looked even smaller. The poor thing looked rather lost and forlorn on the plate, because besides a few potatoes there was nothing else. I looked at it with remorse and vaguely wondered if pigeons had souls. Would it become a ghost and haunt me? Was its spirit fluttering around the cold dark room looking at me with reproachful eyes even now? For once I wasn't hungry. The scene was one of spooky gloom, and unforgettable in its wretchedness.

Mother finally cut the pigeon up with great care, and everybody got a tiny sliver. The lion's share, which didn't amount to much, went to my sixty-two-year-old grandfather. He had not been feeling well ever since some young Russian soldiers beat him within an inch of his life in broad daylight when he tried to protect his wife. That was when I took a really good look at him and noticed how poorly he looked. He was such a quiet man that I had not realized that there was something seriously wrong with him. Of course there was no medical help available after the beating he took. Our hospitals had been bombed in spite of the large red crosses painted on their roofs. Doctors were also very scarce, because so many had lost their lives during the war or were still working in prisoner of war camps.

About a week after this fine sliver of pigeon, I met an older girl I knew on my way home from school. She stopped me, and without preamble said: "Your grandfather is dead!" Deeply offended, I told her: "That's not true. Don't tell me terrible lies like that."

"You'll see," she said, and without further comment she went on her way. I didn't believe her, because grandparents and parents weren't supposed to die now that the war was over. It just couldn't be true. The thought that my grandfather could be dead wasn't one I wanted to contemplate, but the encounter with the girl left me with an uneasy feeling in the pit of my stomach.

When I got home, I found my grandmother sitting on our dilapidated couch dissolved in tears and wailing pitifully. Both my parents were very upset and looked like they had been crying too. So it was true after all. The girl hadn't lied to me. I stood stunned and found it difficult to comprehend what had happened. How could it be?

My parents sadly informed me that my grandfather was operated on that very morning in a makeshift hospital. I was told that it was an emergency operation to look for an intestinal blockage, because he had scarcely been able to eat since his encounter with the Russian soldiers. Drugs, anesthesia, and blood were in short supply, or not available at all. By the time my father was sent for to give blood, my grandfather was gone. He died of shock on the operating table. I didn't even want to think about my poor grandfather going through such an ordeal.

The last time I saw my grandfather was in the tiny bare room of a little house, which was part of the cemetery. He was laid out on a primitive slab on a sheet of paper and covered with paper. Since there was no electricity for refrigeration, he already showed signs of decomposition and the pungent odor of putrefaction was overpowering. It almost tore my heart out to see this fastidious man under such miserable conditions. But this was the best that could be done under the circumstances. I remember there was not even a coffin when he was buried. They just put him into the ground wrapped in paper, but at least he had a grave. Thousands who had been buried in mass graves had no graves of their own.

I mourned my grandfather's passing and often stopped at the cemetery on my way home from school to spend time at his grave talking to him. I never realized how much I loved him and how much I would miss him. Sadly I remembered the happy times we spent together drawing pretty pictures when I was very young. Grandfather opened my eyes to the beauty of color and form and the inner satisfaction derived from creativity of any kind. I learned to see in an entirely different way, which enabled me to perceive beauty even in ugliness. This kind and gentle man with beautiful white hair, which I always tried to braid while he patiently endured, was no more. Yet in a way he lived on for me, because his influence enriched my life and made it much more rewarding. I still think of him often and always remember him with love and gratitude!

*   *   *

Chapter 22

The Ice Palace

Plauen, January 1947

It was a year and a half since the end of the war, but once again Christmas passed unnoticed this very cold and snowy winter. New Year's Eve slipped by the same way. The coming year only promised more of the same: no food, no water, no electricity, no heat, and no decent shelter. We had absolutely nothing to look forward to. All we had was the same Russian occupation and Communist oppression without any hope of change. Surviving near starvation and the freezing cold in our bomb-wrecked house absorbed all our attention and energy. I was so hungry that I was constantly hallucinating about food all day and most of the night too.

The mountains of rubble in our devastated city were now mercifully covered with a blanket of snow and ice. The bent girders were festooned with long icicles, which glistened brightly on sunny days. Icicles in the empty windows of the standing facades looked like long teeth in gaping mouths, while the smoke-blackened ruins made a stark contrast to the almost obscene whiteness of the snow. When it snowed, the ruins appeared through a white veil like specters in a surreal landscape, hiding their loathsome ugliness and the terrible memories they evoked. The snow and ice had turned the ravaged city into an abstract dreamscape, which presented a macabre kind of beauty. The abysmal ugliness of the destruction was transformed as if by magic into a strange world of frosty, silent wonder, where the all-pervasive odor of charred debris heightened the impression of its alien character.

The badly damaged roof of our house, which I called our "Ice Palace," allowed water to run down two stories to settle on our bedroom walls in thick sheets of ice. Gusts of wind blew ice and snow through the empty window openings, whining and wailing through the house. Sometimes it sounded like the plaintive cries of lost souls. At times I thought I could see them within the swirling snow, their insubstantial, shadowy forms invading our stairwell with the wind, leaving more ice and snow in their wake. But I wasn't afraid; their distress in the twilight of their existence was to be pitied, not feared. I just wished that they wouldn't bring so much snow into our house.

The ice-and-snow-crusted stairs and landings had to be continuously scraped and covered with ashes. But since coal and firewood were very scarce, these resources had to be used very sparingly, so the stove was only in use when Mother was cooking our scanty meals. The rest of the time it was so cold in our apartment that we could always see our breath, which at least proved that we were still alive.

Getting around on the slick, ice-covered streets, which never saw a plow, was an exercise in agility. That's where our thin bodies, which didn't have an ounce of fat, were of great advantage, because it helped us to manage our errands without breaking our necks.

Once, against my mother's wishes, I tried to ice-skate to school on a pair of skates someone had given us. Stubborn as usual, I insisted on trying them out. It was a complete disaster, because there wasn't a smooth surface anywhere. It wasn't very good for my only pair of shoes either, because the skates screwed onto the shoes, and tended to rip off the soles. They certainly did a number on my shoes. Heels and soles were hanging by a few shreds. Mother was beside herself when she saw the state of my shoes.

"Didn't I tell you not to use those skates?" Not for the first time I heard, "Can't you ever listen?" Look at your shoes now! You better hope that they can be fixed, because I don't know where to get you another pair!"

When the shoemaker saw the sorry remains of my shoes, he shook his head at my folly but promised to do his best to repair the damage. He certainly had to use his most powerful magic to stitch the soles back onto the shoes, because there was no rubber or leather available for new soles. I'm still surprised my mother didn't kill me after this little episode! Not surprisingly, the ice skates disappeared after that, never to be seen again. Those shoes were deposited every night next to the stove in the hope that they would dry out, but of course they never did. Every morning my wet shoes were lined with fresh newspaper, which was worn to mushy shreds by evening. At least those Communist propaganda "newspapers" were good for something besides toilet paper.

One day we heard that the slaughterhouse not far from our house was scheduled to receive some beef. Not that I knew exactly what that was, or what it tasted like. My mother acted immediately by sending me there with a milk can to see if we could at least get some beef broth, because she knew that the chances of seeing any of the meat or bones were slim to nonexistent. It was no use speculating where the meat would go or who would get it. So off I went, full of hope and expectations, happily swinging my milk can. Ever-hungry, beef broth sounded good to me.

When I arrived, there was already a long line of people waiting with all kinds of receptacles. I joined the line snaking along several blocks of smoke-blackened ruins, where we had to wait for hours in the subzero cold until they were ready to distribute some broth. Most of those standing in line didn't have warm clothing and were a sorry sight. They were bundled up in whatever rags they had. Not that I looked much better. I was wearing a coat my mother had made for me from an old army blanket, which unfortunately was getting too small. An old wool scarf wrapped around my head completed my cold-weather outfit.

Like the body of a snake, the line was in constant, undulating motion as we stamped our feet and blew on our hands to prevent them from getting frostbite. White vapor issuing from all these mouths made it appear like a herd of strange, mangy animals had taken over and fogged up the street. There was very little talk or complaining, even though it was a long wait in the freezing cold. Everybody kept their mouths shut, not only to conserve as much body heat as possible, but also to avoid being denounced to the authorities for an innocently uttered remark. You never knew who was listening. It was not a cheerful assembly.

It was already getting dark and it started to snow again when they finally started to ladle out the broth. Everyone was looking for some fat "eyes," the round globs of fat normally swimming around on top of broth, but there were none. Some people remarked sarcastically that there were more eyes looking into the broth than there were looking out.

Somebody in front of me grumbled: "What did you expect? Real beef broth? First our liberators killed half of us with bombs, and now the Communists are finishing the job by starving the rest of us to death." This sentiment was expressed by a foolhardy soul who was unable to contain her frustration and anger, consequences be damned.

Others walked away silently with stony, resigned expressions on their faces, while still others were disgusted and angry.

I could hear some mumbles: "This is what we had to wait hours in the freezing cold for? What kind of shit is this? They call that beef broth? Looks like water to me." And there were other, less polite, remarks.

But everyone was anxious to get out of the cold and hurry away with the thin broth to whatever makeshift shelter they had. That included me! What I had in my milk can after so many hours of waiting in line in the freezing cold was better than nothing, and at least it was hot. Frozen to the bone but grateful, careful not to spill a drop of the precious liquid, I took my share home to our "Ice Palace." Mother was of course also looking for some fat eyes, but she couldn't find any either, no matter how hard she looked. That watered-down broth and a slice of bread was our dinner that night, and we were grateful to have that.

We muddled along as best we could that winter, trying to stay alive with very little food. I didn't know what was worse, starving to death or freezing to death. From what I heard, to die from starvation was miserable and slow. Freezing to death, which was not uncommon in our wrecked city, was quicker and seemed preferable. But my parents did their very best to have us avoid both, and valiantly struggled to keep the wolf away from our door.

I learned Russian in school with limited success since I didn't try very hard, while I made good progress with my secret English lessons. At least it kept me busy and my thoughts away from food, because just thinking about something to eat caused my stomach to growl and complain.

I had made one friend since our move back to Plauen. Magda was in my class and we felt the same about most things, like having to learn Russian. She and her mother lived in a ruin around the corner from us, so we went to school together, slipping and sliding on the ice, which was fun, but not too good for our only pairs of shoes. Luckily the soles didn't fall off our shoes with this rather enjoyable activity, so we didn't feel too guilty about it.

Magda's father died in Stalingrad and since they were refugees from East Prussia, they had no family or friends to help them. They had lost everything people hold dear and were all alone among strangers in an unfamiliar city. Magda never talked about the circumstances of their flight, or how they came to Plauen. Everybody kept their tales of misery to themselves.

Her mother was a "rubble woman" who supported herself and Magda by cleaning up the ruins and digging out dead bodies. This was terrible work for a woman at any time, but much worse in the midst of winter, when all the debris was frozen solid. Next to nothing to eat and insufficient warm clothing made the job even more difficult, but people did what they had to in order to survive. Both mother and daughter were extremely thin, if not skeletal. Magda, who might have been called pretty in normal times, looked very delicate and unhealthy. Her skin, stretched tight over her cheekbones, was tinged with a waxy, grayish color. They were in really bad straits and I often felt very sorry for my friend. I was so lucky to have my parents, cousins, aunts, and grandparents nearby.

One thing I learned really well was to keep my mouth shut and to be very careful not to say anything that would get us in trouble. I didn't even trust my friend Magda enough to tell her about my English lessons. Any carelessly uttered word could land you in more trouble than you could imagine. There were enough whispered stories about people disappearing overnight, never to be seen or heard from again. Friends of my grandparents who lived in another ruin around the block disappeared like that. We heard that they had received a small package from their daughter in West Germany, who had used a West German newspaper to cushion its contents. Someone visiting them had seen the newspaper and denounced them to the authorities. We were not allowed to receive any Western reading material. That was another very dangerous no-no. Our Communist government in its "caring wisdom" didn't want us tainted by the terrible corruption and lies of the West. They were protecting us! According to what we were told, we should be grateful to live in the DDR, because unlike us, people in the West were starving to death.

The news of my grandparents' friends' sudden disappearance and other stories like it were enough to silence even a defiant blabbermouth like me. So this extremely harsh winter, together with our Communist government and the Russian occupation, froze us into a silent submission of sorts. What else could we do? Our mental landscape mirrored the bleakness and hopelessness of our reality. It too was frozen, like our surroundings.

* * *

Chapter 23

The Mystery of the "Eels"

Plauen, February 1947

As if we weren't miserable enough, this unforgettable winter was bitter cold and there was no end to the ice and snow that nature bestowed on us. Life became so difficult that I was almost glad that my grandfather was gone, and that he was now safe in God's hands. Living at bare subsistence level in what was left of our bomb-wrecked "Ice Palace" was a daily challenge, which required all the resilience and stamina of youth.

But we were glad to have shelter, such as it was. Many people lived with the rats in basements under the ruins of what had been their homes, so we were comparatively well off. At least we were above ground. Only God knows how many people did not manage to survive. Hard as it was, my parents did their utmost to ensure our survival, often taking chances that could have cost them their lives.

Even though the back wall of the house was rebuilt, everything in our house was makeshift, including the windows and doors in our rooms on the second floor. Most of the doors in the building were ruined, but we used the least damaged doors we could find, and replaced any missing wood paneling with the remnants of other broken doors. The French style front doors, which missed all their paneling and glass, were artistically held together with a rusty old chain my father found in the rubble. Making do with sparse materials and lots of ingenuity had become a way of life. But all our creativity couldn't solve the problem of the severely damaged roof. There simply was no material to repair it with. It leaked so badly that water ran down two stories to settle on the bare brick walls of our bedroom in sheets of ice, which were getting thicker by the day. Our bedroom door was so iced over every morning that my father had to use an ax to hack off the ice so that we could get out. This had one big advantage—if we couldn't get out, nobody could get in at night either.

Drunken Russian soldiers looking for vodka and women often prowled our pitch-dark house during the night and things would have gone very badly for us had we been discovered. Rape would have been the least of it. We would have been lucky to escape with our lives. So we cowered in the dark, holding our breath, hoping to stay undetected. Hollering and yelling what sounded like curses, the Russians stumbled around the dark stairway. When they found our door, they rattled and pounded on it, accompanied by more expletives. But the ice and some boards propped against it held fast. They usually left when it dawned on their alcohol-fogged brains that there was nothing to be had in this wreck of a house. It was nothing short of miraculous that they didn't break their necks on those dark, icy stairs, or fall down the open shaft. It would have been a big problem for us to explain dead Russian soldiers in our house. The Russian authorities might have assumed that we had killed them, and the consequences would have been catastrophic. Our liberators had given us a curfew, but it was really they who should have had a curfew, if only to keep them from killing themselves in one of the ruins.

Going to our hole-in-the-ground bathroom in the basement at night was another scary part of life. Despite all our resourcefulness, we couldn't do anything to improve our bathroom situation. Where each floor's toilets had been there now was nothing but a deep, open shaft within the rebuilt wall, with a black hole yawning at its bottom. A flimsy, wobbly railing on the landing was all that prevented you from hurtling down into the black pit we used for a toilet. One misstep and you could wind up with a broken neck, which wasn't a very pleasant thought. So I always stayed as far away from the railing as possible.

If on occasion it was absolutely necessary for me to use the toilet after dark, it was a harrowing trip down iced-over stairs. The feeble glow of my flickering cup candle threw ghostly moving shadows on the walls, where they loomed large and menacing. I would see spooky apparitions everywhere, reaching for me with grasping fingers, trying to pull me into their frightening darkness. Fearful of the unknown horrors that lay in wait for me in the dark, my visits to the pit at night were as few and as short as possible. What made it even worse were the stories my cousin

Inge told me. According to her, that hole was the lair of the devil and all kinds of frightful monsters waiting to pull me into their smelly depths. Nobody would ever see me again, she said, for I would be with all those unimaginable horrors for all eternity, provided they didn't eat me first. I did have some doubts about that, but since she was older, she knew everything! She wouldn't lie to me! Looking into that dark pit, I could very well believe it. Even though I didn't see any devils or even an ugly monster, the opening wasn't only smelly, it looked incredibly disgusting too. I couldn't imagine why any self-respecting devil would want to live there. But then, who knew what monsters liked? It was definitely better to be safe than sorry, and avoid that scary place at night.

Going to bed at night in our ice chamber wasn't something to look forward to either, because the sheets were always icy and damp. It took quite a while for a heated brick wrapped in a towel, plus our body heat, to warm them enough for us to fully stretch out. All four of us slept in our only bed, which kept us from freezing to death. Thank God Mother had managed to save two of our feather beds, but unfortunately they weren't large enough to cover all four of us, so old blankets had to fill in the gaps.

Getting dressed in the morning was also a major production. First you tented the feather bed, then reached out to pull the clothes in piece by piece to get dressed within the warmth of its shelter. After that was accomplished, you had to brave our freezing-cold room. The kitchen/living room wasn't any better, for the rusty old iron stove we had rescued from the debris was only used to cook what little food we had. It was never used for heat, because coal and wood were almost impossible to find. Since everyone in town was looking for firewood, miles and miles of rubble had been picked clean of every stick of wood, and the woods surrounding the city looked like someone had gone over them with a vacuum cleaner. The situation was so critical that hardly a day went by when we didn't hear of people who had frozen to death during the night.

Then one night when we were sitting in our freezing kitchen by the feeble glow of our homemade candle, I heard my parents discussing something in hushed tones. Very unusual! What was going on? I pricked my ears; my antennae were on high alert. I swiveled them in all directions, but no matter how hard I tried, all I could pick up was something about eels. An eel? I knew that an eel was some sort of slippery, snakelike fish. FOOD! Something to eat!

Smoked eel was considered a delicacy in Germany, but of course I had never tasted one. I had heard about it, though, just as I had heard about many other things, like mayonnaise, whipped cream, bananas, and real coffee. The adults talked about these things with longing. Could they have gotten hold of an eel on the black market? Eel did not appear all that appetizing to me, but since I was always hungry, I was ready to try anything. I pictured a very long eel, crispy brown and about the length of our table, big enough to feed all five of us. My mouth watered in anticipation. I could already smell it!

When we were sent to bed, I went gladly for once without giving any of my usual arguments. Curled up under the feather bed, I was thinking happy thoughts of a fine eel dinner the next day! Of course I was also wondering what the eels had to do with my parents' mysterious behavior. Why wouldn't they tell us about such a lucky find? I finally decided that maybe it was supposed to be a surprise! Looking forward to a fine eel dinner the next day, I went to sleep with a smile on my face.

The following morning I got up with great expectations. Since I had never seen an eel, I couldn't wait to get a look at one. When I saw nothing even remotely resembling an eel, or what I thought it would look like, my curiosity was out of bounds and I started to ask questions.

"Where is the eel you were talking about last night? Can I see it? I've never seen one. Are we going to eat it today?"

"You weren't supposed to be listening," my mother said, heaving an exasperated sigh. "Your ears are way too big for the rest of you. Can't we keep anything a secret around here?" But then she relented and told me what I wanted to know, and she took me to the basement, where I finally got to see the eels.

The story Mother told me, and what she showed me, certainly was a surprise, but not the kind I expected! In spite of the curfew, my parents and a couple of relatives decided to take a chance and venture outside. This was very dangerous, because if they were caught by a Russian patrol, they could be shot on sight. In an effort to minimize the chance of getting caught, they left in the darkest hour of the night. Hugging the darker areas of the street, they pulled sleds up the hill to the unused railroad tracks. The Russians had already dismantled and transported part of them to Russia, like they did with a lot of other things—toilets for instance, not to mention people.

Once they got there undetected, my parents and our relatives immediately started to dig out the wooden railroad ties from under the tracks. How they managed to get them out of the frozen ground I'll never know, but desperation makes us do the most impossible things, and these were desperate times. Unfortunately they were surprised in their dangerous endeavor by a German Communist guard, and they found themselves in an extremely sticky situation! I am sure they already saw themselves in some gulag in Siberia, or in front of a firing squad. Luckily they were able to talk their way out of their predicament by offering to dig out a few railroad ties for the guard. Even the Communists were freezing! After several hours of backbreaking work in the freezing cold, they finally came away with six oily wooden railroad ties, three for us and three for our relatives. They brought the incriminating evidence home without further incident and immediately stashed them in the darkest corner of our basement, ensuring that we wouldn't freeze to death like so many others.

After hearing the tale of my parents' dangerous activity during the night, I stared at the three smelly chunks of dark brown wood resting in a corner of the cellar with mixed emotions. By the dim light of a cup candle, I looked at what Mother called "eels" with astonishment and more than a little confusion. They definitely weren't what I had expected. My eavesdropping had certainly led me astray this time. On the other hand, it was a good thing that my trusty antennae couldn't pick up on all of my parents' whispered conversation the night before, because, aware of the risk it would involve, I wouldn't have slept a wink. I realized with a jolt that the night's action might have been a costly one for all of us, had our guardian angels not been with us once again.

So these hunks of wood were the mysterious eels! They were certainly nothing that could be eaten, but they cooked what little food we had, and kept the kitchen warm at least part of the time that winter. My parents called them eels because these railroad ties were dark and oily, like smoked eels. It was also a code word, so nobody would know what was really hiding in our basement. Therefore they were always referred to as "eels." Of course I was warned not to tell anyone about our secret in the cellar, which wasn't really necessary, because the past had already taught me when to clam up.

I was rather disappointed that my vision of food had come to nothing, but having something burning in the stove was just as good, and probably even better. Those unforgettable, wonderful eels helped us survive that terrible winter. Yes, eels in the stove were definitely better than eels on the table for one night!

* * *

Chapter 24

Rays of Hope

Plauen, March–April 1947

We managed to get through February thanks to the eels we had stashed away in the basement, where they kept our resident rats company. Split into smaller, more manageable pieces, they cooked our meager food and provided us with just enough heat to keep us from freezing to death that winter.

One day my usually fearless mother came running up from the cellar screaming: "Help! A huge rat jumped me and tried to bite me! Somebody come and kill it!" She had gone there to get a piece of wood when she was attacked. The rats had become very large and aggressive toward humans after two years of feeding on the corpses buried under the ruins. We heard stories of people being attacked in the streets in broad daylight, so we took precautions by taking a big club with us whenever we had to go into the basement. No rat, no matter how big and aggressive, was going to take a bite out of us and get away with it! Not after all we had been through.

March proved to be a very eventful month. My maternal grandparents, who had spent the winter in a rented room on the outskirts of town, were allowed to leave our "workers' paradise" and emigrate to the United States. Their deliverance from our dreary existence was an event of monumental joy for all of us. My uncles in the United States made use of their status as veterans to enlist the help of their congressman in order to bring their parents to the United States. They were allowed to leave because our Communist government was happy to get rid of people who were over sixty-five. The state considered them a burden and had no further use for them. As far as they were concerned, the West could take care of the old people. The authorities only wanted the productive young people, whose developing minds could be filled with Communist ideology.

So everything went very quickly. Since my grandparents lost most of their possessions in the bombings, there wasn't much to pack. They left with our prayers and good wishes for a safe trip and a better life in the United States. As happy as we were for my grandparents, we also knew that we would miss them terribly. They had been pillars of strength for all of us during those terrible war years. The last news we had from them before they arrived in the United States came from Berlin. We were informed that what little luggage they had was stolen, along with everything of sentimental value they had taken with them. But they arrived in the United States safely to a joyous reunion with their sons, daughters-in-law, and the grandchildren they had never seen.

Later that month we received more good news. The Communist government finally allowed us to receive packages from abroad. So we waited with bated breath for the first packages from our American relatives to arrive. We knew that they would do everything possible to help us. Since my grandparents were now in the United States, they could give my uncles firsthand information about our situation and what we needed most.

When we were finally notified that two packages were waiting for us at a post office on the other side of town, we were delirious with joy, and we went there full of excitement and anticipation. On arrival, we saw that the packages had already been opened and completely taken apart. Everything was laid out on the counter. Every item was inspected to make sure that nothing was missing, but everything noted on the invoice was there. The postal employees looked at these things with longing, but to their credit nothing was stolen. I think they were as curious and anxious as we were to see what the packages contained.

Oh God! All those cans of food, cocoa, coffee, chocolate, and cigarettes were things my parents hadn't seen in years. Of course for Margit and me much of what was in the packages were things we had heard about but had never seen, and we were beside ourselves with excitement and curiosity. We couldn't wait for the postal employees to finish their inspection, so we could bring all those wonders home.

We were happy as can be and felt like we were dreaming when we could finally take our treasures home. We spread them out on the kitchen table to admire each and every one of the items separately. It was like all the Christmases we had missed rolled into one. We couldn't stop looking and marveling at all those wonderful things. There was flour, sugar, tea, and cans of something called spam. Opening one of the interesting-looking cans, we found it to contain a pinkish meat. Mother said that it was ham—whatever that was. I had a lot to learn about different kinds of food, especially when it came to meat.

This was also the first time in four or five years that my mother had a cup of coffee! For her it was pure happiness, because she loved coffee. Mother was in seventh heaven. Coffee! I couldn't figure out what all the fuss was about. What was so special about coffee? I was more interested in the chocolate, but what I liked best was the thick and sweet condensed milk. I liked it so much that Mother had to hide it from me, otherwise there wouldn't have been any left for anybody else. We shared some of the things with our relatives and the rest was carefully rationed. Every time a package arrived, the day was celebrated like a holiday.

God bless my uncles in the United States who kept us supplied throughout the year. I never forgot their generosity, which brought such joy and hope to an otherwise dreary existence. It alleviated the food shortage for us and we now could barter for other desperately needed items, like shoes. Since nobody in our family smoked, my mother made good use of the cigarettes on the black market. American cigarettes in particular were of high value after the war. So were the clothes, since many people had lost most of their clothing along with all their other possessions. Everything from socks and underwear to outerwear and shoes was sought after. Even essentials like soap, toothbrushes, and toothpaste were impossible to come by and were extremely valuable bartering items.

I remember Mother altering an American dress for a young woman who had a Russian boyfriend. These kinds of women were frowned upon and ostracized, of course, but they were widowed and did what was necessary to keep themselves and their children alive. Thanks to the woman's Russian boyfriend, Mother received some sausages in payment for the dress. Mother prepared the sausages with care, and we savored every bite with great appreciation.

Then one day, to our great surprise, a poorly translated letter arrived from the United States. It was from a lawyer in Baltimore informing us that my great-aunt Marie Gross, who had given me the golden heart necklace, had passed away and left all her earthly goods to her relatives in Germany. As I did so often, I fingered my necklace and its golden heart, which was by now as badly dented as my psyche, and I thought about the long-ago day when my mother fastened it around my neck. Little did I know then that the little heart would share my life for years to come. I had to admit that chewing on the heart when I was hungry or afraid hadn't improved its looks, but I loved it just the same.

I felt saddened by my great-aunt's death, because I knew that now I would never be able thank her. I thought of her often and wondered what she looked like, because I had never seen a photo of her. Was she dark-haired and dark-eyed like me? In my imagination I saw her as very beautiful, as only a woman with such a generous heart could be. I was deeply touched that this wonderful woman in a faraway land had remembered us in her will. Her bequest would have been heaven-sent, but receiving an inheritance from the capitalist United States in Communist East Germany was impossible at the time, and nothing more came of it. Months later we received a postcard from her American lawyer, who was enjoying himself in Paris. I felt as if he was laughing at us and rubbing salt into our wounds.

The end of March brought warmer temperatures. The melting snow and ice enveloped the city in vaporous mists hovering over the ruins and fields of rubble. Sometimes the breeze gave life to the mist, which morphed into ghostlike apparitions writhing through the ruins like the lost souls of our city. The shape-shifting forms moved in a languid dance, licking at melting icicles here, caressing a blackened chimney there, and dissolving, only to reform in another spot. The cloying wet mist invaded our stairwell through the empty window openings, probing it, as if looking for victims to absorb into its misty gloom. It permeated everything it touched with its malodorous wetness as it crept through the house, drifting into every nook and cranny. My home felt and looked spookier than ever, the haunt of ghosts and other figments of my imagination.

When the March winds started to blow, the thick fog gave way under their onslaught. Bits and pieces of the fog tried to hang on, clinging to the ruins to no avail. It disappeared like last night's dreams and was replaced by welcome sunshine and clear blue skies. The dark gloomy days, which made us feel even more hopeless and depressed, were finally gone.

Our "Ice Palace" was now in a meltdown phase. Water was running down our walls and stairs, and large chunks of ice slid off the roof, shattering on the ground into millions of glittering shards. The icicles dripped water relentlessly, and they were soon gone too. The ice on our bedroom walls melted, but it left them covered with a black, velvety fungus. It looked like expensive flocked wallpaper and it made some interesting patterns as it grew and spread, creating ever-new, interesting shapes and forms. Fungus bloomed all over our "Ice Palace" in all its many wet places with an unusual dramatic effect.

We tried to scrape the fungus off our bedroom walls, but it kept coming back. The conditions for it to flourish with nothing to impede its growth were perfect, because we had no heat. The walls were just too wet and cold for them to dry out. Summer and warmer weather couldn't come soon enough for us. We had no choice but to live with the fungus until then. Since it didn't attack us or try to bite us like the rats, we simply ignored it.

The "Ice Palace" was gone, and in its place was a very dilapidated, waterlogged house, where black fungus bloomed in profusion. Everything was a soggy mess and smelled awful. As the walls slowly dried and the fungus finally died an ignominious death, it left interesting gray patterns on the walls as a reminder of the thriving existence it flaunted not long ago. I can't say that anybody regretted its demise.

The sun now had a warmth which it had lacked during the long winter months. I still remember sitting in a patch of sunlight coming through the window one day and how much I reveled in it and enjoyed its all-but-forgotten warmth. A feeling of well being spread through me, reminding me that happiness could still be found in life's small things. The sun shedding its glorious warmth over me after a terrible winter when I never felt warm was one of them. It is often the inconsequential things that we remember a lifetime later.

But the warmer days deprived the ruins of their covering of snow, so they looked bleaker and more depressing than ever. Their loathsome appearance was fully exposed and hard to ignore. Awareness of the ugly reality of our world returned with full clarity, but we took it in stride like everything else. It was what it was, and nothing could change that.

Reeducation of the population was now in full swing. With some like us it was a wasted effort. We were incorrigible gulag candidates! We were already suspected of harboring treasonous thoughts because we received mail and packages from the capitalist United States. So we had to watch our step if we didn't want to disappear overnight. We learned very quickly what was necessary to survive the ever-present threat. That included forcing myself to show more enthusiasm in Russian class. I knew what was at stake, so I managed to put on my very best act, and stopped being a nuisance. I worked a bit harder at memorizing the vocabulary and practicing reading and writing the strange Russian alphabet. To my teacher's delight, I became a model student in Russian class!

Thanks to our relatives in the United States we had more to eat, and with more food, life didn't seem quite as menacing as before. We cautiously dared to hope for better days ahead. Spring couldn't be far away and with it would come our return to our little country cottage and the garden. We could once again make believe that our world was whole and the ravaged city and the terrible winter would seem like a bad dream. The woods and the flower-laden meadows would again gladden our lives and allow us to dream of the glorious warm summer days to come.

We went to the garden cottage on weekends as soon as the weather permitted so we could get things ready for the coming season, for there was always a lot to do. It seemed strange, though, not to find my grandparents there. They were usually the first ones to arrive. We thought of them often and were always very happy whenever one of their letters arrived with news about their lives in the United States. All their letters were happy and upbeat; nevertheless we surmised that at their age it couldn't be easy for them to be transplanted into a foreign country with a different language and different customs. But at least we knew that they were safe and well taken care of, and we didn't have to worry about them.

April came and with it the second anniversary of Plauen's final days as a viable city. We tried not to think of that terrible night of April 10th, 1945. There was enough for us to worry about as it was!

* * *

Chapter 25

Vanished into the Night!

Plauen, May 1947

Sometime in May we had another big surprise. One evening a friend of my father's whom I had never seen before came for a visit. That in itself was unusual, because we very rarely had visitors. Since my father was back on rubble cleanup duty, I assumed that it was one of the men from his crew. Nosy as always, I tried to follow what seemed to be a weighty discussion, but I couldn't make heads or tails of it. Something was going on, but what? My mind was spinning with all the possibilities.

When I woke up the next morning my father was gone! But where to? I just couldn't figure it out, because my mother didn't seem particularly perturbed. Nervous, yes! Upset, no! So it couldn't be that the secret police came to take him during the night. That would have caused a big commotion and I'm sure I would have woken up. I just couldn't figure it out. My mother would only give me very evasive answers when I pressed and pestered her about my father's strange disappearance. That was very curious too! What was she hiding? I was very bewildered by the whole thing. It was frightening to suddenly be without a father again. My fertile imagination ran away with me, picturing all kinds of fantastic scenarios, none of which seemed to fit. Why would my father disappear overnight without even saying good-bye? Why would my father do that? Mother obviously knew something she wasn't telling us. But what?

A few days later, my mother broke her silence and told me in the strictest confidence that my father fled to West Germany, where the Americans were! I was shocked and elated at the same time. I knew that this was a very dangerous undertaking and that many people lost their lives trying to get across the border, but according to a message he sent through my mother's friend in the West, he made it safely. Thank God! My father was safe!

My mother carefully instructed me not to tell a single soul about it. "Nobody must know!"

"Not even Inge?" I asked.

"Not even Inge, not your aunts, not anybody," she replied.

That was big news indeed. None of my imagined scenarios could equal that. I was shocked and elated at the same time. West Germany! Occupied by the Americans, it was a Germany where people could feel free. Even though we were told by our government that, unlike us, people in the West were starving to death, it was astonishing to hear how many people risked their lives to go to a miserable place like that. Somebody wasn't telling the truth. Aware that Mother had trusted me with dangerous information, I was very careful to avoid betraying our secret by a slip of the tongue. I became even more closemouthed than I already was. From then on Mother kept me in her confidence, but she only told me what she thought I needed to know to keep me mindful of our dangerous situation. All correspondence was done in coded messages through my mother's friend in the West. That way nothing could be traced to my father and endanger us if the Communist authorities found out. That's also how we learned that he had found work at a chemical factory in Southern Bavaria.

My mother eventually told me why my father left so precipitously. The foreman of his work crew had informed him in confidence that his name was on a list of men to be shipped to a uranium mine. He had moved my father's name to the bottom of the list of chosen unfortunates to give him time to get away. I also found out that another friend gave my father instructions on where to cross the border, how to get asylum in the West, and where to find work. It was amazing to see how people helped each other in these tough times and how well this underground network functioned. It was good to have friends in times like those.

It didn't take long before the authorities started asking questions as to my father's whereabouts. My sister Margit and I had strict instructions to answer all questions with: "He ran away with another woman!" So I lied with a very sad face every time the secret police asked me questions. When they asked me, "Who is the woman he ran away with?" I just shrugged my shoulders and said, "I don't know." That's all they got out of me, no matter how they phrased their questions. The same story was told to our relatives and friends. The truth was too dangerous not only for us, but also for them. I'm sure that some of them suspected the truth, for those who knew my father would have known that the story of his infidelity couldn't be true. It would have been completely out of character for my father.

For the next few weeks and months the secret police visited us periodically, but they were unable to get any information out of us. We pleaded ignorance with straight faces. Necessity and fear of reprisals made us accomplished liars, and we played the betrayed, forsaken family to perfection. It was always quite scary when they came, looking very stern and official, to question us and to snoop around our one-room apartment. They were searching for anything that would give them information about my father. We always heaved a great sigh of relief when they were gone without finding anything that could be used against us.

Mother told me that we too would go to the West to join our father when the time was right. Among many other things, that depended on how long it would take Father to get settled and make his preparations for our arrival, not to mention how long we would be under heightened surveillance.

In preparation for our flight later that year, Mother got busy packing some of our belongings in two-pound packages and sending them to her friend in the West, who forwarded them to my father in Bavaria. Two pounds was the maximum weight we were allowed to send. She even managed to send the few remaining pieces of her good china, one plate at a time. This went on all summer and into the fall. I don't remember how many packages were sent, but there were a lot of them. To avoid detection, Mother used different post offices for her mailings. Every time the secret police came to check on us, there was a mad scramble to hide the packages and all evidence connected to them. Luckily there were many good hiding places in our bomb-wrecked building.

For the first time in two years, we had a few hours of electricity every day, from 5 p.m. to 8 p.m. It was great not to have to burn our sooty beeswax candles at night. Now we could listen to our radio, which we kept hidden under some old blankets. We usually listened to music, which we hadn't heard for a long time. The pleasure of hearing the familiar tunes of Strauss and Lehár's operettas lifted our spirits and temporarily freed us from our worries.

When summer came we spent a lot of time in our garden cottage as usual, but it seemed strange without my grandparents and without my father. Our family was getting smaller. Things were very boring in the garden without them. Even my cousin Inge, my companion in mischief, wasn't around anymore. She and her mother had moved in with relatives in another small town. I sure missed Inge! Between the two us, we never ran out of interesting things to do, which gave our parents more stress than they already had. To get me off her back, Mother allowed me to go to one of Plauen's swimming pools on a rusty old bike that somebody had given us. The bike was a grown man's bike with a crossbar, and my legs were too short to sit on the saddle and reach the pedals. So I learned to ride it by holding the bike on an angle and sticking one leg under the bar to reach the pedal on the opposite side. It worked out all right, even though I must have been a strange sight. I really became quite good at it and it was certainly better than walking.

The swimming pool, where I met a lot of my classmates, was on the outskirts of the city and therefore less damaged by the bombings. It was none too clean, which didn't bother us in the least. No chlorination sullied its murky-green invisible depths, which was excellent for playing hide-and-seek in the water. If you could hold your breath under water long enough, nobody could find you, and your chances of winning were greatly enhanced. So I practiced holding my breath, because I didn't like losing.

I spent many hours in the water in my determination to teach myself how to swim. When after untold tries I finally succeeded in swimming across the narrow end of the pool, I was proud of my accomplishment, and thought it time well spent. The pool was always full of children of all ages and the lifeguard was usually the only adult present. Since there was never any fighting, bullying, or accidents that I can remember, the lifeguard didn't really have much to do. Everybody got along just fine and a good time was had by all!

The pool also had a very interesting fenced-off section for nude sunbathing. It was for adults, who made use of it after work and on weekends. We took great delight in looking through holes in the fence, giggling and laughing at the naked people relaxing there. People really looked funny without their clothes. Some of the adults must have complained, because our fun ended when they filled in the holes. That really was a shame!

Toward evening, after a fun day at the pool, I pedaled through the woods back to the garden. I biked as fast as I could to avoid the drunken Russian soldiers who used the woods as their hangout. This wasn't all that difficult because they were always very noisy. They were so busy yelling and singing that they probably paid scant attention to anything going on around them. Only to hear them thrashing around the bushes, whooping and hollering, was enough to give my bike wings. Of course I never told my mother about that. If I had, she wouldn't have allowed me to go to the pool anymore.

I was reasonably happy that summer, mainly because I had become inured to Plauen's ruins. I saw it dispassionately and refused to allow my emotions to entangle me in their depressing reality. To perceive it with full comprehension would have been much too painful. The garden and the pool insulated me to some extent and gave me a partial sense of normalcy. My focus was on the garden, the woods, the pool, and my friends. But somewhere in the future was the adventure of our planned escape. It was exciting just to think about it, even though I knew that we could get killed in the process. I was uncertain as to how we would accomplish it, but I had faith in my mother's resourcefulness.

I felt that life was what it was, and I dealt with it as well as I could. I was often reminded of something my grandmother used to say: "To be human means to be a fighter." So I fought my past and present fears and didn't allow them any space in my life.

That summer was like a reawakening, as I realized fully that life went on, no matter its difficulties and vicissitudes. I took pleasure in the small things that nature gives us freely—things like blue skies, the sun warming my limbs, the wind giving voice to the trees, and even the rain, which washed the woods with fresh color and cleaned the air. They couldn't take that from us like they took everything else.

* * *

Chapter 26

A Summer Carnival—Communist Style

August 1947

A well-remembered event took place in late August when the Communist Party announced an afternoon of fun and games for Plauen's children. There would be carnival rides and sweets, culminating in a torchlight procession through Plauen and its outskirts. That sounded great! I was all excited and couldn't wait for the appointed day. Mother was less enthusiastic, but didn't try to talk me out of it.

When the day came, I left our garden with happy anticipation as I made my way through the woods to the place in Plauen where we were supposed to meet. A large group of children had already gathered there by the time I arrived. Two officious-looking men in suits were busy directing the children to form a line, which I was told to join. I didn't know any of the fifty or so boys and girls who patiently waited on the sidewalk for what was to come. The men, with pencils and pads in hand, busily went from one child to the other, asking their names, addresses, and ages. I vaguely wondered about the purpose of all these questions, but in the excitement of the day I didn't pursue this line of thought.

The men tried very hard to appear friendly, but I sensed that it wasn't their customary mode of behavior. Their faces looked like they were more used to frowns and their lips didn't seem to be in the habit of smiling. I thought them rather intimidating and I suppressed a giggle at the thought that their faces might crack under the strain of producing all those smiles.

I didn't pay much attention to a small ticket they gave to each of us, because I was more interested in what came next, which was the promise of a cookie. After they were done gathering their information, each child was rewarded with a small cookie. It wasn't at all what I imagined a cookie should taste like. It really wasn't very good, but it was the first cookie I had eaten in a very long time, so it was better than nothing. It was food, after all.

Then we were told that at the end of the afternoon, we would each be given a lantern with a candle inside for the torchlight procession, which would take place in early evening after the carnival closed. We were instructed to sing the children's songs we all knew once the procession was under way. I felt a little silly at this point. It made me feel like a sheep that had to be marched singing to its destination, which usually was the pasture or the slaughterhouse. I hoped it would be the former, where a lot of cookies and sweets might be waiting for us. But now that I was there, I had no choice but to go along. It was too late to leave without having to answer more questions.

After they were done giving all their instructions, the column of children paired in twos slowly began to move. Herded along by the men, we trooped past some of the smoke-blackened ruins until we came to the small fairground on the outer edge of Plauen.

When we arrived at the entrance, my excitement mounted by leaps and bounds. I could hear the music from the carousel calling me to come quickly and share in the delights it offered. I couldn't remember the last time I had seen or been on one. This was the first time in a long time that I felt like the child I still was.

Occasionally there had been a carousel years ago in a vacant lot near my grandparents' house, and I would wheedle dimes out of Mother so I could go there. I used to love riding in a swan or on a horse, which took me around the carousel's garishly decorated center to the sound of the ubiquitous organ. What I liked even better were the seats, which lifted off and whirled me high in the air, going around and around at a dizzying speed. It made me feel like I was flying like a bird while the world below spun by. It was always a letdown when the ride was finished and—unless you had another dime—you had to get off. Mother was never too generous with coins, so my small hoard was quickly used up and I was reduced to watching other children enjoying themselves.

With this memory of bygone days and past pleasures, I entered the carnival ground with great expectations. Aside from my group, there were many other children, who were already enjoying the different rides, happily laughing and screaming with joy. I watched as some of them were led around on ponies by the men, which really looked like fun and something I would have liked to try. But there also were many other children who were aimlessly wandering around, looking somewhat lost and bewildered. I was one of those children looking with longing at the rides, anxious to try any one of them. But you had to wait for one of the men to help you get onto one of the rides. For some reason, which I couldn't figure out, I didn't seem to be able to get any of the men to help me. It crossed my mind that maybe the ticket I had been given wasn't any good. Then I noticed that the men only seemed to be helping certain children, and I definitely wasn't one of them. I was ignored throughout. Wondering what the problem was, it occurred to me that maybe only children with Communist backgrounds were singled out to enjoy the rides. The promised cookies and sweets didn't materialize either, at least not for me. Were these small-minded men really callous enough to do something like this to children?

Feeling lonely, dejected, thoroughly disgusted, and disappointed, I decided to leave. Nobody stopped me or even noticed my quiet departure. It was a long walk back to the garden, and because it started to get dark, I decided to take a shortcut, walking on what I hoped were unused railroad tracks. I needed time to deal with my disappointment, so I took my time dawdling on the way. A lot of thoughts of what I had observed swirled through my head; I had a lot of thinking to do.

Deep in unpleasant thoughts, I almost missed seeing the children's torchlight procession across the meadows in the distance off to my right. The long line of children carrying lanterns looked very pretty in the gathering darkness. The orange, glowing orbs of their lampions seemed like a strange, alien animal with a glittering body bobbing along. The lights winked at me in a show of defiance, telling me about all the joys I missed. I could also hear the faint sound of their singing carried by a light breeze. Captured by its charm, I stopped and watched the glowing line meandering along until it disappeared among the trees. Only the children's songs drifting across the meadow remained until they too ceased, and I was all alone on the railroad tracks.

Darkness was descending fast now and I was in a rush to get to the safety of our cottage. When I finally came trudging into the garden after dark, Mother was so relieved to see me that she didn't even scold me for my tardiness. She immediately saw that something was wrong. She asked me how it was and did I have the fun I expected. I told her some of it, but left out my suspicions about the preferential treatment of certain children and what I thought of the men in suits.

I could hear the sympathy in Mother's voice as she said: "I'm sorry that it wasn't what you expected. I could have told you so, but I didn't want to spoil your day and burden you with my doubts. I hoped that I would be wrong."

Mother's soothing words made me feel much better. But once again I learned that life just wasn't fair! A little wiser, I decided not to let this experience ruin any more of my days. I tucked it into a corner of my mind as a reminder for the next time life's unfairness reared its ugly head.

So summer passed into fall without any major detrimental incidents. When school started in September, I kept up my act and I was still that good model student in Russian class and a teacher's delight. What a chore that was! My acting ability was stretched to the limit.

The secret police seemed to have given up on us. Their visits finally stopped, but I'm sure someone was keeping an eye on us, and that could have been anybody. It might be an acquaintance, someone we thought was a friend, or the people who moved into the dilapidated apartment on the ground floor. The most logical person was the single man the Communist government had moved into what had been our fungus-decorated bedroom, because they felt that one woman and two children didn't need it. One room, our kitchen, had to be sufficient for the three of us. So we lived and slept in the one room left to us. As far as I was concerned, the man was welcome to the "Fungus Room." Surviving a winter there was a rather daunting experience, and I didn't envy him in the least. Nevertheless we were very careful, especially of the new boarder in our former bedroom!

Since my grandfather's death the year before, my father's stepmother, with whom my mother was not on particularly good terms, lived alone in the one other livable room on our second floor. I couldn't quite understand what the problem was, because she was always nice to me. She even taught me how to do very intricate embroidery on her one remaining embroidery frame, which had miraculously survived the bombings. Adults were often very difficult to understand.

The packages from the United States, which now came regularly, improved our lives tremendously, and life became much more bearable. The news we received about Father in the West was also good, so there was no need to worry about him. We just had to be careful and bide our time until we could try to make our escape. Since we were already under a cloud of suspicion, it was very important not to arouse more of the same. Any hint of our plan to defect would have been disastrous. It was a very critical time for us, and we had to behave as normally as possible.

Our planned flight was always on my mind and I thought of it with great anticipation and a lot of apprehension. I often tried to imagine what the West would be like. What did it look like? Were its cities as devastated as Plauen? Was there really more to eat? I couldn't wait to find out.

* * *

Chapter 27

Escape to Freedom

December 25, 1947

The big day of our planned flight to freedom finally came in December of that year.

For many months my mother quietly laid plans for our escape to the West. Why she waited until the middle of winter for our escape I don't know, but she must have had good reasons. Maybe we were too closely watched until then. She traded cigarettes our American relatives had sent us for a ride close to the border. Everything had to be done in utmost secrecy, because the penalty for trying to flee East Germany was severe. She chose Christmas morning as "The Day" because she reasoned that maybe, just maybe, the border might not be as strictly guarded as usual. Small as my mother was, she had a will of steel and the courage to match. Even though she trusted me with some secrets, there were many things she kept to herself. All this must have been very hard for her. I can't imagine how she managed to keep everything under control without slipping up. But she did!

Me, my mother and sister, Margit

So it was Christmas morning at 3 a.m. when Mother, my little sister Margit, and I crept down the dark, icy stairs of our bomb-wrecked house out onto the snow-covered street. The car Mother had arranged for us was already waiting by the curb. I turned and saw my dear paternal grandmother standing there crying. There was one last hug and one last good-bye, which we knew would be our last. With our nervous excitement mounting, we quickly and silently piled into the car, and our journey began.

My last memory of Plauen was this drive through its desolate streets, where streetlights had long since become a thing of the past. Avoiding the large holes in the street, we drove past block after block of nothing but heaps of rubble and the grim facades of burned-out buildings. Often the only things still standing were chimneys reaching up into the night sky like admonishing fingers, as if to warn of the dire consequences of war. Black, empty window openings, icicles clinging to them like long sharp fangs, yawned like sated carnivores. Large rats scurried away at our approach. It was a nightmarish scene, especially for me with my vivid imagination. You couldn't even close your eyes and pretend, for there was the smell of decay that even the new snow couldn't hide.

This drive is forever burnt in my memory, because saying good-bye to my beloved city in ruins was much harder than leaving it as the beautiful city it had once been. It was not only the destroyed city we were leaving behind but also destroyed lives, misery, cold, hunger, and fear. It was as if we were leaving a deathly ill relative to his fate. I felt pain and sorrow not only for my dead city, but also for all the people I loved who we were leaving behind. For them the nightmare continued. There was a great deal of anxiety concerning our escape plan. Would we be able to cross the border safely? We knew that we would need all the help that God and our guardian angels could give us in our dangerous undertaking. Many people lost their lives in their attempt to reach the West, but Father and freedom beckoned like a beacon in the dark of night. I remember when he fled to the West six months earlier after a friend told him that he was to be sent to work in a uranium mine, which would have been an almost certain death sentence. Thoughts of past and present fears mixed with hope swirled through my mind on this drive through a fateful dark night.

By and by we put the city and its sad face behind us, and the nocturnal landscape of fields and woods drifted by. The trees, which stood like sentries along the road, were dark silhouettes in our headlights against the white snow. Their snow-laden branches swaying in a light breeze seemed to wave us on, and like ghosts, they were quickly swallowed by the darkness as we sped along. Finally the car stopped beside a field. We hurriedly said good-bye to our driver, who immediately disappeared in the direction from which we had come. It was still dark and freezing cold. Our only source of light was the snow, which was deeper here in the country than in the city.

We started to walk along the snow and ice-crusted road, and then across the fields. The harsh sound of sudden gusts of wind chasing ice pearls over the snow made us feel even colder as we shivered in our shabby clothes. Our faces stung as the wind pelted us with tiny ice particles, which attached themselves to our clothes and eyelashes. It wasn't easy for us children because in many places the snow was over our knees, and after breaking through the top layer of ice our feet sank deep into the snow, making our progress slow and difficult. When we flagged, Mother spurred us on with: "Come on, you can do it, you have to be brave. Soon we'll see your father!" So we struggled on as best we could. Our old, secondhand shoes, stuffed with newspaper, were quickly soaked, and our coats were soon covered with ice.

The morning, Christmas morning, began to gray, and our surroundings slowly gained color and form: black for the woods, white for the snow, gray for the cloudy sky and the windswept fields. Groaning with exertion, we worked our way up a steep hill, trying to reach a pine forest, which stretched along the horizon as far as the eye could see. Halfway up the hill we had to rest, because my little sister could go no farther. She had been very brave, but now she sat in the snow with tears running down her cheeks.

After we had rested a little, and after many encouraging words from Mother, we prepared to go on. But as we looked up, we saw what at first looked like a long black snake coming toward us across the white expanse. To our horror, this black snake was composed of people who were held in line by soldiers with rifles. Desperate, we searched for cover, but aside from a small bush without leaves, there was none. We crouched down into the snow in an effort to hide, but to no avail. We had already been seen, and two soldiers separated themselves from the column to intercept us. They had us quickly, and checked our identification papers in a brisk, efficient manner. Then we were gruffly told that we would have to march fifty kilometers in the snow with the other prisoners to a collection camp. From there we children would be taken to a state home and our mother to a work camp or worse. Trying to flee the "Workers' Paradise" was a criminal offense, and punished accordingly.

When my sister and I heard this, we started to cry. We cried and wailed even more when the soldiers tried to separate us. We refused to let go of our mother, and held on to her for dear life. Tears ran in floods and our screams were heard far and wide. My seven-year-old sister, who was small and undernourished for her age, really looked pitiful. Her woeful little face was blue from the cold, and frozen tears hung on her eyelashes. Maybe my sister's pitiful state touched their hearts, for the soldiers relented and decided to hand us over to the Communist mayor of the next village. But first my mother received a tongue-lashing for trying a border crossing with two young children in the midst of winter. She had to promise not to try it again.

Luckily the mayor and his wife, who most likely were Communists for survival purposes only, took us in and treated us kindly. They helped us dry our shoes and clothes as much as possible, gave us something warm to drink, and even a piece of bread. Then instead of sending us back to Plauen as they had been instructed, they told us the exact route to take to the border and the approximate time the guards on the watchtowers changed. The towers were spaced at regular intervals all along the East German border, and the guards manning them had orders to shoot anyone trying to cross to the West. Toward noon, armed with our new information, we put our damp shoes and clothes back on and tried once more.

When we resumed our trip, this time we reached the forest undetected. We made our way through deep snow, thick bushes, and undergrowth, always mindful of cover. Finally, after a long struggle, often on all fours, the forest gave way to a clearing approximately the size of a football field. Peering through the pine boughs we could see the watchtowers, each manned by soldiers with machine guns. To the right of one of the watchtowers grew an area of young firs flanking the clearing all the way to a mature forest. It was those distant woods we had to reach. Mother pointed and whispered: "We'll try to cross the clearing under the young firs. They'll give us the best cover, but we have to be very, very quiet. We can't afford to get caught again." This was our moment of truth. We looked at the watchtowers and the distance we had to cover, took a deep breath, and with a silent prayer we began this most difficult part of our journey.

We went down on all fours again and crawled under the dense branches of the young spruce trees, careful not to dislodge any snow that might give away our presence. Sometimes we had to stop because branches snagged us, and we had to quietly and carefully disentangle ourselves from their grasp without attracting the guards' attention. This stretch of about one kilometer seemed like a hundred. Finally, after a long struggle, we came to a small stream, which was the demarcation line between East and West.

We had just waded through the stream and entered the forest on the opposite side of the clearing when shots fired in rapid succession rang out. Bullets tore off branches and cracked against tree trunks as we threw ourselves on our stomachs, fear and panic forcing us to move faster than we thought possible. We were still on our stomachs when all of a sudden a soldier's boots appeared before us. Our breathing almost stopped and our hearts fell. Could our struggle have been in vain? Did we get caught again?

Looking up, it took us a few moments to realize that this was an American soldier. Placidly chewing gum, he looked at us three miserable creatures. "Oh dear God help us," we prayed. "What if he sends us back?" Mother pulled out a letter from her brother in New Jersey, ready to negotiate or beg. But the soldier only gave the letter a quick glance with a rather bored expression, then with a casual wave of his hand and an "OK," he waved us away from the border—direction west! Relief flooded over us. We had made it! We were safe! Thank God!

Happily we turned our backs on the watchtowers and moved along a narrow path through the forest, unafraid now but still shaken. We walked and walked, I don't know for how long. Darkness descended on the forest with an eerie quiet as it started to snow again, enfolding the tall, dark pines in a soft white veil. My little sister was so exhausted by now that we could barely keep her going. So we sat down in the snow with swirling flakes softly settling on us, and Mother told us the story of

Mary and Joseph and their flight to Egypt. That was how she got us going again and again until we reached a road. There we sat with chattering teeth on an iced-over milestone on the side of the dark road. I was so cold and frozen that I felt as if I would crack and splinter into a million shards of ice if I moved.

A passing truck driver, who saw us in his headlights through the driving snow, stopped and gave us a lift to the small town of Hof in West Germany. It had been dark for a long time when we finally arrived at my mother's girlfriend's apartment, where Father waited for us. He had been waiting for us at the border during the day, but after waiting several hours in the cold with no sign of us, he went back to Hof to wait for news of us there. He knew that something must have gone wrong to account for our delay.

So when we finally showed up well after midnight, he was incredibly relieved. The joy of seeing each other again was enormous as we fell into each others arms crying happy tears. Icicles fell off us and broke on the floor, where they turned to puddles. At last we were able to take off our stiffly frozen clothes and shoes. There was ice and newspaper pulp inside my shoes and even between my toes. We stayed there for the night, sleeping on the couch and on the floor.

Before drifting off to an uneasy sleep, I kept thinking how lucky we were that our family was intact and unhurt, that at last we were safe. This was the best Christmas of my life.

* * *

Chapter 28

Freedom At Last

Burghausen, December 26, 1947

West Germany! We were in West Germany! I still couldn't quite believe that we had made it, and that we were really in the West. Our guardian angels had been with us once again, and it occurred to me that we had been keeping them very busy in the last few years. Hopefully they would get a rest now.

After thanking our friends for all their help and hospitality, we left early in the morning to continue our journey. Still numb with exhaustion, in defrosted but damp clothes and wet shoes stuffed with fresh newspaper, we boarded a train for Southern Bavaria. My father had found work there in the small medieval town of Burghausen. The most memorable thing about this ride was that the train was heated. I was still so frozen to the bone from our thirty-hour flight through ice and snow that the heat felt absolutely heavenly. I reveled in it, and felt like crawling into the train's radiator, which ran along the floor below the windows.

The warm cocoon of the train and its gently rocking movements lulled me into a half sleep, with a kaleidoscope of memories whirling around in my head—the bombings, the horribly devastated city of Plauen, the garden, the flight to the West, the soldiers who caught us, the ice and snow, the shots ringing out from the guard towers, and most of all the ever present fear. These memories surrounded me like nebulous specters evolving and merging with each other in a realm where dreams mesh with reality. There was also a vague dream of hope for a new beginning and a better life in the West, even though it was hard for me to imagine what that might be like. But whatever it would be, it had to be better than the life I had known in Russian-occupied Plauen.

Of course we knew that there was a huge flood of refugees everywhere in the West, and Burghausen would be no exception, so our expectations were very modest. West Germany not only had to house and feed people like us, but also the millions of Germans who were expelled from Germany's eastern lands in the huge ethnic cleansing that took place after the war. West Germany was hard-pressed to house and feed all these traumatized survivors, especially since many of its cities were damaged almost beyond recognition. Living accommodations for all these destitute, homeless people were close to nonexistent. Consequently refugee camps were established all over the country to cope with the catastrophic situation, and people had to make do with whatever they could get. Food was rationed and conditions were still very chaotic, even though two and a half years had passed since the war ended. Only small towns in out-of-the-way places like Burghausen remained unscathed.

It was another cold and snowy night when we finally arrived in Burghausen. I was dead tired, but I had to shake myself awake after the long journey, because it was still a half-hour walk through a dark, snow-laden forest to reach our destination. Our new home turned out to be barracks on the outskirts of town, close to the chemical factory where my father worked as a laborer. The barracks, supplied by the factory for its workforce, were set up in rows with large open spaces in between.

Our lodgings were far from ideal, but they were much better than what we had to contend with the last few years in Plauen. We moved into two rooms at the end of one of the barracks. One small room became our bedroom. The other room had a huge stove in it because it had once been a community kitchen. The best thing about the barracks was that they had steam heat, so they were cozy and warm. Not only that, they also had electricity. After so many years without heat or electricity, we thought we had died and gone to heaven.

Of course our rooms were almost completely bare of furniture. Aside from the big black stove, the kitchen only had an old table with an even older bench sitting on a floor of dirty-gray wooden planks. The bedroom boasted one old, dilapidated locker to hang our clothes, but since we only had the clothes we came in, one locker was enough for the four of us.

Besides the locker, the bedroom had two twin-size iron beds that were pushed together. They had wooden boards instead of mattresses, but once again, necessity was the mother of invention. To make our beds more comfortable, my father managed to get yards and yards of bicycle inner tube tires from the chemical plant where he worked. He filled them with air, tied them into a mattress of sorts, and placed them on the boards. These fine, ingenious mattresses were then covered with a blanket.

Completely exhausted, all four of us just fell into bed and were asleep in seconds. I slept closest to the wall, which I had picked as the best spot, because I could only get kicked from one side. However, it wasn't long before I suddenly woke up, itching all over. When I scratched, it not only itched even more, but it also burned. Nevertheless I couldn't help scratching. Of course it didn't take long before I had everybody up with my frantic, nocturnal activity, which shook the bed. Groaning at being so rudely awakened, my parents put on the lights to see what created the commotion and to get a look at me. What they saw was enough to scare even the bravest. I was covered from head to toe with angry red welts, which I was scratching like someone possessed. What terrible disease had their daughter suddenly come down with? At first they didn't know what to make of it. Finally they decided to inspect my side of the bed and the wall where they discovered the terrible truth. My mother yelled: "Oh my God, bedbugs!"

"Bedbugs!" I let out a loud wail. From what I knew, only dirty people had bedbugs. We weren't dirty, were we?

They were in the wall and my body heat brought them out in droves. Only God knows how long they had waited there for such a delicious meal. All those welts on my body bore witness to how much they adored me. I was their promised land! Or was I their Christmas present? I could almost hear them celebrating in the wall. Actually I would have preferred it if they had taken their adoration to someone else, like my sister, for instance. Never having made the acquaintance of these little, bloodsucking pests, I thought them absolutely disgusting, and vented my anger by killing as many as I could. They not only left bloody splotches when they were squashed, but also gave off an awful stench. Even dead they were disgusting.

I contorted myself to scratch in hard-to-reach places. Mother warned: "Don't scratch, the bites will get infected and then you'll have ugly scars." I tried not to scratch, but that was easier said than done. I was one big, itching mess. At this point, growing up ugly concerned me less than the agonizing urge to scratch.

In between scratching, I let out a howl: "Yuck, there's one on my arm!" I quickly squashed it, leaving a bloody splotch were it had been gorging itself on my blood. Mother, turning her attention back to me, told me to hold still so she and my father could check me for more stray bugs. They found a few more, which immediately went back to where they came from—hell! Of course it was impossible to get any sleep for the rest of the night.

Now the bedbug hunt was on. They paid dearly for the audacity to pick a fight with us WWII survivors. The only trouble was, no matter how many we killed, there were always more where they came from. It was a fierce fight for survival! It was us versus the bloodsucking little beasts! How could these little brown devils that were no bigger than an apple seed create such havoc? Lucky Margit, who hadn't been bitten, watched me with big eyes, wondering if her big sister had gone crazy, as I angrily and frantically squashed one bug after another. Feeling that I was being picked on, I became a regular killing machine, only stopping to scratch now and then.

That's how we spent our first night in our new home. Our cozy, warm refuge already had tenants who waited patiently for their next meal, which happened to be us—me in particular!

The next morning we moved the beds against the outer wall of the other room. Unfortunately the bugs made the move with us. They weren't giving up so easily. Well, neither were we. Of course we didn't get much sleep between the bugs and our fancy inner tube mattresses, which kept deflating, but as always, we managed. It was all-out war against this formidable foe until the barracks were fumigated a week later, after my father put in a complaint with the factory's administration. When the exterminators finally came, we greeted them with great enthusiasm and high hopes that our sleepless nights would be over. They proceeded to seal all the windows and doors before placing their chemicals. We had to stay away from our barrack for a day, and inconvenient as it was, that finally put an end to those miserable little creatures. That was a very happy day, and I couldn't help gloating over their trip to hell, where they belonged. Hell became a lot worse with the arrival of our bloodthirsty little vermin.

In the meantime we familiarized ourselves with our new surroundings. The bathrooms, which were communal, were in a building some distance away. Not great, but much better than the hole in the ground we had in our bombed-out "Ice Palace" in Plauen. At least there were real toilet seats with lids. So what if we had to walk a block to go to the bathroom.

Water, which to our delight ran hot and cold, had to be hauled from a small building in the center of the complex. This structure also doubled as a place for washing and general hygiene, and the smell of soap, toothpaste, and shaving cream emanated from its door. In one room there was a long row of washbasins where people could take care of their morning toilette. Another room had large wooden tubs that had to double for taking baths and for the women to do their laundry. The water, supplied by the chemical factory, had a very weird smell, but who cared, hot water on demand was an almost forgotten luxury. I remember taking a hot bath in one of those big wooden tubs, the steam swirling around me and turning the room into a fuzzy, dreamlike world. It felt so good I didn't get out until my mother banged on the door and told me: "You have been in there long enough. How about giving the rest of us a chance?" Even though I would have liked to stay in the tub much longer, I reluctantly obeyed. What luxury after years of having to wash in basins of ice-cold water.

Next Margit and I decided to beautify the kitchen with pine boughs from the surrounding woods. We brought in armfuls of spruce branches and stuck them all around the kitchen, wherever we found a likely spot. Their wonderful, pungent scent immediately spread, covering the musty odor of dirt and neglect. Since it was still the Christmas season, we adorned the branches with little stars we cut out from newspapers, and we were quite proud of our decorating skills. We thought that bringing the forest into the kitchen was a great idea. At least it added a pleasant scent and a friendlier atmosphere to the otherwise bare and dismal room. Our beautification spree kept us very busy, and gave Mother time to get acquainted with some of the women in the neighborhood, where she could get the necessary advice and information about life in our new home. We were destitute, and any advice they could give us was more than welcome. Since all who lived there were in the same predicament when they arrived, they understood our situation and helped us as much as they could. As it was, we lacked just about everything. Mother even had to borrow pots from neighbors to cook our scant meals until we could get our own. Brooms and pails to give our new abode a necessary cleaning were also on loan from the neighbors.

We did our best to make our accommodations more livable. But the immediate, most pressing problem was food. We didn't have permits to stay in the West, and therefore we couldn't get ration cards. This meant that we had to make do with the one ration card my father had, with whatever our relatives sent us from the United States, and with neighbors' donations.

Most of them, if not all, were expellees who lived to tell about their expulsion from their ancestral homelands. They told us heartbreaking stories about the millions of German women and children driven west on foot in forced marches, their trail of misery into a truncated Germany marked by the shallow graves of those who succumbed to abuse, injuries, starvation, and cold. They also mentioned that many others died in Polish and Czech transit camps of exposure, starvation, disease, murder, and mass rapes by those who took over their farms, businesses, and homes. Millions of women and children lost their lives in this euphemistically called "resettlement." I would listen to these tales of misery with mounting horror. My mind couldn't grasp that this mass murder continued for three years after Germany's surrender, which meant that for millions of Germans the war didn't end until after 1948. For them peace was a word without meaning. A lot of the expellees who reached West Germany alive were in such deep despair that mental breakdowns and suicides were common. Compared to the fate these people suffered, we had actually been lucky. Our experiences were bad enough, but at least my memory pit didn't have to store the abominations I heard about.

The greatest danger was that we could be sent back to East Germany with disastrous results. We felt like we were living on borrowed time. Eavesdropping on my parents' conversations, I felt insecure and worried about our illegal status. Just the thought of having to go back to East Germany and the ensuing punishment gave me nightmares.

Once again our relatives in the United States came to our rescue. My uncle got in touch with his congressman, who used his influence with the occupation authorities to get us permission to stay, and with it the desperately needed ration cards. It took about six anxiety-ridden weeks for these precious documents to arrive.

When they finally arrived, we hugged each other with joy! We wouldn't have to go back! We were here to stay! We were safe! All was well with our world, and I can't express how grateful we were. We had official permission to stay, our ration cards, and a roof over our heads. What more could we want? Finally we had found a safe haven after so many years of fear and turmoil. Strangely enough, it took some getting used to. It was very difficult to shake off the deep-seated fears we lived with for so long. The feeling that someone would come and get us or that we had to run for our lives stayed with me for a very long time. It had become part of my psyche, encapsulated in every part of me. The same could be said for sharing my thoughts or voicing my opinion. An ingrained fear of reprisal kept me tongue-tied for half a lifetime, which often earned me a reputation of being aloof.

For my parents it was another beginning from scratch, but we were used to that. To have nothing but the bare necessities was no novelty to us.

*　*　*

Chapter 29

Fairy Tale Burghausen

1948

Once we had settled in, we began to reconnoiter the medieval town of Burghausen. In contrast to my poor, destroyed Plauen, the fairy tale town of Burghausen, built over a thousand years ago, and unscathed by war, emanated a peace and tranquility we had not known for many years.

Translated into English, Burghausen means Castle Home, and true to its name, it is the home of Germany's longest castle. The castle stretches for a mile along the narrow back of a mountain ridge overlooking the town. The old town nestling at its base is bordered on the opposite side by the swiftly flowing Salzach River, which divides Germany and Austria.

It was an hour's walk from our barracks home through the new part of town, with its scattered houses and fields, to where the land suddenly dropped off. A steep, winding road running along the ancient castle walls took us down to the river's edge and into the heart of Burghausen.

There the town slumbered in the pale winter sun, its red-tiled roofs partially covered with snow, waiting for the kiss of spring to bring it back to life. Seeing this idyllic town for the first time, I was wide-eyed and dumbfounded. It was like being placed in midst of a fairy tale that had suddenly come to life. This enchanting, storybook town was the epitome of every fairy tale I ever read. I thought I was dreaming. This couldn't possibly be real. It was unbelievable but true. I felt like I had stepped through a door into a long-ago past, a time of kings and beautiful princesses, of witches and dragons, and of knights in shining armor.

I imagined jeweled princes and princesses in sumptuous furs and gold-embossed velvets with richly dressed nobles in attendance, riding though town in a festive procession. As they passed, people in homespuns of browns, rusts, and greens respectfully bowed and doffed their hats. Children, laughing and shouting, ran to avoid the horses' hoofs in this colorful tableau. My imagination was in high gear and was fed by an ongoing festival, where to my delight the town's people, taking part in the reenactment of a historical event, walked around town in medieval dress.

Pastel-colored houses of many different hues, from pinks and pale yellows to light blues and greens, clustered around the cobblestone market square graced by old chestnut trees. A large fountain at one end of the square added its charm to this enchanting picture.

The bell tower of an impressive Romanesque church, consecrated in AD 1140, stood like a sentinel dominating the southern end of the square, reminding the faithful to come to pray and repent their sins. Passing through an archway decorated with a large mural of a family breaking bread, a narrow cobblestone road flanked by fifteenth-century houses wound its way along the river to the other end of town.

The river Salzach, as its name implies, once brought barges loaded with salt from the mines near Salzburg to Burghausen's quays. After paying a toll, this precious cargo was transported to inland destinations. Since salt was worth as much as gold in the Middle Ages, it brought great wealth to Burghausen, and allowed it to grow into a very charming town. The thought that I would now live here was beyond all my fondest dreams. A feeling of peace and serenity enveloped the town like a comforting blanket. After all the bombings and running for our lives, it was as if I had escaped from hell and entered heaven!

Burghausen, in all-Catholic Bavaria, was of course an all-Catholic town complete with a nunnery, a monastery, and a seminary. Nuns and priests were a constant presence in the town, enhancing its air of tranquility. The nuns also ran a boarding school for girls, and they could be seen walking their charges in pairs, with two nuns in the front and a nun or two in the rear to make sure none of the girls took a forbidden detour. That was something I had never seen before, and I wondered what these young girls were being protected from, for aside from imaginary demons and evil sorcerers, I couldn't see danger lurking anywhere in this enchanted realm.

The castle was first built as a wooden fortification in the seventh century, and was rebuilt in AD 1255 with huge, three- and four-foot-square stones. Because of the constant danger of invasion, the castle was constantly added to and reinforced until its completion in AD 1480, at which time it represented all phases of the Gothic period. Everything necessary to withstand a long siege was contained within its walls. It sat on the mountaintop as the town's crowning glory, and as a safe haven for the citizenry in times of danger.

In the valley on the other side of the castle was an ice-covered lake running along its entire length. The lake snuggled into the castle's curve, with ice- and snow-laden trees keeping it company all along its shores. The land, which rose again on the opposite side of the lake, was reached through an interesting pathway between two thick, crenelated walls. A safe distance from the castle, the path ended at a round tower where powder for the cannons was kept in bygone days.

There were several different ways to reach the castle from the town. My favorite was a steep stairway behind the church, zigzagging its way upwards. At a point that was even with the top of the church steeple, a roofed-over bench invited weary climbers to rest and enjoy the fabulous panorama. It offered a wonderful view of the town, the wooden bridge spanning the river, and the opposite shore in Austria.

The stairway continued up to the castle, where a drawbridge spanned a wide moat to a gatehouse displaying two coats of arms. One was the Bavarian Lion and the other the Polish Eagle, representing the fifteenth-century alliance between George of Bavaria and Hedwig of Poland. Looking down into the depth of the moat, I thought that it probably once held wild animals, growling and waiting for their next meal. I was always grateful that I stood safely on the bridge and in the present.

It wasn't difficult to imagine fully armed knights thundering over the drawbridge with their colorful banners flying, and soldiers manning the battlements. Big piles of stone balls for their catapults were still sitting around as a reminder that the castle had been built as a fortification. A nearby escape tunnel, which was now closed off, showed that the castle's inhabitants had thought of every contingency. After crossing the drawbridge and passing through the first gate, a spacious court opened up. In the past this court probably teemed with servants taking care of the returning knights' horses. A second gate opened into another spacious court, which held the princely quarters and the lady's bower. There too my mind could see the beautiful ladies of the ducal household in tall headdresses, trailing gowns of velvet and satin trimmed with fur, bending over their embroideries while a court musician entertained them with songs of unrequited love and knightly valor. I imagined them with their veils blowing in the wind, leaning over the parapet, waiting for their loved ones to return from a hunt.

One story, which I found particularly interesting, was that of the Duchess Hedwig, wife of Duke George the Rich of Bavaria. Since she had not been able to bear the duke an heir, he had her confined in a fortified tower. Even though she was kept in the state her position entitled her to, she was not allowed to leave the castle for the rest of her life. She finally died in AD 1502, probably of a broken heart.

That part of the castle is now a museum, housing various suits of armor, weapons, furniture of the period, and paintings. One painting in particular left me incredulous and horrified at the same time. It depicted a hapless "heretic" spread-eagled on the ground, his face in a grimace of pain, while some grim-faced executioners used a winch to remove his intestines through a long cut in his abdomen. So much for the good old days. It certainly gave me second thoughts about wanting to live in that time period.

There was also a beautiful, small, private chapel, which was built in the thirteenth century, with Gothic vaulting and a Gothic altar. Every princely court had its own priest, who was an integral part of the household. He was not only there to hold daily masses and take confessions, but also to keep an eye on the often rebellious princes of the realm and to protect the interests of the church.

In another court I discovered the Torture Tower, complete with a torture chamber. It was joined by an underground passage to the Witches Tower, which used to be the prison. There were a lot of witches in those days who were severely dealt with to protect the good citizenry from their dark arts. Some of the very imaginative ways used in those days to squeeze information or confessions from their hapless victims made me shudder. The Witches Tower's deep dungeons, where prisoners languished and disappeared forever, gave me goose bumps and some rather unpleasant thoughts. It occurred to me that some of the unfortunate inmates may have been heretic Protestants like me. That was an instance when my imagination was a definite disadvantage.

The castle was an absolutely fascinating place and I explored it as often as possible. On my way home from school I often took the stairs up to the castle, walking through its many courts to where it ended at the plateau and the new part of town. The huge building that once stood there had been razed by Napoleon when he occupied the town in 1800 and 1801. A gatehouse still stands there as the only reminder of that part of the castle's history.

There was no end to the enchantment, and my mind often took flights of fancy to this other time so long ago. It too became a part of me, softening the memories of the terrible war years and their dreadful aftermath.

* * *

Chapter 30

The Heathen

Burghausen, 1948

Living in Bavaria presented some unexpected problems. Since the worst effects of the war had passed Burghausen by, there was little understanding by some of the locals for the plight of those of us who had lost everything. There was also a certain amount of resentment that the government had foisted all these poverty-stricken, homeless people on their well-ordered world. In their eyes, we probably were nothing but shiftless drifters looking for handouts. But how could they feel otherwise! We were very poorly dressed, and had to make do with various makeshift accommodations under rather primitive conditions. Even those who had been wealthy were now reduced to poverty. In that respect war was a great equalizer. It was difficult for people who retained their homes, everything in them, and their network of friends and relatives to comprehend our situation. Unless you experienced it yourself and saw the misery the war brought with your own eyes, it was unimaginable.

Our first problem was the language. The Bavarian dialect differed dramatically from the Saxon dialect and from proper German. Some people spoke with such a strong Bavarian dialect that I couldn't understand them at all. Once when my mother sent me to a little store to get milk another customer had to interpret for me when the sales person asked how much milk I wanted. I just couldn't understand what she said and I wondered if I had landed in a foreign country. It took some time to become accustomed to the new sounds and new expressions, many of which were quite funny. Bavarians have a very earthy sense of humor, which is impossible to replicate in any other language.

Our second problem was that the minute we opened our mouths, it was apparent that we were "Prussian" and therefore persona non grata. Bavarians classified anyone who was not Bavarian as "Prussian," and we certainly fell into that category. Consequently I made few friends among the local children. I had several strikes against me. Not only was I a "Prussian," but I also lived in the barracks, which automatically relegated me to an undesirable underclass. That we weren't Catholic didn't help matters either. So we were like foreigners in our own country, and I was quite lonely, but too preoccupied with my new life and my new surroundings to worry about it. As far as I was concerned, being an outcast in an enchanting place like Burghausen wasn't so bad.

Now that we were legal residents, Margit and I were registered in the Burghausen public school system. Thank God my teacher spoke proper German with a charming Bavarian inflection, otherwise I would have been in big trouble. Margit, who was in second grade, wasn't so lucky. She had problems understanding her teacher, who had a strong Bavarian accent. Mother had to explain the matter to the teacher to keep Margit from being put back to first grade.

Going to school in Burghausen was an entirely new experience for me, for aside from the six-day school week, it was very different from the Plauen schools, which had a stern, no-nonsense approach to education. One difference I really liked was that there were no more mandatory Russian classes. I certainly wasn't going to miss them.

It was an hour's walk from our barracks home to the center of Burghausen's old town, where the public school was housed in a centuries-old building opposite the church in the market square. The steps of the wooden staircase in its hushed interior were soft and worn from the thousands of feet that had climbed them over the past five hundred years. It gave me a strange feeling to know that I followed in the footsteps of thousands who had climbed those stairs before me. The wooden floors of the quiet hallways smelled of wax and gleamed with a dull glow under the vaulted ceilings. Children's hats and coats were hanging on hooks in the halls like soldiers on parade.

Since the schools were run and staffed by nuns, they were a familiar sight gliding through those silent halls in their black habits and black veils. No noisy children were seen outside their classrooms, because the teachers changed rooms after each class, not the students. Only the faint voices of the teaching nuns penetrated the thick walls to disturb the sanctity of this quiet house of learning. I found the schoolwork easy, and had no problem whatsoever with it. I didn't even bother to keep track of my grades. But since this was an all-Catholic town, I had to learn a lot of new prayers.

Every morning started with the Lord's Prayer and a Hail Mary. But that wasn't all. Every time we picked up a pencil to write something or to do math, we had to kneel beside our seats and pray for the successful completion of whatever we were doing. Consequently we spent a lot of time on our knees! This was completely new to me and I was absolutely bewildered by this curious teaching method, which was certainly not practiced in the atheistic East German schools. All those prayers should have turned us into geniuses, but as far as I could tell, nobody seemed to get any smarter, no matter how much we prayed. The main result seemed to be nothing but sore knees. Prayers alone just weren't a good substitute for doing your homework.

Nevertheless, the nuns ran the school with smooth efficiency. There was sweet and kind Sister Kunigunde, flitting around the classroom like a bird, her black veils flying around her like wings. For exercise, she made us tiptoe around the bench rows, singing and flapping our arms like a flock of geese about to take flight, while she waved her arms like a conductor to keep us in rhythm. But to her credit she did her best to imbue us with knowledge and wisdom.

Then there was rotund Sister Teresa, the headmistress, who marched in periodically to check up on things. She was not so sweet and kind. She was a tough old bird with a raspy voice, used to issuing orders. Not even sweet Sister Kunigunde escaped her wrath if something wasn't quite up to her standards. Everybody froze to attention when Sister Teresa came through the door, her beady eyes sweeping the room for any irregularities. Sometimes she would ask us questions to test our knowledge and to see if Sister Kunigunde did a good job educating us. Poor Sister Kunigunde, who was visibly nervous and fluttering around the room more than usual, heaved a big sigh of relief with the rest of us when she found nothing to criticize and swept out of the room to terrorize the poor souls next door.

But the real problem for me was Father Venus. Religion was a compulsory subject given twice a week, sandwiched between reading and math classes. Even though I wasn't Catholic, I still had to take part in those classes. As the only Protestant in a class of thirty-five, I felt like a fish swimming in strange, uncharted waters. It was the one class I didn't look forward to. In fact, I dreaded it. Father Venus, with a ruddy complexion and well fed, would lean his big gut over my desk in the front row, look at me sternly down his red nose, and announce in a thunderous voice to make sure the everybody in the class could hear him: "Protestants and non-Catholics are heathens, destined to go to hell and burn in its fires, beset by devils and demons for all eternity! There is no hope for them, unless they see the error of their ways and become Catholic." Since I was Protestant, and one of those despicable heathens, he painted an extremely frightening picture of my afterlife while my classmates, secure in the knowledge that they would all go to heaven, listened in awe with open mouths.

There was a HEATHEN among them! My classmates looked at me as if I had suddenly grown horns and a tail, or as if I had come down with a severe case of leprosy. Some "You are going to hell" remarks came in singsong fashion from their ranks after Father Venus left the room. All eyes were on me as I became the focal point of their attention and whispers, which made me feel very uncomfortable. That was the first time I heard that I, along with all other non-Catholics, was destined to go to hell. But having been forged in the cauldron of a terrible war and Communist oppression taught me to keep my mouth shut, no matter what, so I sat meekly with downcast eyes and let it wash over me. I let it go in one ear and out the other. Sometimes, when it got to be too much, I became angry and my heathen blood was seething, but nobody would have known it to look at me. I had learned my lesson all too well under Communism, and was quite adept at hiding my feelings. My younger sister Margit, more gullible and impressionable than I, was so scared of all the hellfire and devils with pitchforks she heard about in her class that she wanted to become a nun to avoid such a terrible a fate. Of course she changed her mind later on.

Another novelty was the daily walk with my class to the building next to our school, where we were fed. A thin, whitish liquid was ladled out to each of us standing in line between the columns supporting the vaulted ceiling. It was sweet and didn't taste bad at all. The only problem was that there were a lot of worms and little black bugs floating around in it. It was rather disgusting to look at, but we joked that we might be getting some extra meat and ate it anyway, avoiding its unsavory extra ingredients as much as possible. As far as I knew, nobody died from it. I did wonder though, which charitable organization provided us with this protein-enriched soup.

The massive, Romanesque church opposite my school also drew my curiosity. Just entering its dim, hushed interior by the huge doors made me feel insignificant and like an intruder. It almost felt as if I was suspended in time, and entered a mystical realm removed from the sorrows of the real world. It felt as if those who had brought their hopes and tears to this church over the last thousand years had left an imprint of their fleeting existence. The atmosphere seemed filled with their prayers and their disembodied presence. The flagstone floor and the high, vaulted ceiling carried the slightest sound. Even a whisper was too loud. My footsteps echoed and even my breathing seemed to rebound from the walls. Tall stained glass windows scattered the light over the worn pews. There were ancient stone grave markers of citizens gone from this earth ages ago and statues of saints lining the walls among the many columns supporting the roof. A beautifully carved altar rail separated the apse from the rest of the church. On the opposite side a huge organ, rising from a balcony to the ceiling, commanded the nave of the church. But most intriguing were the glass coffins in the side aisles, in which rested the bony skeletons of departed saints. Their yellow-gray bones, clothed in rich brocades, were lavishly encrusted with gold and precious jewels. Empty eye sockets in bejeweled skulls stared hollowly from their magnificent glass prisons. Yellowed teeth in cavernous mouths were frozen in perpetual, benevolent grins and long, skeletal fingers clasped crosses and rosaries. Dried flowers, colorless from age, surrounded the saints in this macabre tableau. I thought it positively ghoulish and spooky, but to the locals the skeletons were venerated relics.

A visit with my class to a small church in a neighboring hamlet was an experience that left me perplexed and uncomfortable. Before entering the beautiful baroque interior of the church, we had to pass through a small vestibule where one of its walls displayed a huge mural illustrating the tortures of hell in vivid detail. Devils and demons plaguing their hapless victims with grim satisfaction were very realistically rendered. It had a strong visual impact designed to produce revulsion and fear. The phantasmagoric quality of the mural achieved by the artist caused my heart to skip a beat, mainly because it evoked my memories of the war.

My interpretation of what I saw was that you had to go through hell before you could enter the beauty of the kingdom of heaven. Considering what I had seen of life so far, it seemed to fit. In my case, Father Venus's opinion notwithstanding, going straight to heaven should be a cinch.

So I learned a lot again. In East Germany the Communists could come and get us; here it was the devil. As far as I was concerned, the devil was by far the lesser of the two evils. I had been to hell already in the last few years and survived, so all those sermons about devils and hell didn't scare me at all. Poor Father Venus labored in vain in his attempt to convert me. I was a lost cause!

* * *

Chapter 31

Life in the Barracks

Me, my mother, my sister Margit, and my father

Spring 1948 brought more good changes for us. We were able to move into another barrack, which gave us more living space, so now we had a large kitchen and two bedrooms. However, the bathrooms and the water supply were still in the other buildings, about the same distance away as before. We were so happy to have heat and electricity that we considered the lack of a bathroom and water in our living quarters as nothing more than a minor inconvenience.

Mother did her best to make our new apartment as pleasant as possible, using old furniture left there by the previous tenant and some of our meager belongings. Since there wasn't much to work with, it was a job for a magician. An iron bedstead, upholstered with a sack stuffed with cellulose and an old blanket, served as our couch, a shelf to hold our few cups, plates and pots, an old stove, some ancient, scarred chairs, and an old table comprised our entire kitchen furnishings. It wasn't exactly a decorator's dream, but it was the best she could do at the time.

My parents also worked out a way to make our beds more comfortable. The wooden boards with their bicycle inner tube mattresses were taken out and replaced with netting they wove with strong one-inch plastic ribbon. The netting was then covered with the ubiquitous sacks of cellulose, all of which were items my father picked up at work. It really wasn't too bad, except when the spaces between the netting spread and our arms, feet, or butts would hang through the holes. But this was easily fixed, and it was definitely a huge improvement over the wooden boards covered with the constantly deflating inner tube mattress.

Life in the barracks wasn't bad. The people living there, all refugees like us, were very nice, and many enduring friendships were forged. There was a great sense of camaraderie, and problems were usually solved together with lots of good humor.

One well-remembered episode took place some time in August of that year. My mother had to go to the Burghausen Hospital for a week to repair double hernias that were the result of all the heavy lifting during and after the war. While she was gone, we had to shift for ourselves, with my father, who was completely useless in the kitchen, trying to do the cooking with me as his equally useless assistant. We survived our culinary efforts, even though most of what we ate was burned to a crisp. Even the well-meant advice of neighbors didn't improve our cooking skills. But who cared? So our food was well done. At least it was something to eat. Nevertheless, we were very glad when my mother came home and took over the reins of the household again. Unfortunately, one of her precious pots was missing, and since she only had two, this was a real misfortune.

"Where on earth is my other pot?" Mother asked, all upset. "What did you do with it? What am I going to do with only one pot?" Father met Mother's questions with an innocent face and: "I have no idea. I can't imagine where it went. I'm sure it's around somewhere." Mother searched everywhere without results.

When Mother questioned me, she met with a similar response; I didn't know either. Nobody knew what happened to it. Replacing it wasn't as easy as going to a store and buying a new one, because even in West Germany such things were still scarce. That was aside from the fact that we were so financially strapped that every penny counted. So Mother was once again reduced to borrowing pots from neighbors, who smirked when they heard about the vanished pot. My father continued to plead ignorance. The pot had simply disappeared! Where to was a big mystery. Months later we found it badly burnt under a stack of wood in the small shed that came with our apartment. It was the only place Mother never thought to look, and my father had a hard time explaining the charred pot and its strange hiding place. Of course everybody living in the barracks heard the story of the pot and Father was teased about it mercilessly for a long time. Nobody ever trusted him with pots after that.

Since soap for doing laundry was also in short supply, Mother and several other women tried to make soap from spruce tree sap. Everybody laughed and thought they were crazy when they began to collect sap in small tins. "Whoever thought of using tree sap to wash clothes? What makes them think that that sticky stuff could be a substitute for soap? Who or what on earth gave them that idea?" were some of the comments I heard. The result of the women's ingenious endeavor was a large vat full of a gooey, brown substance, which contained only God knows what else besides the tree sap. Nobody laughed anymore when they used this weird-looking, syrupy mixture to do their laundry. I don't know how well it worked, but it was probably better than nothing and I can't remember wearing dirty clothes. We may have been poor, but dirty we were not. Mother made sure of that. Making do with lots of imagination and ingenuity was a way of life for all of us in the barracks. We understood each other's problems of coping with a difficult present and a past too painful to remember, but too hard to forget.

Annie, a pretty newlywed with dark hair and eyes, lived in a barrack opposite ours. Even though she was much younger than my mother, they bonded and became good friends. Annie had gone through some very rough times in her young life after she was expelled from her home in Silesia when it was ceded to Poland in 1945. Yet she was always good-humored and in good spirits. Since she loved children but was unable to have her own, she was always happy when Margit and I came to visit. We went there often and loved sitting in her tiny kitchen, listening to stories. Sometimes she even had a rare, home-baked cookie for us, which of course was another reason we liked to go there.

Since food was still rationed and not plentiful, Mother often sent us into the woods with Annie to collect berries or mushrooms so she would have some extra ingredients for our next meal. These excursions into the forest were so much fun that we didn't consider them a chore. We were always happy and proud when we came home with a milk can full of berries and mushrooms to contribute to our food supply.

Annie's husband Luggy, a tall, lanky, six-foot-four-inch man, was very quiet, if not morose, and never had much to say. The awful things he experienced as a soldier during the war still had a hold on his mind and severely affected his outlook on life. Nevertheless, he and Annie seemed to have a happy marriage. Annie's upbeat personality and happy disposition was just what Luggy needed to bring him out of his dark moods.

Since Luggy loved cucumbers, he decided to grow some himself. Every day, as soon as he came home from work, he visited the spot where he had put some small seedlings into the ground. He didn't want to miss the first sign of cucumbers appearing on the plants. But when time passed and no cucumbers showed themselves, he became very downhearted. To get Luggy out of his doldrums, Annie managed to get some fully- grown cucumbers from God knows where, and fastened them to the plants. I don't know what his reaction was to seeing fully ripe cucumbers appear over night, but he was happy to get cucumber salad, his favorite dish, for dinner. Annie's ingenious way of lifting his spirits was cause for much amusement among the rest of us.

Annie also was the culprit who snuck out in the middle of the night to the small plot where my father had planted tomatoes. She removed all the ripe tomatoes from their vines and replaced them with pinecones. When my father saw his tomato plants the next day, he was extremely upset and angry with the hooligans who had done this dastardly deed. Of course the news of my father's strange crop traveled through the barracks like wildfire, and everybody had a good laugh. Father was mollified when Annie brought back the stolen tomatoes and all was forgiven. Annie's mischievous sense of humor was like a ray of sunshine that brightened all our lives.

But there was one family living in the barracks that none of us were very fond of, mainly because of the way they treated their twelve-year-old daughter Ingrid. Her father, a giant of a man, had re-married after his first wife died during their flight from Prussia, and the second wife treated her stepdaughter like an indentured servant. Her life was devoid of all kindness and made miserable by a cruel stepmother who had no pity for a child who lost her mother under tragic circumstances.

I liked Ingrid, and felt sorry for the poor girl. Her clothes were no more than rags and she looked like she didn't get enough to eat, but got plenty of beatings instead. She was skin and bones and had a very pale complexion. Of course she was never allowed to play or spend time with the rest of us because she was kept busy with interminable chores, while her stepmother, who was more than well nourished, expected to be served morning, noon, and night. The father who was completely under his new wife's thumb seemed to be oblivious to his daughter's plight, and unfortunately none of us could do anything to help her. She was a real-life Cinderella, a very sad little girl. The only difference was that there was no prince on a white horse to come to her rescue. Then one day Ingrid vanished. Her parents refused to say anything about her disappearance, but we heard rumors that she was given shelter by the nuns, and I hoped that her life would take a turn for the better. I was rather gleeful that her stepmother had lost her servant and now had to do her own housework. It crossed my mind more than once that Margit and I were very lucky to have parents like ours, who loved us and allowed us to be the children we were.

In a wooded area within walking distance from our barracks was a nice pool where Margit and I spent many wonderful summer afternoons. The pool was an amenity supplied by the chemical plant for its workers, and to my delight, it had a twelve-foot slide. We would slide down sitting on top of each other and wind up in the water in a jumbled heap, screaming with laughter. Two six-foot-long, smooth wooden logs floating in the pool were another opportunity for more fun and mayhem. When manned, they became battleships, which warred against each other. Each team did its utmost to throw the other team off its log. The last person who managed to stay on their constantly rolling log was the winner. Even though I almost drowned a few times defending my "ship" among flailing arms and legs, I enjoyed those water fights tremendously. If there were any lifeguards, they certainly did nothing to curtail our fun. After a great day at the pool, I usually came home sunburnt and tired but happy.

The summer brought other memorable occasions for us barracks' dwellers. On nice summer evenings there was always someone sitting outside a barrack on one of the benches, playing a zither or an accordion. The bewitching sounds of familiar old melodies drifting among the barracks created wistful memories of better days and a wonderful end to a busy day. Some of the children sang along as they crowded around the musicians, watching their nimble fingers producing wonderful sounds, while others who didn't know the words watched with openmouthed fascination. To say that it was a great improvement over the last few years would be an understatement. Even though we were as poor as church mice and food was still scarce, life began to be good again.

When the wind blew from the east a thick white fog belching from the smokestacks of the chemical plant blanketed our barracks. But not even that could squelch our happiness at having finally found a safe home. So what if the visibility was only twenty feet on bad days, and made you feel like you were wading through a world of white cotton. Luckily the wind usually blew from the west, away from us, so we took those few bad days in stride. We never gave a second thought to what it might do to our lungs.

The quality of water supplied to us by the chemical plant wasn't exactly that of a mountain spring either. It had a weird, unpleasant odor and an odd taste, which wasn't so easy to shrug off. But since nobody seemed to get sick from it, we ignored it, as we had to ignore a lot of things. Eventually our noses and taste buds became accustomed to it, and we didn't even notice it anymore.

* * *

Chapter 32

A Wonderful Surprise

Sometime toward the end of the school year my teachers brought up the subject of tests for admission to the Gymnasium or the Realschule. The Gymnasium had a curriculum that included classical languages like Latin and Greek besides the core subjects. The other choice was the Realschule, which was basically the same, except that there was more emphasis on math, the sciences, and modern languages.

I didn't pay too much attention to it, because I thought that my chances of going to a school like that were nil. There was no way my parents could afford the tuition, small as it was. So I never even bothered to bring up the subject at home. They had a hard-enough time scraping by as it was. Sending me to a school, which required tuition and would also prevent me from earning my keep, was definitely not high on their agenda.

I had already resigned myself to staying in public school, which only went to the eighth grade. After that it would be an apprenticeship in a trade with a small salary, while continuing my academic education at night. Mother's plan for me was an apprenticeship with a dressmaker, which I wasn't particularly enthusiastic about. So the time when the better students in my class took the entrance exams for the school of their choice passed me by, and I thought no more about it.

That's when fate intervened once again. My mother's hernia operation in August led to a very important event that was to alter the course of my life tremendously. The minister of our small Protestant church visited her in the hospital, demanding to know why I hadn't taken the tests for either of the advanced schools, since my grades were very good. I couldn't imagine how he could have known that, especially since I paid scant attention to my grades. He told her that she would be committing a terrible sin by not giving me the opportunity for an excellent education, and embarrassed her to such an extent that Mother relented and agreed to let me go to one of the schools. The guilt trip he put her on was very effective, with far-reaching, beneficial consequences for me. She gave me the astounding news when she returned from the hospital. Now I was very excited and happy, because I knew that it meant a wonderful education, which would be of great value to me for the rest of my life. That I had the minister of the tiny Protestant church to thank for it really baffled me. But after some thought I realized that he was a true representative of faith who cared for everybody, not just for the parishioners who attended his church regularly.

This surprising development seemed like a miracle to me. It once again gave me the feeling that the influence of a benevolent higher power guided my life.

So just before school began, Mother took me into town to take the exams they had especially arranged for me at the Realschule. On the way, I received a long sermon with dire warnings. "If you don't keep up your grades or get too conceited, I'll pull you out immediately. You'll have to go to work and learn a trade. You know how hard it is for us to pay the tuition, so there will be no playing around." I knew she meant it and I was ready to promise anything.

When we entered the the Realschule's old building I was a little nervous, because I didn't quite know what to expect. After a short interview, I sat all by myself in an empty classroom where I was tested in German, math, and English. That was when my secret English lessons in Communist East Germany paid off. Not only did I pass all the tests, I did well enough to skip a grade and start school at a higher level. So I started a new life in a fine school, which was a great opportunity for me. Without the intercession of the clergy, nobody could have embarrassed my mother into making this decision, which channeled my life in a wonderful new direction. It was another one of my life's unexpected surprises!

My first introduction to the school was the reading of the statutes. It was a yearly, mandatory event that all five hundred students were required to attend. It consisted of the reading of all the school's regulations and standards of expected behavior, including the penalties for disregarding them. One of the rules I distinctly remember was the 8 p.m. curfew during the school year. The reading was done by the school's director in the presence of the entire teaching staff and took about an hour and a half. There were many rules we were expected to follow and I felt a little intimidated.

The next day classes began. I now had a lot of homework and I really had to work. We were told that if I could maintain a B average, the town would pay my tuition. Aware of our financial situation and Mother's threat, I did my best and I was able to get that B average, even though Bs were very hard to get and As were almost unthinkable. Mornings still started with the Lord's Prayer and a Hail Mary, but except for the twice-weekly religion classes, that was all the religion for the day. Since there were only about a dozen Protestants in the entire school, we received our instruction from the Protestant minister in a small room, separated from the Catholic majority, who took instructions from Father Venus.

My class of about thirty-five students consisted mainly of girls boarding with the nuns at the cloister next door. My classmates were quite a varied group from many different backgrounds. They came from all over Germany and from places like Austria and Switzerland. Some were the children of old aristocratic families, but most were from displaced refugee families, who arrived by train every morning from outlying villages. None of us ever spoke about the terrible things we had experienced during the war. It was as if a huge void existed where happy childhood memories should have been. We kept our nightmarish wartime pasts hidden away in the farthest corners of our minds.

Sometimes when I looked at my classmates, thoughts that disappeared as quickly as they came swept through my mind. What terrible memories were behind the smiles of all the fresh young faces like mine? We joked and laughed like other young people our age, and pretended that everything was normal. Yet, how would our pasts affect us later in life? Would we have the mental fortitude to deal with it? For now, life was good again. The skies were blue and no dark clouds threatened our days in fairy tale Burghausen. Young and guileless, we embraced life and all our new world had to offer. We refused to think beyond that.

Karin, a very pretty girl from Estonia, became my best friend. Her father was killed during the war, so she, her mother, and three other siblings lived with their uncle, who had taken them in after their flight from Estonia. Since she was a talented artist, we spent a lot of time together drawing and painting after we finished our copious homework. Karin was not only pretty with classical features, bright blue eyes, and white blond hair, she was also extraordinarily intelligent. She was the only one in my class who would consistently produce As, which didn't win her any popularity contests. Unfortunately the perversity of our competitive human nature is such that it isn't kind to those who excel, and she certainly did.

Every year more subjects were added to our curriculum, and once added, they stayed there. With each added subject our homework grew proportionally, demanding more and more of our time. Since frequent unannounced tests were the norm, skipping homework wasn't a good idea if you wanted a decent grade at the end of the year.

The third year, which was my second year at the school, French was added as a second foreign language. Math became algebra and geometry and later trigonometry, statistics, and calculus. Physics and chemistry were added in the fourth year, when our math proficiency enabled us to do the math required for these subjects. This brought my course load to ten, not counting religion, music, art, and sports. Everything was mandatory. Choice of subjects didn't exist. They kept us very busy juggling all these different courses within a six-day school week, and no time was wasted by students changing classrooms. When one teacher left the room, the next one entered, barely giving us time to change books from one subject to another. This not only eliminated crowded halls, but also gave us the full forty-five minutes of instruction. Homework was a chore of several hours every day, including weekends. The only time off was three weeks for Christmas, three weeks for Easter, and the six-week summer vacation. There was no rest in between!

As time went on, my class kept getting smaller and smaller, dwindling down to eighteen, as students who couldn't keep pace dropped out, or were advised to leave for schools with easier requirements. There was no such thing as summer school or tutoring. Almost all of our teachers had doctorates in the subjects they taught and were well equipped to answer questions or explain difficult theories. Their attitude was that if you needed tutoring, you didn't belong there in the first place. There was also no favoritism! Even the wealthy countess of such and such would be asked to leave if her work wasn't satisfactory. A princess wasn't treated any differently than the child of a poor laborer. Merit was the only criteria you were judged on. Wealth and social status were irrelevant.

A rather interesting thing happened one year. A girl in a class ahead of me became the talk of my school when she went to the United States as an exchange student for a year. We all envied her and thought how lucky she was to spend a year going to school in the fabled United States, an unattainable dream for the rest of us. When she returned after a year, she proudly showed off her American grades, which were straight A. Since she barely made the grade in our school, this was nothing less than astounding. How could this be? However, after she was tested, she was told that she would have to repeat the whole year she spent in the United States, because she had fallen behind. But rather than repeat a year, she decided to drop out. So she wasn't so lucky after all, and it certainly gave us second thoughts. This incident left us wondering about the American school system and its reputation for excellence.

My pen pal Abdul Aziz Al Futaih

As another part of our education we were encouraged to take up correspondence with students from foreign countries. The aim was to foster better understanding and friendly relationships between the young of different nations, and to practice our foreign language skills. So I sent my photo with personal data to a central agency in Munich, which facilitated these exchanges. It wasn't long before I received a lot of letters from different parts of the world. There must have been at least a dozen, including one from the French Foreign Legion. All came with photos of nice-looking young men looking for pen pals.

Since I couldn't possibly write to all of them, I finally decided on a student at Cairo University. His photo showed a dark-skinned young man with finely chiseled features, close-cropped, dark, curly hair and kind, dark eyes. I picked him because his letters had charm and I sensed an innate kindness and warmth, which I found very endearing. I called him Abdul, which was the first name in his mile-long name. So we began a lively correspondence, exchanging ideas and learning about each other's countries. I even pressed plants and sent them to him as examples of our fauna. My intuition proved me right, because it turned into a lifelong friendship and he was to play a very important part in the course of my life. He was to become another of my life's magical surprises.

An event of major proportions took place with our initiation into the adult world when we turned fourteen. Up to this point, we were considered children and addressed with the informal "*Du*," while adults were addressed with the more respectful "*Sie*." We were now considered adults and addressed with the formal "*Sie*." Braids disappeared, and short hair and permanents took their place. The childish look gone, we suddenly looked like young adults. It was very strange yet very exciting to be addressed as equals by people in stores and by our teachers. It made us feel very grown up, and we were expected to behave accordingly. I can't say that this was always the case. We were still the same teenagers as before, who experimented with life, and we pushed our new status to the limit, frustrating parents and teachers alike. This official induction into the world of adults was yet another interesting aspect of the world we grew up in. It was an added boost to our self-confidence and self-esteem, so necessary in the competitive world we would soon enter.

*   *   *

Chapter 33

The Potato Bug Hunt

As we did in East Germany, we went to nearby farms to augment our rations. Of course the results of these forays were much better than the ones in our other life under the Communist system. The bread, baked in outdoor brick ovens, and the fresh butter we were able to get from the farmers on rare occasions, were absolutely delicious, and our starved taste buds relished them. Nevertheless, the daily struggle for food was still a very important part of all our lives. Consequently anything endangering our food supply was a potential calamity.

Our second summer in Burghausen was a memorable one for many reasons, not the least of which was the arrival of a terrible pest—the potato bug and its larvae. They were threatening to devour and ruin all the potato plants in the fields around Burghausen, depriving us of our most important food staple. It was a previously unknown plight and nobody seemed to know where it came from. There were of course all kinds of rumors, but none that could be established with certainty. Since rationing was still in effect and food was still very scarce, this was a looming catastrophe. Strong measures were called for to combat and defeat this voracious enemy. So the town fathers in their wisdom declared an all-out war on the bugs, and ordered all children over the age of twelve out into the fields to do battle with this fiend. That included me and my class. We were given a day off from school to go on the potato bug hunt. We certainly weren't unhappy about this aspect of the town fathers' plan. As far as we were concerned, missing a day of school was no great misfortune.

None of us had ever seen or heard of a potato bug, so before setting out, we received a description of the criminal and its progeny. The bug was about three-eights of an inch in length, yellow with black stripes on its back, a black head, and six skinny, black legs. His children, much larger than the adult bug, were disgusting-looking, fleshy white grubs. Everyone received a glass container to hold any of the bugs and their larvae we would find. The school's blessings and a reminder of the seriousness of the situation came with the receptacles. We were also told to make good use of the jars and leave our allotted field bug-free.

It was a beautiful, hot day with the sun bright in an azure sky when we were sent to one of the nearby potato fields. Clutching our jars, none of us had much enthusiasm for the planned foray. Bugs weren't exactly on top of our list of favorite things. I for one would have preferred to spend the day at the lake. The only good we could see in this situation was that we could skip a day of school. We were only too happy to escape French, English, math, or any other tortures our teachers had planned for that day.

The field we were assigned to was just over a ridge opposite the castle, so it didn't take us long to get there. It was rather large and its sheer size was intimidating. Looking at it, we wondered uneasily how much time we would have to spend there with the bugs. Supervised by two of our professors, we began our search-and-destroy mission, accompanied by a lot of moans and groans. If that didn't scare the bugs, nothing would. Every bushy plant had to be checked individually and delivered of its voracious pests. It wasn't an easy job, because these little guys were fast. Not so for the disgusting larvae hiding beneath the leaves, eating themselves into oblivion. They were gorging themselves on the succulent green leaves, and some plants already showed the results of their gluttony. The ugly miscreants hung onto their food source with incredible tenacity. We had to pry them loose carefully, for accidentally squashing one of them between our fingers was unthinkable. The thought alone was nauseating. They were so disgusting that nobody even wanted to touch them.

Time and again we heard: "I got one! Somebody come and get it; there's no way I'm going to touch it!" This definitely wasn't a job for the squeamish.

"Get over it! And get on with the job," we were told. "You like to eat potatoes, don't you? Besides, do you want your class to be known as too lazy or too prissy to catch a few little bugs?"

"Where on earth do these miserable little beasts come from?" we asked.

Somebody said: "I heard that the Americans dropped them from their planes when they ran out of bombs."

"No, it was the Russians who brought them," was another opinion. "Everybody knows that they have all kinds of crawly things."

Then a girl yelled: "You're all wrong! The devil did it!" as she crossed herself. "Only the devil could dream up such horrid little creatures to plague us."

"Yes," came a reply. "I think you're right. These bugs are abominations that could only come straight from hell. The devil must be jumping for joy to see his little demons give us such a hard time."

"Good heavens, what an idea! What else are we going to blame on the devil? I could almost feel sorry for the poor guy," came a mumbled response from an irreverent soul. "In that case, they should have sent Father Venus with holy water instead of us." I wisely kept my mouth shut.

At that, one of the professors cut them off: "Enough of that nonsense! Do you have to believe every stupid rumor you hear? Get on with it. Stop wasting time." So, gingerly and with gritted teeth, we started to round up the offenders and put them into our jars. Some seemed stunned by their sudden change of fortune. They just sat there, looking at the glass walls of their prison, while others desperately tried to escape, so the lids had to be closed very quickly. The larvae, completely disoriented, moved around their jail blindly, groping for the nice, green food, which had suddenly disappeared.

Just holding the jars with their wriggling inmates was disturbing and repugnant.

Yet there was no choice. Bringing back an empty jar simply wasn't an option. That would have resulted in disparaging remarks, a blot on the reputation of our class and on our character. After all, we survived a terrible war and had seen much more revolting things, so being repulsed by some little bugs just didn't make sense. So we suppressed our loathing of these foul creatures as we put one bug and one larva after another into our jars. It was a matter of who would eat, them or us, and we were determined that it would be us!

Occasionally our activity would come to a sudden halt when somebody screamed: "I got one on me! It's running up my arm!"

"Don't be such a ninny!" came back from some hardier soul. "Brush it off and kill it! Send it back to hell and let the devil deal with it!"

But eventually even the most squeamish among us conquered their disgust and got used to this distasteful job. We even began to stalk our prey with enthusiasm, and it became a race to see who would catch the most of these little villains. When a receptacle was full, it was emptied into a larger container held by one of the professors, and the hunt began anew with an empty jar.

There was no shade anywhere and the sun's rays showed us no mercy. We were sunburnt, sweaty, and dirty, not to mention that our backs hurt by the time we were done clearing the field. That's when it dawned on us that a farmer's life was a tough lot, and we all agreed that farming wasn't an option to be considered for our future.

Our mission accomplished, the potato harvest and our food supply saved, we felt positively virtuous and very good about ourselves. But there were no medals for the victors and the successful completion of our mission, even though a few potatoes or some bread would have been a nice reward. No such luck. Our heroic deeds had to remain unrecorded and unsung. With big sighs of relief, we happily turned in our last jars, hoping to never see them and their odious contents again. This wasn't our idea of a nice day in the country.

Of course we probably missed some bugs here and there to reproduce the following year, which wasn't a very comforting thought. We fervently hoped that there would be no repeat of the bugs and larvae competing with our professors to make life difficult for us. Since it never happened again, we assumed that we had done a thorough job. It could also be that the farmers had devised a better method to save their crops. Either way, we never had to go out into the fields again, thank God!

Given a choice, we thought it preferable to sit in math or English class than to spend a day in the hot, dusty fields hunting bugs, and that's saying a lot!

*   *   *

Chapter 34

The Black Madonna

An interesting experience when I was about fourteen, which left quite an impression on me, was a day trip to Altoetting, a small town not far from Burghausen. Even though I had heard a lot about it and knew some of its history, I had never been there. I don't remember the reason for the trip, but I certainly remember the astounding things I saw there.

Altoetting is a place of pilgrimage, like Lourdes in France, or Magigoria in Yugoslavia, albeit not as well known. It has one of the oldest shrines in Central Europe, dating back to the eighth century, with a venerated statue of the Virgin Mary dedicated to our Lady of Altoetting. She is called the Black Madonna, because her face is black. It was probably blackened over time from the smoke of thousands of votive candles lit by those who came to worship her. Many miracles, which are said to have taken place over the centuries, are attributed to the Madonna's intercession. Tens of thousands came to the shrine in the Middle Ages to call for her help during the time of the plague, the much-feared Black Death, which decimated Europe's population during the Middle Ages.

The shrine, octagonal in form, was originally built as a Roman temple, which became a Christian chapel around AD 680. The hearts of Bavarian rulers have traditionally been buried in the sanctuary since AD 1661, including that of the mad King Ludwig ll of Bavaria. He was the one who built the famous castle of Neuschwanstein, upon which the Disney World castle is based. To this day half a million people, many of them on foot, visit the shrine every year. This is where the faithful go on pilgrimage to pray for relief from physical or spiritual ills, for forgiveness of sins, or to fulfill a vow made in moments of great distress.

Since I had always been curious about Altoetting, this promised to be a very interesting trip. When I got on the train, my car was full of nuns and priests accompanying the many people going there on pilgrimage, and this Protestant "heathen" sitting in their midst felt rather out of place. Many of my fellow passengers sat there quietly praying the rosary, while I prayed to remain inconspicuous, so I wouldn't have to answer any uncomfortable question like: "What church do you belong to? Who is your priest? Do you go to Mass and confession regularly?" Some priests and nuns could be very inquisitive in a kindly sort of way. After all, that's why they are called caretakers of souls. The condition and salvation of our souls is of utmost importance to them. In the austerity of their world, the forces of darkness are ever-present, looming large and dangerous, and forever poised to corrupt our souls.

When we reached our destination and got off the train, we were met by more priests and nuns. They helped to arrange the new arrivals in a long line. I noticed that some were in wheelchairs, others had difficulties walking, and many wore troubled, sad faces. It definitely wasn't a cheerful group. When everybody was finally assembled, this solemn procession of about seventy people, dressed in dark clothes, proceeded to slowly make its way through Altoetting's streets. A priest carrying a large cross led the procession in prayer, the singing, praying crowd following sedately behind him. Curious as ever, I walked along, observing the proceedings with astonishment and great interest.

When the procession reached a cobblestone square, it started to circle the small chapel dominating its center. The low hum of Hail Marys echoed through the square, and the very air seemed to vibrate with the sound of prayers. The constantly repeated Hail Marys, with an unvarying cadence, had a hypnotic effect. Not wishing to be caught up in this altered state of consciousness, I closed my mind to its lure.

Several people carrying large, heavy crosses on their shoulders moved painfully around the chapel on their knees, their faces grave and mournful, with their lips moving in silent prayer. Was it to do penance for a sin, or the fulfillment of a vow? There was no way to tell, and I couldn't help being affected by what I saw. I had never seen anything even remotely like it, and I watched incredulously. Nothing in my past prepared me for anything like this. I felt like a fish out of water, snapping for air.

Feeling like an impostor, I eventually managed to get through the throng and enter the chapel. It was very small and filled with the smoke of candles and incense, imbuing it with a pious atmosphere. The low murmur of fervent prayers of those around me heightened the aura of sanctity and mystery surrounding this simple place of worship. After dipping my fingers into the font with holy water and crossing myself, as was customary, I stood in line waiting for my chance to approach the small altar with its effigy of the Virgin Mary. Many people knelt before her, praying and leaving small tokens of faith. When it was my turn, I followed their example and knelt before the Madonna, whom I saw through the misty twilight of the shrine, resplendent in a dress and a crown studded with precious stones, holding the infant Jesus in her arms. I looked at her with curious, questioning eyes, hoping to find an answer to the mystery surrounding her, but the eyes in her beautiful, dark face only gazed back at me with dispassionate serenity. I said a prayer, crossed myself, as I had seen others do, and left to make room for the people pressing in behind me.

I took the time to inspect the walls in a roofed-over pathway surrounding the tiny chapel. The walls were covered with hundreds of drawings and letters, which were testimonies of people whose prayers had been answered. There was an outpouring of love and gratitude for the Lady of Altoetting, who had healed them or saved them in times of great peril. I looked at them, and after reading some of their heartbreaking stories, I considered myself blessed and lucky to stand there on my own two feet, to be able to walk, hear, and see. A feeling of immense gratitude stole over me, and it occurred to me that this was a lesson for everyone to learn, but I also wondered how many took heed.

I absorbed the intensity of feelings surrounding me with a sense of confusion and awe. I was awed by this very public exhibition of faith, but also confused, because I thought of prayer as a private affair. I wondered why all the fervent prayers said by those who died in the terrible war, or by those still languishing in gulags in Siberia, yielded no results. Why some prayers were answered while others seemed to fall on deaf ears was a big mystery to me. Why did some live and some die, regardless of their prayers? What perplexed me even more was that more often than not the innocent suffer and perish miserably despite their prayers, while the evil sometimes seem to flourish. It was something about which I could only speculate. It seemed to me that we are helped on occasion through the intercession of forces beyond our understanding. We often call an unfortunate outcome of a situation bad luck, but is it really? Who knows? As usual, my whys were endless. I concluded that prayers give hope and the strength needed to endure life's many misfortunes. "Thy will be done" in the Lord's Prayer would give solace and the peace of acceptance to those whose fate doesn't change.

Ringing the square were churches, monasteries, nunneries, and souvenir stores filled with religious items, where the faithful could buy all sorts of things promising to give them protection from evil and life's adversities. Of course I checked them out. Their windows displayed bibles, catechisms, crosses, rosaries, candles, and statues of the Virgin Mary in all sizes and price ranges. There were also books on the lives of saints, whose inspirational messages undoubtedly gave comfort and courage to people. Watching all these stores doing a brisk business gave me some very mixed feelings. In my naïveté, I felt that mercenary pursuits shouldn't coincide with worship. What if someone was poor and couldn't afford the comfort the items offered? Would some charitable entity provide them with some of the holy objects?

On the other hand, if some of these articles gave hope to those who had none, they were worth any price. I found this to be a rather complicated problem. It certainly gave me a lot to think about on my way home on the train, which I now had all to myself. The feeling of this place of worship stayed with me as I pondered what I had seen. I could still smell the incense, I could still feel the magic of the unassuming little chapel and the pure and simple faith of the people who came to pray for the Madonna's help. Whatever their reason for coming, they probably left with hope and their spirits lifted.

I in turn left with the feeling that all those letters of gratitude on the chapel walls were a message to be remembered on days when dissatisfaction or unhappiness over some trifle shadowed my day.

* * *

Chapter 35

On the Road to Recovery

Our lives began to improve slowly but surely after a major currency reform, which took place in June 1948. This important change was to help West Germany become a thriving country again. It was a new beginning for all of us, which held the promise for a brighter future.

For a start each person received sixty deutsch marks for sixty of the old reichsmarks. For everything over sixty, the exchange rate dropped to one deutsch mark for ten reichsmarks. It was bad news for those who had substantial savings, and for those who had amassed fortunes trading on the black market, but it didn't really affect people like us, because we had no savings.

The Russians also issued a new currency in their occupied East Germany, which became known as the east mark. But since they printed large amounts of east marks, they had in effect inflated the currency. The official exchange rate was ten east marks for one deutsch mark, but of course the street differential was much greater.

The terms East and West Germany didn't exist until after the war, when Germany was carved up into four zones of occupation. The American, French, and British zones became known as West Germany, while the Russian zone became East Germany. It effectively divided the two parts of Germany according to their forces of occupation. The Allies combined their three zones into one democratic entity called the Bundesrepublik Deutschland or BRD. In response the Russians established the Deutsche Demokratische Republik or DDR in their zone of occupation. This created two separate Germanys with opposing political systems; one Communist, the other a capitalist democracy—not a good recipe for a cake or world peace!

Shortly after the currency reform tensions between East and West came to a head with Russia's Berlin blockade, which effectively cut off Berlin from the West, bringing great hardship to its people. For the duration of the blockade all supplies, including food, had to be flown into Berlin by the Allies, which became known as the famous Berlin

Airlift. Our news was full of stories about the heroic American actions on behalf of the people of Berlin. We held our breath and worried about the possibility of further conflicts between the two factions, with Germany caught in the middle. Of course it occurred to us that Russia might be poised take all of West Germany, and we weren't sure if the United States would consider us worth defending. It wasn't so long ago that we had escaped East Germany, so we knew better than most what could be in store for us. This was one scenario hovering in the back of my mind, which I suppressed with all my might. Yet I realized that it was a very stressful time for West Germany and the Allies, and like everybody else, I was relieved when the hostilities were peacefully resolved almost a year later.

Older now, I was aware of all these events, but they passed me by without disturbing my equilibrium too much. The same could be said for the sins of the former political system and the Nuremberg trials, which had started in 1945 and were winding down in 1949. My friends and I were heartily sick of the politics of war, and we ignored everything and anything connected with it. We had already lost our childhood, and if we wanted to save our teenage years, we couldn't allow ongoing events to destroy them too. All we wanted was a normal life with the normal interests of young teens.

Not long after the currency reform, previously unavailable goods started to appear in West German stores, so we slowly began to acquire much-needed items. And we needed almost everything. My sister Margit and I were growing, but unfortunately our secondhand shoes didn't grow with us, so shoes were one of our most pressing needs. The shoes our US relatives sent us were fashionable, high-heeled shoes, but as beautiful as they were, they were definitely not practical for walking long distances or on cobblestone streets. To make use of them, my mother had a shoemaker cut down the heels to about an inch. The result was very odd-looking, out-of-balance shoes with the front sticking up, but it didn't occur to me to complain. It was better than going barefoot or wearing the crude vinyl shoes that were produced in limited sizes where my father worked. The vinyl didn't allow air to penetrate, constantly leaving our feet uncomfortably wet with perspiration.

Of course the quantity and choice of shoes now appearing in Burghausen's only shoe store was still meager, but at least there were some available, so we could finally retire our old, worn-out shoes. I was happy as can be when Mother bought me my first pair of new shoes. After years of ill-fitting hand-me-downs, this was a special day to remember. The shoes she bought for me were flat brown leather shoes with crepe soles, and very comfortable for walking the long distance to school.

Even fabrics became available in limited quantities, which enabled people who had been wearing the same old patched, second and thirdhand clothes for years to replenish their wardrobe. Since what my father earned working at the chemical factory was barely enough to cover our living expenses, Mother, who was a very good seamstress, helped out by sewing for people. We bought a secondhand sewing machine as soon as we had saved enough money, and Mother was in business.

Sometimes people brought her two old dresses and Mother made one dress out of the two old ones, using the best parts of each. Mother had learned to extend the life of clothes, and became quite inventive and imaginative at making them last. She also altered the American dresses sent to me by my uncles in the United States. I was always well, if somewhat unconventionally, dressed. I guess you might say that I stood out, which I wasn't always happy about. But the dresses were so pretty and different from anything else seen in Burghausen that women started coming to my mother with fabric, requesting dresses styled just like mine. She now sewed dresses that were modeled on those sent to us by our US relatives. So she was extremely busy, and I was often pressed into service to sew seams, or to sew on buttons, after I had done my homework.

I also made some pocket money by repairing runs in newly available, but extremely expensive, nylon hose. They were so expensive that it was cheaper to have them repaired than to buy new ones. It was a very tedious job and hard on the eyes, but luckily I had good eyesight, and although I didn't earn much, it was better than nothing.

As soon as we could afford it, we bought a secondhand bike, which made shopping for food a lot easier. Heavy packages didn't have to be carried the long distances from the stores anymore, because they could be stowed on special racks behind the seat or hung on the handlebars. I also started to take the bike to school with my books safely stowed on the bike's rack.

In 1951, six years after the end of the war, food rationing finally ended, and we were able to get foods we hadn't seen in a long time, or in some cases had never seen before. The only thing that kept us from gorging ourselves on meat, butter, and pastry was lack of money, not to mention our shrunken stomachs. But after many years of deprivation, our wants were still modest. Just to go to a store and buy milk, eggs, meat, or vegetables in any quantity without ration cards was a new and pleasant experience, which we had no problem getting used to.

Imported items like citrus fruit and bananas were still things we could only look at, because of their exorbitant prices, but just knowing that they were available gave our spirits a lift. Unbelievable happiness was to be able to buy an occasional ice cream cone. We were very appreciative customers when Mother was finally able to bake her wonderful apple crumb cakes and plum cakes again. Her long-forgotten talents in the kitchen, which had been wasted all those years, began to resurface. She could now cook delicious, balanced meals, even though we were still on a very tight budget.

We were also able to travel freely within West Germany or to any other Western country. The only criterion to see the world was a passport and money. Of course that left us out, since we had no money, but at least it was something to strive for. For the first time in years we felt free, as if the shackles of fear and oppression we had worn for so long had been struck off. This sense of freedom after long periods of want was sweeter and more intoxicating than the strongest wine. I savored this new freedom from fear and want with wonder and gratitude. The very air seemed to whisper "Free, Free" as I sped to school on my bike. For the first time since early childhood, I was happy again. This indescribably beautiful feeling life had bestowed on us was a treasure to be cherished.

People rediscovered long-missed pleasures, and finances permitting, made up for lost time. They grasped at newfound freedom with joy and abandon, as if they feared that they would disappear again. Burghausen was no exception, and life there took on new dimensions. Young and old danced on Sunday afternoons to the sound of a small band at a café in town. I went there occasionally with my parents to enjoy a small ice cream or a piece of cake, and had fun dancing and flirting with the boys.

My parents in turn enjoyed pleasant conversations with friends and acquaintances who happened to be there. Young and old didn't always go their separate ways then, as they seem to do nowadays. A lot of things were done together, and it kept the old young, while the young benefited from the experience of the old. It bridged the generation gap and helped us to acquire social skills through observation, which was good practice for later in life. Being accepted in the adult world made us feel grown up and mature, and we tried our best to appear as such, though not always successfully. Of course it was merely self-delusion, because we were far from mature. Nevertheless it was a big boost to our self-esteem. Toward evening we walked home and felt that it had been an afternoon well spent.

Then there were monthly bus trips to the refurbished opera house in Munich to see operas and ballets, which enriched our lives. These trips were sponsored by the chemical plant where my father worked. Since the cost was nominal, I took advantage of it as often as possible, even though it was a three-hour bus ride. For me, the wondrous classical music transcended whatever troubles visited the world. Listening to Beethoven or Mozart transported me to other dimensions, which made me forget the past, and that Munich, like other large cities, was still a heap of rubble. I especially loved ballet and I would have loved to become a dancer.

On spring Sundays, we took long walks in the woods along the river to pick the wildflowers growing there in profusion. We brought them home with us and the scent of the woods and of spring filled our barracks apartment, announcing that summer wasn't far away. With summer came delightful afternoons at Burghausen's lake, which became my favorite place and my home away from home. Our pleasures were simple and, for the most part, cost next to nothing. Even though we still lived in barracks and lacked many material goods, it was a simple but good life! We considered ourselves blessed to live in West Germany, and we were quite happy tucked away in this quiet little corner.

Meanwhile the news we heard about East Germany was not good. The Communist system did little to improve the life of its citizens.

Severe shortages of food and consumer goods were still a fact of life. It was common knowledge that thousands of people still risked their lives trying to escape the "Workers' Paradise." To stop this drain of manpower, the Communist government made escape ever more difficult. All along its borders they added mined death strips to the barbed wire fences and manned watchtowers, making escape almost impossible. But desperation caused people to invent the most improbable escape routes—all of them dangerous. Some lucky ones succeeded, but most were killed in their attempt to escape. Some lost their lives in the minefields, others were shot outright. Those who were caught and arrested landed in jails for many years to atone for their crime of attempting to flee. This made the DDR's citizens virtual prisoners without hope of escape. Thank God we fled East Germany when we did.

* * *

Chapter 36

A Butterfly Comes to Life

As Germany recovered, so did we. Our lives had improved tremendously, and the past seemed more like a bad dream. Burghausen was like a peaceful island that the war had passed by. It slumbered in the past, as if waiting for a kiss to bring it into the present. I reveled in its serenity and the beauty of the surrounding meadows and woods. It was an idyllic place for the teenager I had become.

One day, on my way home from school, I decided to take the more enjoyable route through the forest. On a narrow path meandering between towering pines, I was stopped by a very old woman with a cane who was making her way painfully and awkwardly through the woods. Leaning on her cane, she looked me up and down and her old face creased into a smile: "So, the ugly little caterpillar has turned into a beautiful butterfly!" she said. Then without another word, she went hobbling on her way. I had never met the woman, but she must have known me or seen me around. I was rather perplexed, and I couldn't imagine what she meant. When I thought about it later though, it dawned on me that it was a compliment, and a nice one at that.

There's a time in all our lives when we are neither children nor adults. We are somewhere in between as we teeter on the brink of adulthood. The period of transition from one stage to the other is generally not an easy one. Some are chubby with leftover baby fat, while others are all arms and legs as the maturing process takes place. But then seemingly overnight, a metamorphosis occurs, and the ugly ducklings transform into sleek swans in a way that is often nothing less than miraculous. This metamorphosis is particularly pronounced in girls as their bodies undergo a change just before and after the first menstruation. Their bodies fill out in all the right places and soft curves replace angles and flat planes. Since we didn't pay too much attention to our appearance, the transformation took most of us by surprise.

Unfortunately my generation was given little or no warning by the adults as to what to expect.

I remember the big commotion at school one day when one of my classmates ran screaming from one of the bathrooms: "Help! Someone help Ossie, she's bleeding to death!"

Ossie was a Chinese-German girl who boarded with the nuns, and was slightly older than the rest of us. The teaching staff came running and poor Ossie was whisked away to the director's office, and then sent home to the cloister. This incident left us completely bewildered and worried about our classmate's state of health. She was back in school the next day very much alive, acting as if nothing had happened, and nothing further was said about the incident. There was no explanation, even though we were all very curious and would have liked to know more about the terrible disease Ossie had come down with. Even Ossie remained silent and wouldn't answer any of our questions. It was a big secret about which we could only speculate. In Catholic Bavaria the subject seemed to be one big bad taboo! Certain things just weren't talked about, and this was one of them.

When I came down with the same thing a few months later, and Mother told me that this would now happen every month, I realized that Ossie didn't have a disease after all. It was nature's way of letting us know that we had become women. I can't say that I was happy about this aspect of being female. It was just plain horrible! Our bodies were changing, and dealing with this new state of affairs was quite unsettling. All I could think of were the days I wouldn't be able to go swimming or take part in sports. But it also explained the old woman's comment, and why I suddenly began to draw the attention of boys. That was the only plus I could see in this new situation. Or maybe it was my new, homemade bathing suit? Even though conditions in Germany had improved, many consumer goods like bathing suits weren't available yet. So I used wool remnants to knit myself a bathing suit. Because there was little wool to work with, I had barely enough for a sedate, two-piece suit. Beige with green trim, it really turned out quite nice, I thought. The only problem was that after wearing it a few times, it shrank drastically and I wound up with my first bikini. Could that have had anything to do with all the attention I suddenly drew from the opposite sex? But if any of the boys wanted to take me on a date, they would have to ask my father's permission first. I thought it a very good arrangement, because it took courage on the young man's part to brave my father, even though he was by no means a difficult ogre. Since it was a long walk to our barracks home, it also required an extra effort, which was further proof of his affection. Before permission was given, there were all kinds of questions, followed by instructions on what time to bring me home. However, except for the occasional Saturday, dating was infrequent, because the workload at school didn't leave us much time.

Then there was my school's 8 p.m. curfew during the school year to consider. Of course that didn't apply to the girls boarding in the cloister, for they were always under lock and key. But it didn't prevent the girls from flirting with the town's young men behind the nuns' backs when they were marched through town on their daily afternoon outings.

I became the local post office with the official title of "*Postillon D'Amour*" for the girls boarding with the nuns, since their mail was monitored, and they weren't allowed to receive mail from boys. I was tremendously popular on the days when I brought mail from their lovelorn admirers. Some of the girls had admirers in town and communication took place at night when the nuns were sleeping. Young men would gather under the girl's third-floor dormitory windows and letters were passed up and down on strings. Where there's a will, there's always a way!

One of the girls in my class boarding with the nuns successfully eluded them on their daily outings by using her passport to cross the bridge into Austria to a cozy little wine tavern while the nuns were frantically looking all over town for her. After it happened several times, the nuns' patience was exhausted, and she was asked to leave the cloister. Her unhappy parents had to look for new accommodations for her. She wound up boarding with a family in town after my parents politely rejected the idea of hosting her. They weren't looking for extra trouble. They had enough trouble keeping me under control.

Those of us who didn't live in the cloister managed to get around the curfew by hugging the darker sides of the streets and sneaking into the movie theater after the film had begun and the lights were out. It was always a challenge, because sometimes school staff monitored the two movie houses in town. Of course a successful flouting of the curfew only added to our enjoyment of the evening.

Thankfully we didn't have to worry about our school's regulations during our summer vacation, so we took full advantage of our freedom. On late summer afternoons, a group of us would take our bikes to a nearby village, where the farmers made delicious wine from currants. A successful harvest and the new wine were duly celebrated with live music in vine-covered outdoor booths. A small dance floor served those who were inclined to dance. We sampled the wine, danced, flirted, and laughed until nightfall. Biking home in the coolness of the evening through meadows and woods, laughing and singing, was always a great conclusion to a fun-filled day.

Unfortunately the summer was over too quickly, giving way to fall and my school's odious restrictions. Nevertheless we usually managed to avoid getting caught when we were out and about after our 8 p.m. curfew.

However, there was one occasion that landed me in a lot of trouble. It was carnival time, and one of the big events in town was the annual masked costume ball. Since I had just turned sixteen, my parents decided to let me go with them and some of their friends. All excited, I readily agreed to their condition that we would leave at 11 p.m. So my mother made me a gypsy costume and this butterfly barely escaped from its cocoon was absolutely thrilled to go to her first costume ball. Alcohol restrictions for minors didn't exist in Germany, so that wasn't a problem. Since it was readily available and there was no challenge in obtaining it, most young people like me showed scant interest in it. Of course in my excitement I forgot all about my school's regulations.

The ball took place in the hall where our school's statutes were read every September, but entering the building through its large doors, I hardly recognized the place. The wide stairway leading up to the hall was decorated with balloons and streamers. Part of it was taken up by a slide for revelers who wanted to go downstairs to visit the cozy bar on the first floor, where a small combo played popular tunes. They came sliding down in groups, screaming with laughter as they wound up in jumbled heaps at the bottom.

The spacious hall was completely transformed. Vine-covered booths lined the walls around the dance floor and balloons in large nets with colored streamers hung from the ceiling. An orchestra played lively tunes, which added to the festive atmosphere. Masked costumed people filled the dance floor and the booths. Nobody knew who anyone was because the masks hid their identities, and depending on their acting ability, they assumed the personality of whatever character they represented. Losing no time, I delved into the crowd of weird creatures with gusto.

Of course I paid absolutely no attention to the clock. I was having too much fun dancing up a storm, and wearing out one partner after another. Like a butterfly flitting from blossom to blossom, I didn't stay with any of them too long, unless they were good dancers. I was having the time of my life. But as usual when pleasure clouds the senses, time seems to accelerate, and it raced toward 11 p.m. at lightning speed. So eleven o'clock came and went, as I continued to enjoy myself with carefree abandon. If my parents were looking for me at the time, their chances of finding me in the swirling, happy crowd were slim, and I did my best not to be found.

Then all of a sudden, it was midnight! By the stroke of twelve, all music and dancing stopped. The nets on the ceiling opened up and all the balloons and confetti floated down on the happy crowd. It was also time for everybody to remove their masks. That included me and the frog I was dancing with at the time. There was a lot of laughter and merriment when people discovered who had partnered them on the dance floor. Except me! I wasn't laughing! I was in shock! My blood turned to ice and my knees turned to mush! It wasn't because the unmasked frog had suddenly turned into an ugly monster, it was because of the couple that took their masks off right next to us. To my horror, one was the director of my school! Belatedly I remembered my school's regulations. I was wishing the floor would open up and swallow me or that I could become invisible, but unfortunately none of these things occurred. The director didn't say a word, but gave me such an icy, withering look that I felt like I was disintegrating on the spot. What miserable luck!

After everybody had removed their masks the music and dancing continued, but unfortunately without me. I left the hapless frog unceremoniously on the dance floor and immediately sought out my parents, who were sitting with friends in one of the booths. Greatly agitated, barely able to speak, I spilled the story of this terrible mishap.

My parents were as upset as I was, and my failure to come back at 11 p.m. so we could leave was duly noted. Recriminations abounded: "Where were you? We were looking all over for you. Now you see what you have done."

Mother angrily shook her head: "This isn't the first time your willfulness got you into trouble. This is quite a calamity. You know that you're in a lot of hot water now, don't you?"

"You'll be grounded, and for a long time," was my father's terse comment.

What could I say; it was my fault. I only had myself to blame, for had we left before the unmasking, nobody would have been the wiser. Who would have known me behind my mask? My presence at the ball would have gone undetected.

We left for home immediately in a very subdued mood, while the ball and the merriment continued into the wee hours without us. It was a long walk home, which was painful in more ways than one. Even my feet hurt badly, because I didn't give them a rest all night, except when I visited the little bar downstairs with one or the other of my dance partners. This butterfly was now caught in a net from which there was no escape.

The next day, a Sunday, I was dead tired after a sleepless night, but I forced myself to do the homework required for Monday. It was a good thing that I made the effort. The first class was history and I was thoroughly quizzed. The professor's eyeglasses glittered as she squeezed me for every last bit of my knowledge on the subject.

To my surprise, Ilse, another girl from my class, was caught at the ball as well. When it was her turn, her quizzes went very badly, and it was obvious that she hadn't even looked at her homework. That's how it went the whole morning, class after class. Ilse and I were the victims of merciless, hostile quizzes, spiced with caustic remarks. Then both of us were called to the director's office, where we were read the riot act and threatened with expulsion for our transgressions.

A formal letter was sent to our parents asking them to appear for a conference. At the appointed time our parents were also castigated for their disregard of school regulations by allowing us to go to the ball. Then some negotiations took place to determine our fate. In the end we were allowed to stay, but now had a formal reprimand and were basically on probation. This was serious business! We had to become prim and proper model students and carefully avoid any further infringements on the school's regulations.

Aside from that, I was grounded, stuck fast in the net I wove myself. Now I had to turn down many invitations to parties and leave quite a few young men disappointed. Carnival season, which had another two weeks to go, unfortunately had to go on without me, which pained me no end. This properly humbled butterfly had to go into hibernation, impatiently waiting for the time it could leave its cocoon again. But the memory of the ball was well worth it!

* * *

Chapter 37

The Enchanted Lake

Among Burghausen's many attractions was the Woehrsee, a lake that was the center of many of our activities. Whether it was summer or winter, the lake that ran along the entire length of Burghausen's castle was one of my greatest pleasures. The lake's smooth, dark-green surface mirrored the castle perched on top of the mountain ridge to perfection. Every building, every tower, turret, and crenellated wall was flawlessly replicated on its emerald surface, creating a scene of enchanting beauty. On sunny days with intensely blue skies, the lake sparkled where tiny ripples caught the rays of the sun here and there, imbuing the mirrored castle with an air of mystery. It gave the impression of a magical realm where serenity reigned supreme.

Bushes and trees grew in profusion along its western shore, and rushes and water lilies grew in abundance at its undisturbed northern end, which was also home to all kinds of waterfowl. A path running around the lake made it a favorite Sunday afternoon stroll for the older generation, and a lover's lane at night for the young.

At its southern tip were changing cabins, a shed for canoes, and a lush lawn where sunbathers could spread their blankets to enjoy the warming rays of the sun. A small cottage at the lawn's edge offered refreshments to hungry or thirsty guests. All private building along the lake's shores was prohibited, making its pleasures available to everyone. Fortunately, the same applied to powerboats, which would have destroyed the tranquility of this little piece of paradise.

Since so much of my time was spent there, I came to know it in all the many moods it displayed at different times of the year. We went swimming as early as the end of May. Its waters, even when freezing cold, were velvety soft and welcoming. At that time of the year the budding trees covered the lake with a light green veil of pollen, and my friends and I would come out of the water looking like Martians—green from head to toe. We always thought it amusing, and laughed at each other as we went to shower off the green film coating us.

As spring became summer and the weather turned warmer, I spent more and more time at the lake, often doing my homework on its shore. It became my home away from home. I had an old, secondhand bike by now, and getting there was a breeze. Going home took longer, though, because the bike had to be pushed up the steep, winding hill that led from the lake up to the new part of town where I lived.

My time at the lake made me a very good swimmer, but since its half-mile width didn't present much of a challenge, my friends and I would swim the mile to the northern end of the lake, where we relaxed on a huge mossy rock projecting from the shore. We spent time diving off the rock amid a lot of banter and laughter. When we had enough of that, we would run back along the path surrounding the lake and jump back into the water at the southern end.

When I needed solitude, I would swim to the northern end alone. It was on these occasions when I became even more conscious of the lake's bewitching charm. As my arms parted the water, I felt sorry for fracturing the beautiful picture of the castle spread out in front of me. The soft, silky water embraced me lovingly, and made me feel like I was an accepted part of its green, transparent world, where time was endless and had no meaning. The upper layer of water was warm, but sometimes I passed over very cold spots where springs bubbled up from far below, reminding me that the lake was a live entity with a definite personality and character of its own. The hushed stillness out on the water magnified the noise of the water as my arms and legs propelled me along. It seemed like a sacrilege to disturb the peace of this silent world, and I wished that I could be like the water insects, which skimmed noiselessly and effortlessly over the water's smooth surface. Alone, I was fully aware that these were very special moments in my life, which would be unforgettable and treasured forever. I was filled with gratitude to be allowed to experience such joy in being alive.

When I came to the northern part, I sometimes took a shortcut through the lily pads, swimming stretched out as flat as possible to avoid getting my legs entangled in them. Even though this was a little risky, it had its own rewards, because close up, the lilies were another beautiful aspect of the lake to be enjoyed. Arrived at the rock, I sat basking in the sun in utter contentment and couldn't help reflecting on the blessings given to me after so many years of sheer misery. My golden heart necklace glittered as it caught the rays of the sun, and it seemed to join me in singing the praises of this paradise.

On weekends, when it was more crowded, I escaped the noise and the unwanted attentions of some of the young men by swimming out onto the lake to go ashore wherever I wanted. It was true freedom, because restrictions didn't exist. You had to know your own limitations, because you were completely responsible for your own actions. After negotiating the muddy shore bottom at the selected spot, I sat among the high grasses, so hidden from view that I felt as if I was alone in the world. I was able to observe the activities of small insects, study all the interesting grasses around me, and still enjoy a view of the lake with the reflected castle. At peace with myself and at one with the world around me, I felt myself merging with the high grasses softly whispering in the breeze, the water lilies, and the clouds sailing in the blue sky. It was heaven on earth.

Other times my friends and I had a lot of fun when we went out on the lake in canoes, with the young men doing most of the paddling. We would upset each other's canoes in the middle of the lake. Paddles and seats, which floated away, were retrieved amid a lot of laughter, only to bring them and the canoes back to shore, and then go back out to start the same process all over again.

We also ran the canoes into the rushes, upsetting some of its denizens, not to mention annoying the nuns bathing in their completely enclosed bathhouse at the northern end of the lake. Peeking through the knotholes, we found out that the nuns went into the water fully clothed in what looked like voluminous white undergarments, which billowed around them like balloons. Their white limbs and shaven heads were as white as their garments, which made them appear like some strange, extraterrestrial water plants come to devour the earth. Somebody who remarked a little too loudly: "They look like mushrooms left in the dark too long," was immediately shushed by the rest of us.

"Not so loud, they'll hear us."

"More like poison mushrooms, especially if Sister Therese is one of them," came a whispered comment, which was met with:

"Shut up already. Do you want to get us in trouble?"

We could see that the area of water within the enclosure was very small and certainly not deep enough for swimming, which meant that they were only able to submerge up to their waists. Whispering to each other, we concluded that they were in no danger of drowning or getting sunburned in their secluded, roofed-over bathhouse. But we were all glad that we were out in the fresh air and sunshine and not locked up in that dismal place. Since we couldn't help giggling as the wavelets bumped our canoes against the bathhouse, the nuns quickly became aware of our presence. They were none too pleased, and angry words about young people who had no respect were hurled through the walls. That's when we made a fast retreat, taking our canoes back out onto the lake. It was a good thing that the nuns hadn't been able to see us, because we would have caught hell from the Mother Superior.

One weekend in July the town of Burghausen hosted a festival featuring the castle and the lake, which drew many people from surrounding towns and villages. Bleachers were erected on a meadow facing the lake and the castle. When it was dark, a huge crowd was assembled, with many of them sitting in the grass and under the trees as a band played. Barges lit with lanterns and filled with musicians, ballet dancers, and singers from the Munich Opera House slowly emerged from the darkness. They were gliding along the lake in a dreamlike atmosphere as they sang and danced below the backdrop of the illuminated castle, which appeared like a mirage in the night sky. The evening climaxed with spectacular fireworks erupting over the castle, lighting it up in all its splendor and crowning it with flashing starbursts. Since all this was reflected in the lake, the effect was doubly impressive and beautiful. When it was over, everyone left the lake for the town square and some music and dancing. All the sidewalk cafés and restaurants were serving wine, beer, and food in a festive atmosphere. A wonderful time was had by all, when even strangers became friends.

Come September school started again; the temperatures began to cool off earlier in the day and sometimes a soft haze hung over the lake, signaling the end of summer. Nevertheless we still went swimming whenever we could, even when the red and gold leaves swam with us.

In October and November the lake received a well-deserved rest. I still enjoyed it, though, from the top of one of the high castle walls. I climbed up there through a break in the wall, which wasn't exactly easy, but it was well worth the effort. There I sat on nice days with my homework, very much aware of the reflected castle in the lake spread out below me while the dying leaves of overhanging tree branches softly rustled in the gentle winds.

With December came snow and freezing temperatures. Snow covered the towers, rooftops, and walls of the castle like a confectioner's sugary, prize-winning creation. Now the lake came back to life again clothed in wintry splendor. The ice-covered lake glistened in the sun, with the trees and bushes along its shores bending under their white burden.

When the ice was thick enough, the lake's snowy crust in front of the refreshment cottage was shaved smooth until the dark green water showed through the thick ice. This area was then covered with a thin layer of water, which froze overnight to a glass-smooth, emerald green surface, which was ideal for figure skating and ice dancing.

My group of friends was definitely into ice dancing, so to enable me to participate, my mother made a short, navy blue skirt with white trim for me. I knitted myself a pair of pearl gray tights because, like many other things, they were still not available in stores. Unfortunately I didn't have enough of the light gray wool, so another much deeper gray wool had to be used to finish the project. Consequently I wound up with party-colored hose, which didn't bother me in the least. A red or yellow sweater and a matching scarf completed my outfit. Good skates weren't affordable, so I had to be satisfied with a pair of secondhand, screw-on skates.

During our winter vacation we assembled at the lake daily. We learned how to dance to the strains of waltzes, tangos, and fox-trots, which came over a loudspeaker. Young men came and politely asked for a dance in this open-air ballroom. We accepted with pleasure, especially if a good dancer asked us. When no suitable partner was available, we danced alone. The occasional spill was taken in stride as a normal occurrence in practicing the intricacies of the dance steps—some of which were quite tricky and required a certain amount of agility to perform with proper elegance. Gliding along to the soft rhythm of a waltz with seemingly effortless grace, our shadows followed us like alter egos mimicking every one of our moves, as our skates left glistening patterns on the smooth green ice.

When darkness approached, floodlights reflected millions of ice crystals and silvered the snow, turning our surroundings into a glittering ballroom. Millions of stars in the dark winter sky became our ballroom's chandeliers, their brilliance competing with the splendor of the sparkling crystals on the ground and on the trees around us.

Sometimes, when it started to snow, obscuring the starlit sky, the swirling flakes caught in the floodlights fell on us like a shimmering curtain of white lace. Snow crystals settled on our hair as we danced, jumped, and spun in a fairy tale world of incredible beauty, which normally only exists in our imagination. It was more spectacular and more enchanting than anything I have ever seen. We spent many afternoons and evenings dancing in this hauntingly beautiful setting. Since we were constantly moving, we seldom felt cold. Nevertheless we occasionally went to the cottage for hot chocolate and the warmth of the potbellied stove, only to hurry back out again for more fun.

Around 7 or 8 p.m. we prepared to go home, because that was when the music stopped and the lights were turned off. Most of us had to navigate the steep, very slippery, path leading up to the castle, which usually took us over an hour. We held hands forming a chain, but more often than not, somebody in the chain slipped and fell, taking the whole chain screaming and laughing back down with them into deep snowdrifts. But eventually we made it, and managed to get home full of snow and ice. I certainly slept well those nights! So did the lake, with peace and quiet returned for the night after a layer of fresh water was applied to ready it for skaters the next day.

As winter passed and the ice and snow melted, the lake rested again and slept. With approaching spring, I eagerly looked forward to the reawakening of the Enchanted Lake.

* * *

Chapter 38

Adam and Eve

1952

Even though we loved our beautiful Burghausen lake, we still had an occasional urge to try something different. So one weekend in July my parents allowed me to go on an overnight bike trip to Chiemsee, a large lake about forty miles away. My mother thought it safe since my friend Traudl, who was two years older and already had a good job in the lab of the local chemical plant, was going with me.

We left very early on a sunny Saturday morning with nothing more than our bathing suits, towels, a bag filled with sandwiches, and very little money. Aside from that, all we had was the boundless energy and the optimism of youth.

We biked along country roads with little or no traffic. Often the only traffic, which we passed with ease, was a farmer's horse-drawn wagon slowly ambling along. It was an exhilarating ride with the sun on our faces and the wind blowing our hair. We felt as free as birds trying out their wings after leaving their nest for the first time. We breathed in the scent of the grasses and wildflowers in the fields and meadows we passed. These alternated with stretches of cool, shady forests where the invigorating scent of pine sped us on. We reached the northern shore of the lake after five or six hours of constant biking, and immediately settled ourselves on a stretch of sandy beach bordered by scrub pines.

Chiemsee lacked the quiet beauty of our Burghausen lake, but it had an air of excitement, with the constant sound of waves depositing small pebbles along its shore. It looked more like an inland sea than a lake because of its approximately seventy-square-mile size, and we knew that large steamers plied its waters, carrying tourist to its two islands. After we had rested a little, we jumped into the water to wash off the dust of the road. The water was quite cool and in constant motion, its gentle waves teasing us as they ebbed and flowed around us.

Then it was time to find a place to stay for the night. There was only one hotel in the area and we certainly didn't have enough money for that. The only alternative was to throw ourselves at the mercy of a farmer at a nearby farmhouse and ask for lodging. The farmer took pity on us poor souls, and offered us his cow shed for twenty-five cents each. We gratefully accepted and made ourselves at home with the cows in the earthy-smelling barn. We bedded down next to one of the cow stalls on a pile of straw covered with an old horse blanket the farmer had given to us. It wasn't the best night's sleep we ever had even though we were very tired, but it was better than sleeping under a bush on the beach. At least we had shelter, even if we had to share it with a bunch of cows.

I woke up around 5 a.m. to the sound of a lot of mooing and something wet hitting my face. I opened my eyes a slit and looked up. What I saw was a cow's head hanging over the partition right above me, drooling on me and mooing loudly. The barn's permanent residents were getting restless.

It was freezing cold, and through a space under the door I could see dew hanging like crystal tears on the grass outside. Between the mooing cows, the cold, and the straw poking us through the blanket, further sleep was out of the question. So we shook off the straw, packed our few things, and went to pay the farmer. He and his wife surprised us with a wonderful breakfast of freshly baked bread, homemade butter, and a tall glass of fresh milk. I can hardly remember anything that tasted so good, and all for twenty-five cents.

Since it was too early for anything else, we went to sit on the beach. The morning haze still hung over the water, softening all contours. We watched the sun emerge from the mist, tinting the lake and the beach with a golden light, dispelling the morning chill along with the haze. It wasn't long before a few more people joined us, and suddenly a young man sat down with us and greeted Traudl like a long-lost friend. He turned out to be someone she worked with at the lab who ran into us by accident—as far as I knew.

So now we were three and the discussion turned around what to do with the rest of the day. Since we had more energy than brains, we decided to bike the one and a half hours to Prien, the largest town on the lake. All the steamers left from there for the islands, so it was a very busy town full of tourists. When we arrived, we went straight to the beach since we didn't have enough money for anything else. I had only seven marks emergency money, which I didn't want to waste on anything foolish, and Traudl didn't have much more.

From where we were sitting we could see Herreninsel, the larger of the two islands, off in the distance. It didn't seem too far away, and we eyed it speculatively.

"It doesn't look so far," Alec remarked. "I'll bet we could swim there."

I enthusiastically agreed with him. "*Ja*, let's try it, I'm game. We can't afford the fare for the steamer but it would be nice to see King Ludwig's palace and the formal gardens I heard so much about."

Traudl eyed the distance to the island doubtfully. "I don't know, it may be farther than it looks. Count me out!" Back into the water we went. The gentle waves buffeting us felt good. Traudl swam with us for a short time, but soon turned back. Maybe she was just smarter. Her friend Alec and I continued swimming toward the island.

The farther we swam, the higher and rougher the waves were. It became even scarier when Alec disappeared in a trough and I couldn't see him anymore. But it was too late to turn back now. It was as far to the island as it was back to shore. So I kept swimming in the direction of the island. The waves became so high that I could only see the island when a wave swept me to its crest, before it sucked me back down again into a deep trough. It seemed like a prison with walls of dark green water. All I could see were walls of water threatening to swallow me for the audacity to venture so far into its domain. I couldn't see Alec anymore, and my arms and legs started to feel like lead. I knew that it was literately a case of sink or swim, so I tried to control my breathing and kept swimming, even though my arms felt like they were about to fall off.

When my feet finally touched the muddy bottom, I couldn't believe that I had made it. Visions of my lifeless body being fished out of the lake disappeared with solid ground under my feet. I had no idea where I was. All I could see were bushes and trees. Working my way through the bushes along the shore, I started to look for Alec.I was wondering if he had made it, or if perhaps he had drowned in our foolhardy attempt to swim to an island that sane people took a steamer to visit. But there he was, smashing through the bushes like an elephant gone berserk. The currents had swept us apart, and deposited us in different places far removed from one another. We looked at each other in amazement that we had made it, and had lived to tell the tale.

"When I didn't see you anymore, I thought that you had drowned!" I shouted.

"I thought the same about you," Alec said, "because I couldn't see you anymore either. The waves were just too high and the current sweeping us apart was too strong."

"Hallelujah, we made it. God, were we lucky," I agreed. "We could be at the bottom of the lake with the fish. It's a good thing the lake doesn't have sharks or crocodiles."

"Please don't even mention those things," Alec replied. "The waves were bad enough."

Now we had to figure out what to do next. Swimming back was out of the question. We estimated that our swim took us at least two or three hours, because we left before noon, and to judge by the angle of the sun, it was already midafternoon. Aside from that, we were too tired and certainly didn't want to tempt fate again. So we fought our way through thick bushes to the formal gardens of King Ludwig's Palace, which is an exact replica of Versailles. This was the ultimate goal of the hundreds of tourists the steamers brought there every day.

Alec and I found ourselves suddenly among a crowd of tourists walking around admiring King Ludwig's beautiful gardens, fountains, and statues. Most of the sightseers were Americans who were easily recognizable by their gaily colored shirts and expensive cameras. Some of the women wore a lot of makeup, jewelry, fancy sunglasses, and unnaturally colored hair. When some of them spotted barefoot, bikini-clad Alec and me, they nudged each other, and we heard them say:

"This must be the Garden of Eden! Look, everybody, there goes Adam and Eve! They aren't wearing much more than they did!"

"Who would believe this back home? These two have some nerve to parade around like that."

Another remarked: "You can say that again. Those bathing suits couldn't be any skimpier. Have they no shame?"

Suddenly all attention was centered on us. Some stared while others laughed and snickered at us two soaking-wet, barefoot creatures. We must have looked like denizens of the lake who had come on dry land to confound and amuse them. We certainly looked more than a little out of place. We were no doubt another interesting sight, which added to their enjoyment of the trip, and an amusing story to tell the people back home. Their clicking cameras took home more than pictures of fountains, statues, and Ludwig's Palace. Of course they didn't realize that we understood English and knew exactly what they were joking about. We simply pretended that we didn't understand them, and that our promenade through them in bikini bathing suits was nothing out of the ordinary. We did it with as much nonchalance and aplomb as we could muster, and rather enjoyed shocking all these people who we thought strange.

Finally we made our way to the other end of the island, where a small boat shed stood at the water's edge. There we talked an elderly man into taking us back to Prien in his small motorboat after we promised him twenty marks. Out on the water, we could see a huge bank of black thunderclouds massed off to the west. The wind had picked up, and churned the water, cresting the high waves with white foam. The little boat was tossed like a toy, while showers of frothy spray inundated us. The ride back to Prien was almost as scary as our swim to the island. We found Traudl relaxing on the same beach from which we had left. She had been quite worried, so she was very glad to see us.

"My God, I thought you two nuts drowned." she said. "I can't believe you actually swam to the island. You are lucky you made it back alive."

"*Ja*, well, we almost didn't, but that's a long story," we told her.

"Did you at least get to see Ludwig's Palace?" she asked.

"Sure, but we only saw it from the outside. It's absolutely fabulous. We took a very nice walk through the formal gardens though."

We left it at that. Then we pooled our money to pay the man the promised amount, which left me with exactly nothing.

It was 5 p.m. by now, and we had a long ride ahead of us. We had promised to be home by nightfall, but there was no way we would be able to make it home by then. So we left hurriedly as soon as we had changed into our street clothes in one of the changing cabins. The sun was hanging low in the sky, and the woods we biked through felt quite cool already. It started to get dark by the time we passed the northern end of the lake where we had spent the previous night in the farmer's barn. By the time we were halfway home, night had overtaken us, and it was pitch-dark. There were no streetlights on these lonely country roads, so we had to navigate by the lights on our bikes. The night was quiet and eerie. We could only see what lay within the small circle of our tiny headlights, and the only sound we heard was the whirring of our bike chains as we sped along.

When we came to an uphill stretch, Traudl suddenly fell off her bike and rolled down a steep embankment on the side of the road. When we stopped to help her she told us that she was exhausted and felt sick. So from then on our progress was slow, because we had to walk the bikes for long periods of time to give her a chance to recover.

We finally arrived home well after midnight, where our respective parents stood outside with their eyes glued to the path on which we would arrive. As we came into the homestretch, the storm caught up to us, with torrents of rain and rolling thunder, almost giving our parents heart attacks when they saw us pedaling down the path amidst flashes of lightning.

We had barely out-biked the storm, which now broke over us with all its fury, but the storm outside was nothing compared to what awaited me inside after Traudl and her mother left. My parents had spent many anxious hours waiting for me, and they angrily demanded an explanation for our delay. Feeling very guilty, I told them as much as I could without going into the damning detail of our Prien-to-Herreninsel swim.

The next day my mother quizzed me some more about our trip, and what I had done with the seven marks she gave me. I couldn't very well tell her that I used them to pay a man to bring me back from the island. So I told her the first thing that came to my mind: "I bought bananas!" That started another storm, because bananas were a luxury item and outrageously expensive, practically unaffordable for people like us. My mother was very angry that I spent the money on such an unnecessary luxury.

Of course I was grounded for the rest of the summer. So there were no more excursions for me. I never told my parents about my swimming escapade to Herreninsel. Had they known about that, I would've been grounded for the next few years!

* * *

Chapter 39

Auf Wiedersehen Germany—Hello America

1953

It was now eight years after the war and life had improved considerably. Thanks to Germany's economic upswing there was a lot of construction to provide housing for the millions who had lost their homes, whether through bombings or expulsion from Germany's eastern provinces.

In 1952 we were finally able to get an apartment in a newly constructed building. It was so new that the paint was still damp when we moved in. A carpenter made new furniture for us, and our iron beds with the vinyl webbing could finally be retired. Beautiful white lacquered beds took their place. Sleeping in a bed with a real mattress was a strange new feeling. I had all but forgotten what it felt like.

Even though our accommodations in the newer part of town were spacious and very nice, I missed the friendly camaraderie of the barracks. On the plus side, my trip to school was cut in half, and we couldn't be considered barracks "riffraff" anymore. We were now respected members of the community. Civilized living conditions and a normal life had returned for us in Burghausen, although the badly bombed large cities in the rest of Germany still had a long way to go.

Then in early May 1953 we got a big surprise. After spending five years in fairy-tale Burghausen, we received a letter from the American consulate in Munich regarding our emigration to the United States. We now had permission to emigrate, and we were instructed to present ourselves with all the necessary papers. The letter also informed us that we would have to allow time for complete physical examinations. The news hit us like a thunderbolt. Our excitement ran high! After all those years, we had almost forgotten about our application to emigrate to the United States. At least I had!

Now that it had become a reality, I had mixed feelings about the whole idea of emigration. On one hand I was reluctant to leave my friends and the enchantment of Burghausen, but on the other hand there was adventure and an exciting new life beckoning from across the ocean.

On the appointed day, May 19, 1953, we arrived at the American consulate in Munich. As is usually the case with government offices, we had to sit around waiting for quite some time. I spent the time observing some of the women who shared the waiting room with us. One lady in particular drew my interest. She was heavily made up, had dyed, reddish-orangey hair, and wore a tight blue skirt with a scandalous see-through nylon blouse. She wore high, stiletto-heeled shoes and nylon stockings with a dark seam running down the back. My mother directed my attention to the diamond wristwatch she wore. Since I had never seen diamonds, I found them quite fascinating. Trying not to stare, I looked at her watch as surreptitiously as possible.

Another interesting figure was a man in a long black coat and black hat, with a beard and curls over his ears. He looked a lot like the pictures I had seen in the booklet I picked up on the street a long time ago. I had completely forgotten about this incident, but seeing the man, the memory of that day resurfaced.

Turning toward Mother, I whispered, "Who is that man?"
She replied in the same hushed tone, "He is a Jewish man." That was when I found out that the people depicted in that booklet were Jews. Since I had never met any Jews, I regarded him with fascination.

Finally our names were called and we were interviewed by an American official in the interrogation room. When it was my turn, I was quizzed among other things about whether I had ever worked as a prostitute, which I found extremely insulting! Then it was off to the clinic, where we were checked from head to toe to make sure we wouldn't bring any diseases into the United States. We all got a clean bill of health, so now there was nothing standing in the way of our emigration.

From then on, everything went very fast. Back home the mad scramble was on to get ready for our journey, for we only had six weeks to settle our affairs before our departure. My parents sold all the nice new furniture for a fraction of its cost, and a carpenter made large boxes for all the things we would be taking with us. While all this was going on, I had to study for my final exams, which prevented me from giving my full attention to the work at hand. Mother was extremely annoyed, because she could have used more help than I was able to give. But I wanted to leave school with good grades, so I did my best to divide my time between studying and helping out at home.

Our visas arrived in short order, and so did the tickets that our relatives in the United States had purchased for us on a ship called *Neptunia*. There wasn't much time, and the last few weeks in Burghausen passed in a blur of frantic activity. When the fateful day came, all our friends came to see us off at the train station. There were tearful good-byes, for who knew if we would ever see each other again? It wasn't easy to leave the people who had become such good friends over the years.

The train took us to Munich and then on to Hanover, where the results of the bombings were still very much in evidence. In Hanover we spent the night with relatives, but since there really wasn't enough room to accommodate all of us, sleep was a haphazard affair. Tired as I was, I didn't get much sleep on their couch, because my sister Margit and my cousin Roswitha were having a lot of fun annoying me. They were giant pains.

The next day it was on to Bremerhaven, our port of embarkation, where we spent the night in a facility designed especially for emigrants. My feelings about our emigration were quite mixed. Except for what I had heard and read, the United States was an unknown. My picture of the United States was one of a dynamic, modern country with people to match. In my naïveté, I thought of it as sitting on God's right side in an awesome country that could do no wrong. From the Sears catalogues our relatives had sent us, it surely looked like a land of plenty. Since we had done without for so many years, the amount and variety of manufactured goods available was something to behold, and absolutely astounding to me. So I was excited by the prospect of seeing this fabled country, excited to see my grandmother again, and to meet my uncles and their families for the first time. I was also very curious to see the Indians my grandfather had told me so much about when I was a child. Of course I didn't expect them to be wearing feathers, but thought of them as possible neighbors and friends.

So on July 30, 1953, we boarded the *SS Neptunia* for the ten-day voyage. A band on the quay played a familiar old tune: "*Muss i denn zum Staedtele hinaus* (Must I leave my little town)," which brought tears to many eyes, including mine. That was when I finally realized I was leaving Germany, which I loved with all my heart despite all the terrible times and misery I experienced there. I stood by the railing, crying until I couldn't see German land anymore.

On board ship heading for the United States

Then it was time to settle into our cabin, which slept four. It was tiny, with bunk beds on both sides, and a very small sink, but not much else. That didn't bother me, for aside from sleeping, I didn't intend to spend much time there, or so I thought!

That first day we spent investigating the ship and learning the layout. The *Neptunia* was built in 1919 and had some nice, 1920s-style lounges, which I found very interesting because they were so nicely detailed. There were beautifully polished woods and brass, with plush, comfortable chairs and rugs. After our hard-bitten life, it all looked very luxurious to me. The next day, a gorgeous sunny day, we anchored off the coast of Ireland. The sun glinting off the waves made the ocean sparkle with a million stars. The bay, full of small boats with colorful sails, presented an absolutely charming picture. More passengers were brought out in small boats. That night a brawl broke out on deck. I guess the Irish were celebrating their beginning in a new land. Well, at least it was a lot better than the crying I did.

It wasn't long before I met two young German men. One was blue-eyed and blond, the other was dark-haired with brown eyes. Since I liked them both, it was difficult not to let one or the other monopolize me. But I certainly enjoyed the evenings flirting and dancing, and the afternoons strolling on deck with them. So my first few days passed very enjoyably, but unfortunately the sea began to get rougher. Dancing became quite a challenge, because the movement of the ship caused us to slide from one side of the dance floor to the other. It was rather fun when we slid across the floor and had to catch ourselves on a lally column with a lot of laughter. The constant balancing act to stay upright was an exercise in agility. But a lot of people were already seasick, and the dining room started to look rather empty. The waves rose to unimaginable heights. They were dark green, gigantic walls of water, coming at our little ship as if threatening to swallow it. I spent a lot of time on deck watching the huge waves with fascination. Since I had no fear of water, it didn't frighten me. It was like saying "Hello" to the big brother of an old friend.

Then one morning, maybe our fourth day out, I strolled around the ship and settled in a chair in one of the lounges. An American woman sat in a chair next to me, and we struck up a conversation. I was delighted to be able to practice my English. She wondered why I wasn't seasick like so many others, and told me about some pills she was taking to prevent seasickness. Kindly, she offered me one of her pills. Not to offend her I took it, and one hour later I wasn't even able to eat my lunch. I felt so nauseous, I had to leave the dining room and run for our cabin to throw up.

From then on, I hardly left the cabin, because all I did was vomit. One of my young man friends, who said he missed me, came to take me on deck, hoping that fresh air would help. But all I did was hang over the railing feeding the fish, which must have been very happy to get such gourmet fare. Pretty embarrassing, to say the least! So much for shipboard romance. Since there were a lot of other wan-looking folks wandering the deck hoping that the fresh air would restore their health and good appetite, I didn't feel singled out.

But there was much worse to come. A big storm that had been brewing in the Atlantic hit us full force. Water, my old friend, was about to teach me a lesson I wouldn't soon forget. The ship was pitching violently from side to side. Lying in my bunk bed, I slid down to catch myself with my feet, only to slide back up and hit my head on the headboard. The porthole that used to show sky now only showed dark green water sloshing back and forth, a lot like what was going on in my stomach. It wasn't long before Mother joined me in our cabin, and the two of us were moaning and groaning and throwing up together. We were quite a sight, and not a pretty one either. Our green skin color definitely wasn't very becoming. I thought I was dying, and I'm sure Mother thought the same.

Margit and my father were OK, so they left our smelly cabin every morning as soon as they could. Occasionally Margit would come back to the cabin, and sit right next to me, eating an apple. The smell of the apple and the sound of her teeth biting into it occasioned more violent outbursts of vomiting. I had a sneaky suspicion that she was doing it on purpose, for when I told her to leave, she only looked at me and took another bite. I felt like throttling her, but I was too weak and too sick to do more than groan. When I thought that things couldn't get any worse, they did. The ship was tossed around like a little nutshell. Mother and I had nothing left to throw up, so we just lay there gagging, trying to prevent our stomachs from being thrown up too.

All of a sudden it became ominously quiet. The only noise was the water hitting the side of the ship with loud thuds. In our debilitated state, it took us a while to realize that the noise from the ship's engines was missing. Father and Margit came to tell us that the engines had stopped, and that nobody was allowed on deck anymore because some of the railings had been torn away by the tremendous force of the waves, and some of the sailors had their arms in slings and some were on crutches. Great news! We were drifting without engines in a horrendous storm. Were we destined to drown in the Atlantic after all we had been through? I felt so horrible, I didn't even care.

The next "good" news we got was that the *Neptunia* had sent an SOS to the *Queen Mary*, which was somewhere behind us. I can't say that the idea of winding up in a lifeboat in a roiling, stormy sea was very appealing. Luckily we were spared an evacuation to the *Queen Mary*, because they finally got the engines working again after what seemed like an eternity. A sweeter sound was never heard! It was music to our ears. The storm had finally lessened somewhat and the railings were repaired, so Father and Margit were able to flee the cabin again and go out on the upper deck, leaving Mother and me to our misery.

Slowly the storm abated, and the Atlantic calmed to bearable levels. We were about two days from New York when Mother and I ventured out of our cabin to the upper deck. We had decided that our time to die was not right and that we would rejoin the living. Still feeling queasy, pale as ghosts, and several pounds lighter, we gratefully hung on to the restored railings. The fresh air felt good, and we even started to eat a little. I looked at the water with a lot more respect than before. Big brother—my foot! What I had seen out there in the Atlantic was a gargantuan man-eater we were lucky to escape. The last two days on the ship Mother and I recovered our equilibrium and some of our healthy looks.

As we neared the American continent, two days late because of the storm, our excitement ran high. Many hadn't slept that last night on the ship, and a lot of people stood at the railings, even though there was no land in sight yet. Everybody wanted to be the first to see America! I for one couldn't wait to see New York. Great shouts of joy went up when land was finally sighted, and we began to make our way down the East Coast. We slowly sailed past Long Island, Staten Island, and Brooklyn.

Then suddenly the great island of Manhattan was before us. I was awestruck and speechless at seeing all the tall buildings for the first time. What an incredible sight! Not in my wildest dreams could I have imagined such grandeur. The photos of New York I had seen couldn't compare to the reality. The skyscrapers, washed golden in the morning sun, looked like different-length pencils standing upright. So I dubbed Manhattan the "Pencil Factory." We made our way past the tip of the island, slow enough to give us time to admire the splendid panorama. My eyes absorbed it all in an effort to preserve this precious moment forever.

The elegant "Lady of the Harbor," holding the torch of freedom high in her right hand, appeared on our left. She wasn't only beautiful, but so is what she stands for, freedom for everyone, including the poorest and lowliest of us. Her credo touched me deeply, because it seemed to apply to us. As I saw it, she welcomed us with open arms. Seeing her for the first time was an unforgettable experience for all of us.

Then it was on up the Hudson River to an old quay in Weehawken, New Jersey. After immigration officials checked our papers, which took all morning, we were formally admitted to the United States of America on Tuesday, August 11, 1953. We couldn't wait to disembark and meet our relatives, who were waiting for us among the crowd on the dock. It didn't take us long to spot our relatives among the many people waiting for their loved ones to come down the gangplank. When we were finally able to leave the ship and set foot on American soil, our relatives were immediately at our side. It was a reunion to end all reunions! My mother hadn't seen her two brothers since way before the war, or her mother since 1946, when she and Grandfather were allowed to leave Communist East Germany for the United States.

We were thoroughly hugged and kissed, and torrential tears of joy must have raised the Hudson River's water level by several inches. The only one missing to make our joy complete was my grandfather, who had passed away the year before, and was buried near Uncle Rudy's farm in Pennsylvania. Meeting my uncles Rudy and Carl and their wives, who had done so much for us after the war, was an event of momentous proportions for me. My happiness knew no bounds. I never forgot the care and love they bestowed on us when we were in such dire need.

I hardly recognized Oma. When I last saw her before she and Opa left East Germany, she was nothing but skin and bones. She had put on a considerable amount of weight since, and now looked quite substantial. The stories we had heard in Germany that America was the land of milk and honey must be true, I thought. Uncle Rudy's twins, Robert and Elise, and Uncle Carl's three-year-old, Diane, held back shyly, as children are wont to do when meeting someone for the first time.

After all the first joyous moments of reunion had passed, we piled into their cars and drove up a steep hill and through Union City, New Jersey, which was a disappointment. There was nothing clean or modern about its rather sad-looking old houses. On the way we stopped at a diner for something to eat. I found sitting at a counter for the first time very interesting and efficient, but not too comfortable. Between all the excitement and the unaccustomed heat and humidity, I didn't have much of an appetite. Nevertheless I forced down a liverwurst sandwich on some very odd, spongy, white bread. I had never tasted white bread, so this was another novelty, but I wasn't sure whether I liked it.

There was one thing I found very strange. We were barely off the boat when my aunts were already complaining at length about how tough times had been in the US during the war. Hearing about all the terrible deprivations they had to suffer, how rationing of sugar and other things made their lives miserable, was enough for Mother and I to exchange silent looks, which spoke volumes. I still see my mother rolling her eyes to heaven, and her mouth becoming a straight line clamping it shut. After listening to all their sad stories, none of us ever talked about our experiences during and after the war. How could people who always had a roof over their heads, never went hungry or cold, and never had to run for their lives in constant fear, even begin to understand what our lives had been like?

Now we would have to adapt ourselves to new circumstances all over again. What would the future in a new country hold for us? That thought was in all our minds. How and where would we live? Our relatives had been very secretive about the living arrangements they had for us. Would we be able to master this new life, adjust and perhaps flourish in a completely foreign environment, where even the language was different? The answer of course was that millions of others did it before us, and so would we. In my opinion, after what we had been through, this should be a cinch. As a seventeen-year-old teenager filled with energy and youthful optimism, I saw the United States as a sunlit plain, where happy, contented people lived their lives in security, free from hunger and fear. A true paradise! I hoped that after our long odyssey we would finally find a home where we could spend the rest of our lives in peace and safety under the protective wings of a mighty nation.

* * *

Chapter 40

The Immigrants

Our arrival in the United States of America on Tuesday, August 11, 1953, marked the beginning of the next chapter in our lives. We were given new lives in a country where freedom and liberty were cherished above all else. After our turbulent years during and after the war, freedom of expression and the liberty to pursue a peaceful life was of utmost importance to us.

Of course my golden heart necklace, the guardian of all my memories, made the journey with me, securely anchored at its usual place around my neck. The somewhat-battered heart displayed its history, and every dent told a story of hard times and survival. This was its second trip across the Atlantic, back to its country of origin. The first time it traveled to a foreign land, but this time, after so many eventful years, it was back home. It was a pity that my great aunt wouldn't be there to see how I treasured her gift. But like my grandfather, she was gone. I had often thought about her over the years and would have liked to meet the woman with the generous heart who cared enough to send a little girl she had never seen a token of love in the form of a gold necklace with a little golden heart.

The secret of where we would live was soon lifted. After lunch we entered an area of quiet streets lined with small, neat houses and well-tended lawns in a town called Teaneck, New Jersey. Uncle Rudy and Uncle Carl were beaming as they stopped in front of a small house in a cul-de-sac. Were we ever surprised! After our gypsy lives with mostly makeshift accommodations, our expectations were very modest. So an entire house just for us exceeded our wildest dreams. This certainly was a dizzying turn of events. A dirt road with a treed island in the middle led to our house at the end, just before the road made a U-turn around the island. The name Laurel Terrace suited it admirably. I was glad to have all those trees and the dirt road, which gave the neighborhood a country feeling even though we were only fifteen minutes from New York City.

Our little house, which belonged to Uncle Carl, had some trees in the back of the property and a detached garage. The house itself consisted of an enclosed front porch, a living room, a dining room, a kitchen, and another closed-in porch adjoining the kitchen. The upstairs had two bedrooms and one bathroom. My parents occupied one bedroom while Margit and I not only shared the other bedroom, but also a double bed that was a sure recipe for major squabbling, which wasn't long in coming.

The house was even furnished with pretty-nice secondhand furniture. Fresh paint on the walls and sheer, ruffled curtains on the windows gave it a friendly homey feeling. We even had a small, eight-inch, black-and-white television set in the living room, facing the maroon couch and a coffee table that Uncle Rudy made. We heard later that they had picked up the discarded couch sitting on a curb somewhere. My uncles weren't rich by any stretch of the imagination, so all of this had required quite a few sacrifices, extra work, and expense for them.

My grandmother, who moved in with us, used the enclosed back porch, because at age eighty she had difficulty climbing to the upstairs bedrooms. I was happy to have my grandmother with us again after such a long separation. It was seven long years since we had seen her. Margit and I had grown up since, and Oma had aged a lot.

The first night in our new home, worn out from all the excitement, we slept like the dead despite the heat and humidity. Of course we didn't have air-conditioning, so our little house was unbearably hot.

The neighbors, Evelyn and Ed, came to visit us that first Saturday morning, and we thought ourselves very lucky to have such nice, friendly people living next door. We also spent part of the morning at our uncles' houses, which were only fifteen minutes away by car in the neighboring town of Bogota. Like Teaneck, it was a town of modest, single-family homes, with manicured lawns shaded by lots of trees.

Across the street from my uncles were a few small stores. One of them was a little storefront shop where they beaded Indian moccasins.

My uncle took me there to introduce me to the owners, because as I found out, I was to start work there on Monday. I had never beaded anything in my life, let alone leather moccasins, so I anticipated Monday with some trepidation. It was less than a week after our arrival, so I had little time to become acclimated to my new surroundings.

Father was also scheduled to start work immediately in the sheet metal factory where Uncle Carl worked. Since my father knew absolutely nothing about sheet metal work, he was hired as unskilled labor, but beggars can't be choosers.

Saturday morning we were taken to neighboring Hackensack, New Jersey, which bustled with activity because it was the main shopping center for all of Bergen County. Main Street was lined with busy stores, and people carrying shopping bags crowded the sidewalks. I was not only gawking at the incredible variety of merchandise in the store windows, but also at the way the women and young girls looked. Some of the young girls sported ponytails, which I thought a very attractive and practical hairdo. But many others were walking around with their hair in huge rollers or hairpins covered with pink or light blue nets. They weren't an attractive sight, and I wondered why anybody would go out in public looking like that. Everybody wore lots of makeup, and I almost felt naked and conspicuous with my plain, unadorned face. A lot of girls wore slacks in bright colors and comfortable-looking saddle shoes with white socks, which seemed to be the preferred footwear.

Main Street presented another interesting scene. Cars full of young men were cruising up and down the street, with the young men waving and calling to the girls on the sidewalk, who either gave spirited replies or pretended not to hear them. Young Americans had some very curious habits, which I noted with great interest and astonishment.

We also took some time to reconnoiter our neighborhood, with its neat, one-family homes, and found that we were only one block from a small shopping center with a supermarket and lots of other small stores. There was a bus stop on the corner for easy commuting, which was essential for people who didn't own a car or know how to drive. So for us this was a very convenient and nice place to live. It seemed that my uncles had thought of everything. Margit, who was thirteen, was already enrolled in Teaneck High School, and would be starting in September.

Even though she had only three years of English in Germany, she entered ninth grade, which was appropriate for her age.

Mother was the only one who didn't go out to work immediately. She stayed at home with Oma for a short time.

Sunday afternoon our uncles Rudy and Carl arrived with some German friends, who introduced me to their son, who was about my age. He asked me out for a ride, and drove me to one of the lookouts on the Palisades with a spectacular view of the Hudson River and Manhattan. While our parents became acquainted, I was introduced to something called an ice-cream soda, which was an utter delight. But unlike the ice-cream soda, the young man was not to my liking. I didn't like his condescending manner, and stupid questions like: "Do they have flush toilets in Germany?" and "Do they have radios?" He behaved like I was something that just came out of the Dark Ages and needed to be civilized. Needless to say, I didn't appreciate his attitude, because I didn't think I needed civilizing. Besides that, he made some very disparaging remarks about my golden heart necklace, which I didn't receive kindly. Even my earrings, small silver flowers with a pearl in the center, didn't escape his criticism: "Why don't you wear the kind of jewelry American girls wear?" My lack of makeup seemed to bother him too. Spending money I didn't have on makeup and fashion jewelry was the last thing on my mind. That didn't endear him to me either. I didn't care if I ever saw him again, and I didn't—which was fine with me. So my first encounter with an American male my age was anything but successful.

Later in the day Uncle Rudy took us to Manhattan, and the area where he worked on 33rd Street. I was quite impressed by the height of the buildings, and almost became dizzy looking up at them until Uncle Rudy told me to watch where I was going, because I kept bumping into people, and almost walked into a lamppost. Directing my eyes to the ground, I couldn't help thinking of the old stories told in Germany, where they said gold littered the streets, just waiting to be picked up. Of course that was at a time when the United States needed European immigrants to settle the West and help fight the Indians. So the streets weren't littered with gold, but it did look like the land of unlimited opportunity. After I gave the matter some thought, it occurred to me that the gold wasn't to be found in the streets, but in the golden opportunities they offered to those with incentive and the will to work hard. I liked that, and I was ready to roll up my sleeves and get started.

Looking at the pavement, all I could see were little, glittering mica chips embedded with lots of strange, dark spots. That was chewing gum, my uncle told me. Do people just throw their chewed gum, paper wrappers, and refuse on the street? I asked. The answer was evident. Had they no respect for their exciting city, which rose out of the sea between the Hudson and the East River like a futuristic fantasy? Its buildings were so spectacular that New York City was synonymous with the picture other nations had of the United States that they tried to emulate.

We had a hot dog at one of the fast-food places on a street corner, which was a novelty for us. Notwithstanding the city residents' habit of throwing things on the ground, I looked for a wastebasket of some sort for my used napkin, but didn't see one, so I slipped it into my handbag. I wouldn't contribute to the litter by throwing it on the sidewalk.

The three days following our arrival passed in a blur of new impressions, which needed to be sorted, processed, and absorbed. Aside from the language, many new things waited to be discovered and internalized. I found that American English sounded quite different from the British English I was taught in school, and that took some getting used to. So did the heat and the humidity. There was no getting away from it, and the attic fan in our house didn't help much. Between our combined body heat and the small bed, Margit and I almost killed each other every night. Each of us claimed that the other took all the space, so there was a lot of pushing and shoving and grumbling. We eventually wound up on the floor, where we had more space to spread out, and where it was a little cooler. But there was nothing we could do about the mosquitoes. Oh God, those New Jersey mosquitoes! Voracious and unrelenting, they were bigger than any I had ever seen—and they loved me! What was it about me that made all bugs go after me like I was a delicacy?

I couldn't help thinking how the summer temperatures in Germany rarely went beyond eighty degrees, and the nights were cool enough to need a quilt. It was usually in the seventies with low humidity, so we always wished for warmer weather back then. Now that I had the warmer temperatures, I didn't like it, because I hadn't factored in the humidity. It was definitely a lot hotter than I bargained for, and I thought with longing of the coolness of Burghausen's lake. So the heat and the humidity were probably the most difficult things for me to get used to. I constantly felt like I hadn't showered, and couldn't wait for fall and winter. Once again I was reminded to be careful of what I wished for.

The food was a pleasant surprise. There were a lot of new dishes that I had never heard of, like very tasty egg salads, tuna fish salads, and even potato salad with mayonnaise. Sandwiches with lettuce, tomato, and cold meat were a terrific idea, which I liked, not to mention the many flavors of ice cream and milk shakes. So were cheeseburgers and French fries, all things Americans took for granted, but new to us. Fruits we had never seen before lured the eye and begged to be tasted, and we certainly did them justice by eating nonstop.

There was so much to be learned about a new country, and the new language was the first and most important obstacle to overcome. I realized how hard it must be for older people like my parents and grandmother, whose grasp on the new language was weak. Immigrants leave behind not only the old customs and familiar sights, but also the support system of relatives and lifelong friends. People are like trees. Transplanting an old tree is always a much more difficult and chancy matter, for a lot of their rootlets remained where they grew to maturity.

We experienced what the millions who came before us must have experienced, nostalgia for the familiar past and excitement and hope for an unknown future. These feelings existed simultaneously, side by side. Starting from scratch, working hard, and living frugally were things we had in common with all new immigrants who had brought their talents, skills, and knowledge with them as great gifts for the United States.

Creating a new life and making new friends wasn't always easy, because our accents gave away our origins. With WWII and all the accompanying propaganda still fresh in American minds, Germans weren't exactly welcomed with open arms.

I came to understand why newcomers clustered together in neighborhoods where they could speak their mother tongue and preserve some of their customs. It gave them a sense of security in a land where they were considered foreigners, but it also hindered and delayed their ability to learn the English language, and to become fully accepted as fellow Americans.

* * *

Chapter 41
Greenhorns

1953–1954

New immigrants were commonly called "greenhorns" in the early 1950s, because they made a lot of mistakes as they learned the language and the different customs of their new country. I have to say that we were no exception.

Monday, less than a week after our arrival, was the beginning of my first job in the United States, at the seventy-five-cents-per-hour minimum wage. Unfortunately it came around much too soon to suit me. It took a twenty-minute bus ride from our corner plus a three-block walk to arrive at my workplace. Entering the little storefront shop, a half-dozen middle-aged women and as many strange-looking frames stared at me. I was given one of those frames, a box filled with moccasin tops, strings of colored beads, and a strange-looking implement, which looked like a crochet needle with an extra hook. The needle was similar to the one I had used to repair nylon stockings in Burghausen in what seemed a lifetime ago.

The first day I struggled to familiarize myself with my new tools and how to use them. My nylon repair experience in Burghausen stood me in good stead. The only difference was that I now had leather to deal with, and the beads were fed onto the leather from underneath. This meant that your fingers had to feel and estimate the right amount of beads to execute a pattern. There were several different designs, with names like Thunderbird and Starburst, and small holes punched into the leather determined the pattern for my needle to follow. The unbearable heat and humidity made working very difficult, and the smooth beads kept slipping through my sweaty fingers. The only cooling device was a large fan in the corner struggling valiantly to bring us some relief, but it only managed to move the hot air around.

The radio was going all day long with soap operas and the inevitable advertisements. Soap operas were new to me too. I wondered what all the screaming, crying, and cooing was all about. My ears struggled to understand the words of American English, not to mention the completely unfamiliar slang. The constant gossip going on among the women added to my store of slurred, strung-together words and expressions. The women were generally nice to me, and I had no complaints. My bosses, Elio and John, were also very nice, patiently allowing me to learn at my own pace. So the first few weeks passed in concentration to master a new skill, and I always came home very tired. My shoulders and back ached from sitting in an unaccustomed, hunched-over position all day. Father came home from work dead tired too. It wasn't an easy beginning for either of us.

On weekends Uncle Rudy took us to his farm in Pennsylvania, where he owned about a hundred acres. It was a long ride through the New Jersey and Pennsylvania countryside. I noticed that most of the woods consisted of deciduous trees, with a few lonely pines mixed in here and there. The farm had a somewhat run-down old farmhouse, which nevertheless had a certain charm. I can still hear the squeaking of the screen door when it was opened or closed. The house stood on a little hill overlooking grassland, which Uncle Rudy leased to local farmers for cattle grazing. We were shown sunny fields full of three-foot-tall blueberry bushes. In Germany blueberries grew low to the ground in wooded clearings, and the berries were much smaller. But then, everything in the United States seemed to be bigger. The German blueberries also left blue stains in your mouth and on your teeth, which their much more sophisticated American counterparts didn't do.

We also visited my grandfather's grave on a lonely hill overlooking a valley. Remembering my grandfather's love of nature, I thought this was the perfect place for him, and that he would have been happy to know that this was his final resting place.

Some time in September, all four of us came down with terrible colds and high fevers. Even though we almost froze to death in Germany after the war, this was the first cold I ever had in my life. My whole body felt like it was on fire. I remember Uncle Rudy's doctor coming to our house and going from one to the other, giving each of us a shot of penicillin. This was our first encounter with this wonder drug, which put us back on our feet and back to work in no time. I thought it just marvelous, even though I wouldn't have minded staying home from work a little longer.

With hard work and concentration, it didn't take very long for me to become proficient and quite fast at beading, so I was put on piecework like the rest of the women. Every night I now came home with torn, bloody fingers where the needle seemed to always find the same spots. Wearing gloves or a protective device wasn't an option, since it would have removed the necessary feeling in the fingertips. I worked like a demon, barely taking time to eat a sandwich for lunch. Of course I soon started to make more money than the other women, which didn't sit too well with them. In my best week I earned eighty-five dollars, which was very good pay in the early 1950s. Of that I only kept enough money for the bus, and gave the rest to my parents. I understood that pooling our money was the best way for us to get ahead and to buy the many things we needed. A car was one of our most pressing needs, so Uncle Rudy and our neighbor Ed took time to teach my father how to drive. Once he knew how to drive, they helped him buy a used 1949 Buick, which became our first car.

One Sunday morning in late September, there was a call from New York's Idlewild Airport (now JFK). A voice on the other end said: "Renate, this is Abdul! I just arrived in New York—may I come and see you?"

"Abdul? Abdul, my pen pal from Egypt?" I yelled, all excited.

"Yes, Abdul, your pen pal friend," was the answer.

Of course my answer was a stunned, "Yes, of course! Yes!" Who would have thought that I would actually meet my pen pal from faraway Egypt? What a surprise! Since our emigration went so fast, I only had time to send him our new address in a short letter after we arrived in the United States.

So Abdul arrived in a taxi at our front door in no time, with a beautifully inlaid box as a present for me. Of medium stature, he looked just like his photograph, brown skinned with a handsome, fine-boned face with kind, dark brown eyes and curly black hair. My parents and Margit all liked him immediately. He told us that when my news of our emigration reached him, he changed his original plans to study in Germany and now planned to study in the United States instead. He was enrolled in a Connecticut prep school to polish his English and to ready himself for the college entrance exams. He spent the day with us and left in the afternoon to go to Connecticut, promising to stay in touch. True to his word, he came to visit us whenever he could, and he soon became part of our family.

He told us that he was born in Sana'a, the capital of Yemen, and was brought up by an uncle. In his country the boys were taken from the mother's feminine influence at age seven to be raised by a male relative. One day he brought his native costume of long, flowing white robes with the traditional burnoose headdress. He took some photos of me wearing it, one of which is still around somewhere. Sometimes we would go sightseeing together in New York, where I couldn't miss the frowns and disapproving looks people directed our way. That's when I became aware of how racist my new country was. At that time racial mingling was socially unacceptable, to say the least, and I had a lot to learn on that score.

Then fate showed its hand in our lives once again. Coming home from work, my father struck up a conversation with a man he met on the bus. As it turned out, the man came from the same region in Germany we came from. He owned an embroidery factory where emblems and patches for the police, the army, and professional sports teams were produced. He offered Father a job, and even though it was menial work, it was much more suitable for my father than sheet metal work. From then on, Father worked in the embroidery industry, and soon my mother joined him there. Mother's decision to go to work led to some serious disagreements between her and Uncle Rudy. He thought that she should stay home and take care of the household like his wife did, especially after the hard life she had lived. Angry words were exchanged in heated arguments and Mother threw his well-meant advice to the winds. Of course Uncle Rudy didn't realize that the malleable little sister he remembered had changed, and now was a hard-bitten veteran of WWII with a will of iron. She wanted to help repay our debts as quickly as possible, so off to work she went, no matter what anybody said.

In October the moccasin shop moved, which meant that now I had to take a bus to Hackensack, then walk several blocks to the new location. At this point I understood "American" much better, and could follow the soliloquies of Elio, the younger of my two bosses, who was single, twenty-eight years old, and rather chubby. He would walk up and down the shop and joyfully exclaim to nobody in particular: "Yankees World Champions! Yankees World Champions!"

Who on earth or what were the Yankees he was so crazy about? It didn't take me long to find out, because Elio made sure of that by tutoring me in Yankee lore and a game called baseball. I heard about the Yankees morning, noon, and night! I had no idea that a sport could ignite such passions, but since he was my boss, I listened politely. However, I must admit that most of it went in one ear and out the other. Of course I learned that there were other teams besides the Yankees, which Elio considered mortal enemies. Piously, he wished all of them the worst luck in the world. As part of my baseball education and in an effort to convert me to a baseball fan, Elio took me to New York one Saturday to show me "something very important." Arrived at the important site, it turned out to be a very dilapidated, run-down stadium of some sort. Elio explained with pride that this was a baseball field called the Polo Grounds, which harbored wonderful memories for all baseball fans, including a very famous home run that was hit there a few years earlier. What was a home run? I couldn't see what was so interesting or important about this place. It certainly wasn't the Roman Coliseum. Well, I guess I just didn't understand what drove a genuine baseball aficionado.

And baseball wasn't the only thing I was introduced to. One day my bosses ordered something called pizza for all the employees. They brought in some large boxes containing some rather weird-looking round cakes. Everybody took a slice and started eating that awful-looking stuff. After some urging, I took a slice and gingerly bit into it. Since everybody knew that this was my first taste of pizza, all eyes were on me to see how I liked it. With obvious pleasure, Elio and John hovered over me like two father roosters, so they wouldn't miss my slightest reaction. Well, I thought it tasted awful, so awful that I didn't even chew it. I tried to swallow my bites whole so they wouldn't be in my mouth any longer than necessary. But I didn't want to offend my bosses, who so graciously tried to introduce me to what was a national favorite food. Desperately trying to hide my distaste for what I thought tasted absolutely awful, I lied and told them that it was delicious. After I had swallowed my way through that first slice, I had to swallow a second one to make Elio and John happy. Unfortunately it didn't taste any better than the first slice. I was glad when the boxes were empty and I didn't have to take another slice of that ghastly stuff. Elio and John glowed with the results of their good deed, which I didn't appreciate so much at the time, I'm sorry to say. But they would have been very pleased to know that in time pizza would become one of my favorite foods.

Winter arrived and with it our first Christmas in the United States. We had a Christmas tree, and our Christmas gifts consisted mainly of small, practical things we needed, like stockings and gloves. We were happy to be together and to spend this special holiday with our relatives. My Christmas gift from my bosses was a bottle of Scotch whiskey, which at that time cost about seven dollars. I took it home carrying it like a fragile egg, but when I arrived at home, the bottle slipped out of my cold hands and broke on our front stoop. There was a day's pay flowing down the stairs, making our house smell like the local tavern. My father in particular was very upset, because a bottle of Scotch was a luxury for us, and it would have been nice to be able to offer it to visitors. But there was no use crying over spilled whiskey!

In the meantime Margit had finished her first semester at Teaneck High School. To my astonishment, I never saw her do any homework. When I asked her about it, her standard answer was: "I did it in study hall," whatever that was. But since her grades were good, no issue was made of it. She even got a B in English, which I found absolutely astounding, because in Burghausen she barely managed a C. Unfortunately we were all so absorbed and preoccupied with trying to adapt ourselves to our new work and new environment that nobody paid much attention to Margit and any problems she might have had. She was left to fight her battles alone. I knew she was very lonely, because the kids in her school wanted nothing to do with her. Some even told her that their parents had expressly forbidden them to socialize with her because she was German. The dark shadow of WWII was still with us, following us wherever we went. We were outcasts again! Her self-esteem in shreds, she started to associate with other outcasts in her loneliness.

I was very lonely too and missed the companionship of young people my age, but I was older than Margit and was a little better equipped to handle it, although adjusting to my new life wasn't easy for me either. Since I immediately went to work, I could only observe the habits of my peers from afar, or through movies and TV. Watching the young people my age, I often felt like I came from another planet, an alien transplanted into a perfect world. American teenage girls didn't seem to have a care besides the next fad in fashion and of course boys, dating, and going steady. School and achievement seemed to be a minor nuisance in their lives. They didn't know how lucky they were that their childhood memories didn't include the horrors of war. I often wished that I could be as carefree and innocent as they, oblivious to the misery life can bring. This knowledge made me feel old beyond my years. I dated sporadically, but for various reasons, I had no interest in the young men I met. A few times I went to 86th Street in New York with a young German woman I met. The area was full of German stores and restaurants at that time, and we would go to a place called the "Lorelei," where young singles could go to dance. But getting there on two buses was quite a trip, and it cost more than I could afford, so we didn't go there too often.

Spring finally came, and with it came a new addition to our family. Margit came home one day with the most adorable little puppy, which someone in the neighborhood gave her. After initial resistance, but aware of Margit's loneliness, our parents allowed her to keep it. We named the little brown mongrel Tippy. Luckily Oma was living with us, so he wasn't alone during the day. He quickly grew into a very feisty little dog that was spoiled by all of us. One afternoon, when Oma went visiting and he was left alone, we came home to find our long, sheer curtains in shreds. Tippy had eaten them as far as he could reach. That must have been his way of letting us know that he resented being left alone.

His next escapade was a run-in with a skunk, which as we found out to our dismay made its home behind our garage. There were no skunks in Germany, so this was all new to us. Well, Tippy became an awful, stinking mess, and he didn't seem to like it either. He rolled in the grass and ran in circles in an effort to rid himself of the smell. We finally caught him, but it took all of us to struggle him into the bathtub and wash him thoroughly with soap and water. It didn't help much, except that now all of us stank too. Repeated washings finally made him bearable, and we hoped that he had learned his lesson and wouldn't go near the skunk again. But only after another try to get even with the skunk and more baths, did he finally give up and leave the skunk alone. Unfortunately, whenever it rained and Tippy got wet, he stank all over again. That's how we found out that skunk perfume was extremely powerful stuff.

With the arrival of summer, Elio's next endeavor was to teach me how to drive. He took me to a less traveled road and bravely put me in charge of his fine Cadillac. I managed not to crack it up and got the hang of it fairly quickly. Strangely enough, Elio never made a pass at me. It seemed like he didn't know what to make of me or my reserved stance. So we were just friends, which suited me just fine. Now I could practice driving with our Buick, which unfortunately wasn't automatic like Elio's car. Learning how to work the clutch to shift gears was a formidable task, and I promptly backed our car into a stone pillar at the end of our driveway, incurring costly repairs we could ill afford.

When July came around, Elio and John ran out of work, so we were all laid off, and I had to go collect unemployment. Mother was very unhappy, because the money I contributed to the household was very important. Our new life in the United States was full of unexpected pitfalls, and was by no means easy, but like other greenhorns before us, we were stubbornly determined to succeed.

* * *

Chapter 42

The Apprentice

1954

My first week as unemployed and home for an undetermined time was very pleasant, but soon my mother's caustic remarks and her constant nagging made it less and less enjoyable. She wasn't happy at all with my new state of affairs. Our family work ethic, and our need for money to repay our relatives and to buy the many things we needed, demanded that I get busy and find another job. We still lacked winter clothes and good shoes, for instance.

After a week, without a car to go anywhere, no money, and no friends to pass the time with, I did get rather bored at home. So looking for a job wasn't such a bad idea. It would relieve the tedium of hanging around the house with my grandmother, who was also grouchy and unhappy with my unemployed status. The doghouse just wasn't big enough for Tippy and me.

I thought of trying to make use of my artistic ability, so I decided to look for work as a designer in the lace and embroidery industry. Since I came from Plauen, a city world renowned for its lace and embroidery, and where my ancestors had been in the business since 1800, this wasn't such a bad idea. I would be carrying on a 150-year-old family tradition. So the next logical thing to do was to look in the Lace and Embroidery Manufacturer's promotional yearbook, which listed all the different manufacturers in northern New Jersey. The most prestigious firm in the United States was Stein Tobler, where they employed a number of the best designers.

Optimistic and ever modest, I decided to start at the top. So I put a portfolio of my drawings and paintings together, dressed in my best, and took a bus to their office in Union City, New Jersey. Of course I didn't have an appointment, and didn't even know the name of the company president. Consequently I never made it past the receptionist.

Too young and too inexperienced, it didn't occur to me to try to set up an appointment. This was very disappointing, but I wasn't about to give up.

Shortly afterwards, on a hot and muggy, ninety-degree day, I dressed in my best again, and decided to try my luck at a design studio advertised in the promotional brochure. Unfortunately, their office wasn't on a direct bus route, so my only choice was to take a bus as close as possible and walk from there. It turned out to be an approximately three-mile walk up a long steep hill, down the other side, and up another long steep hill to where the studio was located. By the time I reached the top of the second hill I was drenched in sweat, and my hair hung around my head like overcooked spaghetti. Again I walked in without an appointment, clutching my portfolio. They liked my sketches, but the studio was a small father-daughter operation, and they didn't need anyone else. Kindly, they gave me the name and address of one of their clients, and advised me to try my luck with them. To my relief, I was able to take a bus to the address they had given me.

Once again I showed my sketches, and again they were well received. The only problem was that this firm was something called a "jobber," which didn't employ any designers. When larger manufacturers had more work than they could handle, they contracted their work out to jobbers, who stitched their goods for them. But the owner of the firm really liked my sketches and my enterprising spirit, so he decided to help me. He called up one of his business contacts, told him about me, and then personally drove me to an interview he had arranged for me that same afternoon. The owner of the company looked at my sketches and liked what he saw. Chewing on his cigar, he called in his designer, a tall man in his fifties, and apprised him that he now had an apprentice. The designer wasn't too thrilled at the prospect of an apprentice who would share his room and disturb his privacy. But he had no choice in the matter. The boss had made his decision.

So now I had a job! Even though it paid only forty dollars a week, which was five dollars above the minimum wage, I saw it as an opportunity with good future possibilities. Embroidery and lace designers, who were mostly European, were scarce and therefore very well paid.

My work as an apprentice wasn't very creative. First I had to learn the technical aspects of lace and embroidery designing before I could be useful. I had to use pen and ink to trace the penciled-in patterns, and show every stitch the machine would have to make. It was rather tedious work, but it left the designer free to do the creative sketching. Another one of my duties as an apprentice was to remove all the ink and charcoal stains from the sink. The designer was definitely not happy to have me there. As I found out later, one problem was that I was female in a completely male-dominated profession. It was rather like an old boys club, and they didn't want any females rattling at the walls of their all-male bastion.

While working there, I made the acquaintance of two pretty young sisters who worked in the shipping department. They were twins who looked like Elizabeth Taylor. This was my first contact with American girls my age, but unfortunately boyfriends and clothes seemed to be their only interests. To my astonishment, I learned that they bought a new dress every week from a nearby, high-end store. The dresses weren't cheap at an average cost of fifty dollars each, which was more than their weekly paycheck. I couldn't imagine how they could afford it until I found out that they had a debt of several hundred dollars at the store, which they paid off at ten dollars a week. My mother would have disowned me had I even thought of doing something like that. But they didn't worry about it. Their attitude was that whomever they married would get stuck with the bill.

My apprenticeship dragged on until one fine day when my boss called me into his office. He told me that he felt that my talent was wasted at his place. Their product line was limited to tablecloths and doilies, so the requirement for creativity was minimal. He told me that he had set up an appointment for me with Mr. Weber, the president of Stein Tobler. What a wonderful surprise. Stein Tobler! The same place where I couldn't even get past the receptionist a year earlier. He even gave me the afternoon off so I could go to the interview. Mr. Weber, a man in his early fifties, liked my sketches, and hired me on the spot. Of course it was a minimum-wage salary, but at least I had my foot in the door of the most prestigious lace and embroidery firm in the United States. Another bonus was that I didn't have to take two buses anymore, because Stein Tobler was on a direct bus route. My workday was nine to five now, instead of eight to five, which I liked even better, since I was never an enthusiastic early riser.

So began a new life for me in the creative department of a wonderful company whose designers were recognized as the best in the industry, and whose designs were widely copied by other companies. Stein Tobler had about ten creative designers, and ten technicians who prepared the designs for the machines. At first I worked at a desk in a large room among storage boxes, but soon got my own room like all the other designers. Actually it was part of a three-room suite I shared with Willy Michl, another designer who also happened to be the president of the Designer's Association. He and I got along famously. His eyes always held a mischievous twinkle and I liked his quirky sense of humor. He gave me a lot of good advice and shared his knowledge with me unstintingly. He was a wonderful mentor and never made me feel like a subordinate.

I was always amused when I visited the other designers and they quickly covered up their sketches, thinking I might try to steal their ideas. They guarded their sketches like a horde of gold. Since I never ran out of ideas, this really wasn't necessary, but they didn't know that. What made working for Stein Tobler interesting and fun was that their clientele was very diverse. I designed everything from lingerie, blouses, and children's wear for well-known outfits like Vanity Fair, J.C. Penney, Sears, Dior, and Van Raalte. It was never boring. When my children's designs became big sellers, I wound up designing all their new children's lines. Stein Tobler's large staff of salesmen would take our sketches to clients in New York. Samples were made of their choices, and a price was determined. Often the sketch had to be changed to fit the client's price range. I wasn't too happy about that, because frequently it was pared down to the minimum and it didn't look nearly as good as it did originally. Production began after their final choice went to the technicians, who readied it for the fifteen-yard-long machines. It was always very rewarding to see boxes and boxes of my finished products in the shipping room, and it was even more thrilling to see my designs in the windows of famous Fifth Avenue stores like Lord & Taylor, Bonwit Teller, and Saks Fifth Avenue.

Eventually Willy Michl proposed me for membership in the Lace and Embroidery Designers Association, and I became not only its youngest, but also its first and only, female member. Attending the monthly meetings was always quite unusual. Here I was, a twenty-year-old female, sitting among eighty men over fifty. Some ignored me as inconsequential, while others were friendly but treated me more like a pet.

Even though my salary was greatly increased, I still didn't earn half as much as the male designers. Nonetheless I was satisfied with my progress for now and happy to be a full-fledged designer working for a fine company with a great reputation. I considered myself very fortunate to be able to work at something I enjoyed, and I couldn't help thinking of my grandfather, who used to draw with me when I was three years old. The wonderful design books and sketches I remembered seeing in his studio would have been of great value to me now, but like almost everything else, they had to be left behind in Communist East Germany.

* * *

Chapter 43

The Designer/Student

1954-1958

In 1954 my parents used our combined savings to put a down payment on a small house in a nice residential area at the southern end of town. In order to pay for all our added expenses, which included new furniture, both my parents worked over fifty hours a week. After so many years of homelessness and makeshift accommodations, it was important to them to finally have a nice home of their own.

One day after we had settled in our new house, I returned from work to find my mother all upset. "There was an absolutely huge rat," and here she took another breath. "I never saw one that size. It was right at our front door. Your father killed it with a broom." I'm sure she was reminded of her encounter with a big rat in the basement of our "Ice Palace" in Plauen.

"Where is it?" I asked.

"Over there, behind the garage," she told me, pointing at some bushes. "Go take a look at it if you don't believe me." So I went looking for this big rat. It was indeed huge. No wonder my otherwise fearless mother was upset. Later we found out from neighbors that the "rat" was actually an opossum, and I felt very sorry for the poor thing. So did my parents when they found out the true identity of the "rat." This is the kind of thing that happens to new immigrants.

On nice summer Sundays we would leave early in the morning for Asbury Park, which was a fabulous seashore resort in the 1950s. Its boardwalk, beaches, and public pools along the oceanfront were clean and well kept. We loved the ocean and the sun, which was so much stronger and warmer than in Germany. Soaking up the sun and swimming in the ocean always was the high point of the weekend, and we couldn't get enough of it. The constant motion of the waves depositing sand and pretty shells on the beach, coupled with the smell of the sea, were almost hypnotic. Seagulls screeching and circling over a perceived meal and the blue sky blending with the sea made for a wonderful day.

Experiencing the salty ocean water for the first time gave me quite a shock, but I quickly got over it, and I jumped into the waves with abandon. Not used to restrictions, I was often whistled back by the lifeguards when they caught me swimming too far beyond the ropes.

But I learned to be more careful because on one of those visits to Asbury Park, I almost met my maker. The water was very rough and flags were up, warning people to stay out of the water. Ignoring the warnings, I went in anyway. All went fine, and I swam as far as the ropes allowed without a problem. Smug that I had escaped the lifeguard's attention, I stayed there for a while, enjoying the waves' powerful, back-and-forth motions. But swimming back to shore was a different matter. An incoming huge wave grabbed me, pulled me under, wrapped me around one of the poles supporting the ropes, and ground me into the sand. I couldn't free myself from the pole. The water's pressure held me stuck to the pole at the bottom of the ocean floor for what seemed an eternity. I was running out of air, and I frantically tried to free myself. Finally, and just in time, another wave swept me away from the pole. I was gasping for air, all scratched up and bleeding. Needless to say, I never did that again.

Later we included Jones Beach in our itinerary, but Asbury Park was always our favorite. After getting off the turnpike, even the ride there on Route 9 was enjoyable. It led through farm country and boasted a lot of vegetable and fruit stands along the way. Atlantic City was another great place we visited a few times. We marveled at its wide boardwalks and the fine old hotels along the beach. My people-friendly father usually took long walks along the beach, and we joked that he had talked to everyone on the beach by the time he got back. It was a wonderful time, when everything was new to us. America was a wonderful and fascinating country.

One weekend Margit and I drove to Atlantic City alone, staying overnight in an affordable bed and breakfast. As soon as we arrived, carrying our blanket and towels we set out for the beach, which was only two blocks from our hotel. We happened upon a stretch of beach full of good-looking young men. We looked at each other and we both thought the same thing—paradise! So we put our blanket in the middle of all these good-looking guys and made ourselves at home. But none of the hunks paid any attention to us, which we thought very strange. We usually attracted a lot of attention, mainly because of Margit, who was blond and very well built. Was there something wrong with us? We just couldn't figure it out. Eventually a couple of the men came over to us and said: "Do you girls know that you are on a gay beach?" No, we didn't know, we were just two babes in the woods. Laughing, they joined us on our blanket and stayed with us all afternoon. They were witty, charming, and very entertaining. I never laughed so much in my life. It was an unforgettably great afternoon.

My weekdays were very busy, and sometimes it wasn't easy to fit all my activities into one day. I started to take ballet classes after work at Ballet Arts in Carnegie Hall in New York. It was a long walk from the Port Authority bus station on West 42nd Street to Carnegie Hall on 57th Street, but I was used to walking. Since I sat all day, the strenuous physical exercise of the one-and-a-half-hour ballet class was a good outlet for my pent-up energy. Of course there were times when I could barely walk the next morning, and all my muscles screamed in protest. But I didn't mind, because I knew that it made me stronger and I enjoyed every minute of it. I also enjoyed watching the professional dancers work out.

Soon, instead of continuing ballet lessons, I signed up for evening classes at Columbia University. After my nine-to-five workday, I had to run to get a bus to New York, and then the subway, to be on time for my first class at 6 p.m. When I went there the first time to register, I took the wrong subway. The coaches were chock full, and holding on to a pole, I was shocked when somebody was trying to feel me up. Looking for the culprit among the crowd hemming me in, all I saw were bland, innocent-looking faces. Thankfully I was able to exit at the next stop, but it was already dark when I emerged from the station, and I found myself in the middle of Harlem. A policeman who saw me immediately called a cab and sent me on my way to Columbia. After that experience, I was very careful to get on the right train.

I was happy with my choice of classes in the Theater Arts Department of Columbia University. Classes in history, architecture, drafting, and scenic and costume design were all very interesting and I learned a lot. Of course there was no way I could do all the reading listed on the syllabus every semester. So I took very good notes instead, which worked out fine.

I ran into a problem with my German accent, though. There were times when somebody yelled: "Here comes the German barbarian!" or "Here comes the German whore!" when I entered the classroom. I was genuinely puzzled. I couldn't imagine why anybody would call me those things because I hadn't done anything to anyone and had no prejudices whatsoever against anybody. I didn't understand it. It took me a while to understand that some people hated all things German, including me. It hurt me because I was never taught to hate anybody for who they were. Like my sister Margit at Teaneck High School, I was the recipient of overt hostility from some of my fellow students. I dealt with it by ignoring the barbs directed at me, and concentrated on my studies.

The Brander Matthews Theater was Columbia University's own theater, where we produced many shows. I worked on most of them by painting scenery and designing costumes. That often required me to stay late after class into the wee hours of the morning. A female professor gave me a key to her apartment on campus so I could stay overnight in her guest room. Despite the few hours of sleep, it didn't affect my work during the day. Youth is very forgiving, and nobody at Stein Tobler even guessed that most nights I had only four hours of sleep.

I became well acquainted with how things worked behind the scenes in a theater. It was always a thrill to watch shows we had worked on from the wings and to hear the applause. Once I was drafted to play the part of a dancer in a Japanese play. That's when I learned how actors maneuver to block each other onstage. It was an interesting experience. When I came offstage after doing my little part, other actors pulled me aside. "Didn't you see how so-and-so upstaged you? You mustn't let her get away with it. Next time, do it to her." I tried to follow their advice, but I wasn't ruthless enough. So they finally gave up on me.

Since I was a straight-A student, the department head called me to his office one day. He thought it was time for me to go to school full time and work toward a degree. He told me that they could give me sixty credits for my German education. Together with the thirty credits I already had, that would have totaled ninety credits, just thirty short of the 120 credits needed. It was a very tempting offer, and I appreciated his interest. I would have loved to take him up on it, but it was out of the question financially. It was something I could only dream about. Unfortunately I couldn't afford to quit my job to go to school full time because my parents still needed whatever money I could contribute to our household.

Around the same time my boss at Stein Tobler decided that I was ready to represent the firm in Paris for an extended period. So that was the end of my Columbia University experience, and I prepared to go to Paris instead. Pierre, one of my French coworkers whose parents lived in Paris, informed them of my pending arrival and asked them to help me settle in.

Before I left, I arranged a job at a design studio for my sister Margit, who was a talented artist and due to graduate high school. I remember taking her to the auditorium where the graduation festivities were held. Mother made her an absolutely beautiful dress for this special occasion. Only Margit didn't have a date or a friend to go with. In those crucial teenage years, she was still the German outcast without friends, and there was nothing we could do to help her.

The day before my departure, I had a call from a Fred Stoever: "I'm a college friend of your friend Abdul. He told me so much about you and I would like to meet you. Can I stop by this afternoon?"

I explained that I was busy getting ready for my trip. "You're catching me at a very bad time," I said. "I'm leaving for Paris tomorrow and I'm busy packing."

But then after some back and forth, I finally agreed to let him come over for a short time. He came with a friend for moral support, and Fred turned out to be a very nice-looking, clean-cut young man. As stipulated, they stayed only a short time, with his more loquacious friend doing most of the talking. The next day I left on my thirteen-hour flight to Paris, and didn't give Fred another thought.

The flight to Paris, which was my first, turned out to be much longer than the anticipated thirteen hours. The plane had mechanical problems over the Atlantic, and even though I saw flames shooting out of one of the engines, it didn't bother me in the least. I felt that at twenty-two years old I was too young to die, and that I had a lot more living to do. We finally emergency-landed in Shannon, Ireland, where we had to wait for the next flight to Paris, which wasn't due to arrive until the next day. So we passed the time sightseeing in and around Shannon and sampling the famous Irish coffee. From what I saw of Ireland, it was indeed very green and deserved to be called "The Emerald Isle."

I finally arrived in Paris one day late. Between the time change and the delay, I was dead tired. I had barely recovered a little when Pierre's parents picked me up to join them for the Bastille Day celebrations. Since they had been part of the underground during the war, I had a place on the Tribune d'Honneur with them. When President de Gaulle came around to shake hands, I passed out just before it was my turn. By the time I came to, President de Gaulle had passed to shake hands with others who didn't pass out. That's the only time in my life that I fainted.

Pierre's parents became my unofficial guardians while I was in Paris. Nani, Pierre's mother, was the quintessential French woman. She took me under her wing and showed me how to dress and wear clothes like a French woman. We went to fashion shows together and shopping at the Galeries Lafayette to outfit me with affordable, chic clothes. Jean, her husband, was kind and gentle. They were fine people I'll never forget.

Paris was everything I had heard about and more. I loved everything about it. The Louvre was just down the street from my hotel, the Montpensier, so I spent a lot of time there between sightseeing and exploring. Of course I also took care of my obligations to Stein Tobler by visiting French firms for which I had letters of introduction, visiting the salons of famous couturiers, noted what was in the stores, made sketches, and completed reports at night to send back home. As if I wasn't busy enough, I also attended the Alliance Française to improve my French.

One day I met three American army nurses in my hotel. They were in Paris on furlough. We liked each other's company and began to do some sightseeing together. We went to the Folies Bergère, dancing at the Moulin Rouge, and sat on Montmartre at 5 a.m., having some of the famous French onion soup for breakfast. Two weeks later they took me to visit their army post in Orléans. It was the strangest feeling to be a guest at an American army post. I had to keep reminding myself that the war was over and they weren't the enemy anymore, so it was OK for me to be there. While there, I was introduced to a nice young man called Hank. He came to Paris occasionally, and we had a lot of fun nightclubbing together.

The last time he came to Paris, we went to Montmartre and watched some fire-eaters who were surrounded by a large crowd. When we wanted to go to dinner and nightclubbing afterwards, he discovered that his wallet was missing. He had it in his back pocket, and my guess was that someone in that crowd on Montmartre had relieved him of it. Luckily I had twenty dollars on me so we could at least go eat. After that, I never saw him or the girls again. I was puzzled, and it didn't occur to me until later that they probably thought that I took his wallet. Of course I didn't, but that was my only explanation for the sudden break in our budding friendship.

On a hot August day, I decided to try the pool on a barge in the Seine somebody had told me about. It was a good-size pool surrounded by changing cabins and had a bar at one end. As I sat on my blanket I noticed a group of young people laughing and chatting nearby. I guess I looked as lonely as I felt, because it didn't take long for a pretty young girl to come over to invite me to join them. So I did and she started to introduce everybody. "Meet Jean, he's a dancer at the Lido. This is Gerard, he dances at the Crazy Horse. Maurice here, don't pay any attention to his scowl, he doesn't like women." Then she told me that she was an actress, and that I could come to the movie studios with her. When she took my hand, I decided that it was time to say my *au revoirs*. It was another educational afternoon.

After three months I had to leave France for a short time in order to renew my visa for another three months. So I used my two-week vacation to take a train trip to St. Gallen, Switzerland, where I visited an embroidery factory. I made a short stopover in Burghausen, which was still the same enchanting place, but sadly most of my friends weren't there anymore. From there I flew to Brussels for the World's Fair, and then it was time to get back to Paris.

By October the weather turned very chilly and I caught a bad cold. Since the heat wasn't turned on in Paris until November 1st, there wasn't a warm place to be found anywhere. Every place I went was cold and damp; consequently my cold got worse. My throat was so sore I could hardly swallow.

One morning Amelie, my chambermaid, noticed my flushed and swollen face, exclaimed "*Oh, mon Dieu!*" and had the hotel call a doctor. He came right away, gave me a shot of penicillin, and stuck me in bed. A nurse came twice a day for a week to administer penicillin and hot wraps to my neck. My throat and mouth were so swollen that they had to feed me liquid through a straw. After one week of this, I felt much better and ready to rejoin the world. Nevertheless Amelie would stand there with me every morning, and made me gargle and gargle and gargle. She took good care of me, and was another wonderful human being I met in my travels through life. Of course I was very worried about what all this would cost. But thanks to France's healthcare system, all the wonderful care I received only cost me seven dollars.

In November my six months in Paris came to an end. I had to leave, because as a non-American citizen this was all the time I was allowed to stay abroad without incurring problems with reentry to the United States. So I came home shortly before Thanksgiving. My parents picked me up at the airport after my long flight, and when Manhattan came into view, I was overcome with a wonderful feeling. I was home and I loved it. As much as I liked Paris, I was very happy to be back in the United States, my home.

My boss wasn't too pleased that I didn't stay longer. His only comment when I showed up was: "Why are you back so soon?"

* * *

Chapter 44

Single Life

Even though I loved Paris, it was great to be home again. When I got home my mother told me that I had a call from a Fred Stoever: "You know, the one who came to see you just before you left for Paris. You know, Abdul's friend." I had all but forgotten about him, and I certainly hadn't expected to hear from him again.

I wasn't home very long when he called again to ask me for a date, and he picked me up on a very cold night in December. We went to some place in Greenwich Village and it was a very nice evening, except for one thing. He was driving his father's Oldsmobile, and since he hadn't driven it too much, he couldn't find where to turn on the heat and drive at the same time. So my first date with Fred was a very cold one and I was glad to thaw out in my parents' warm house when I got home. Since Fred was home from college for the Christmas vacation, we saw each other a few more times before he had to go back. Luckily he had figured out how to work the heater by the time he called me again for a date. I gladly accepted after he had assured me that I wouldn't have to dress as if I was taking a trip to the North Pole. Consequently these dates were much more enjoyable, and I was looking forward to the next time he came home from school.

Back at work, I found a new designer had joined the firm and was given the room next to mine. He was a Hungarian aristocrat who fled the Communist workers' paradise, leaving behind his family's confiscated ancestral estates. Luckily he had artistic ability, so he was able to make a living as a designer. Ludwig was a very interesting character who sounded a lot like Bela Lugosi in the old Hollywood vampire movies. I dated him once or twice, but since he was quite a bit older, we ended up just good friends. Eventually he included me, Fred, and Margit in his circle of friends, who were mostly displaced European aristocrats or wealthy cosmopolitan Americans. We had some wonderful times with his loose-knit group of friends at the various tea dances and charity balls we were invited to.

The ball I liked most was the Hungarian Piarist Ball given at the Plaza Hotel. Befitting the Hungarian temperament, it was an elegant yet spirited affair. The women were dressed in beautiful gowns and the men looked splendid in white tie and tails. Distinguished-looking older men wore sashes with many decorative medals bestowed upon them by their respective governments.

Our friend Ludwig was usually the master of ceremonies at the presentation of the debutantes, mostly descendants of old aristocratic families who were partnered for the opening waltz with cadets in dress uniform. Then to everyone's delight, we were treated to lively Hungarian folk dances that set the mood for the evening. After that, dinner was served while an orchestra played and dancing began. There were a lot of czardas and waltzes mixed in with other popular dances. When you were tired of the main ballroom, you could go to another smaller ballroom where a different orchestra played. At one of the Piarist balls, we had just arrived and were going up to the Main Ballroom at the Plaza when we happened to meet John Rothschild of the Frankfurt Rothschilds coming down the stairs. "What a pleasant surprise," he said, upon meeting us.

While Fred was exchanging pleasantries with John, I looked at all the opulence surrounding me.

Here I was among all this super elegance of marble floors, thick rugs, and crystal chandeliers, of men in tuxedos and women in gowns wearing expensive jewelry. I couldn't help but wonder if this was the same girl who only a short time ago was pushing Opa's wagon loaded with horse manure that dripped through the racks and all over my only dress, my only pair of shoes, and me. Wake up, it's real, I told myself.

Once we invited Ingeborg, a fashion designer for Oleg Cassini. She was a striking, raven-haired beauty with very white skin. Always avant-garde, she wore a sequined black gown with a plunging neckline ending at her waist, which was absolutely scandalous for the time. Nosy Fred asked her how she kept her boobies from popping out. "I glued them in," was her bland answer. I had to laugh when I saw a waiter almost drop his tray full of glasses when he saw her. She certainly got a lot of disapproving looks from the women, while the men seemed to approve wholeheartedly. But Ingeborg wasn't fazed in the least by all the attention she drew. In fact, she seemed to enjoy it.

After a great time of dancing the night away, my feet were about to fall off, but who cared? I remember waltzing out of the Plaza's front doors at 5 a.m., taking the memory of a great evening with me.

The Viennese Opera Ball was another ball we liked to attend. It usually took place at the Waldorf Astoria, and was more formal and even more elegant than the Piarist Ball. Friends and acquaintances chatted at the cocktail hour before the ball. Expensively jeweled women were adorned like exotic birds. On one occasion they wore fabulous feathered masks, reminding me of pictures I had seen of glittering Venetian masked balls of past centuries. The men looked very handsome in their white tie and tails, contrasting the colorful, shimmering gowns of the ladies. The atmosphere was festive and exciting, with expectations of enjoyable hours ahead. Singers from the Vienna or the Metropolitan opera companies entertained us with songs from Strauss operettas. Young couples, the men in formal attire and the women in white gowns, opened the ball with a waltz. Fine wine flowed and delicious food flown in from the famous Hotel Sacher in Vienna was served. Happy couples swirled and swayed to the strains of waltzes on the never-empty dance floor. These were wonderful affairs frequented by European nobility, like the Habsburgs and the Hohenzollerns, along with other prominent American and Austrian dignitaries.

As is customary at European affairs, couples were separated to mix with others at the large tables so people could get to know one another. The men dutifully danced with all the women at their table. This added to a congenial atmosphere, and no woman was left sitting at the table alone. When the main ballroom closed after 1 a.m., everybody adjourned to another room where a different orchestra played, and more wine and food was served until dawn for the young and the young at heart.

The summer ball at Tavern on the Green in Central Park was another wonderful affair we attended. Informal "Tea Dances," held at the elegant Hotel Pierre on Sunday afternoons for young singles to mingle and enjoy themselves, usually ended with a party at someone's apartment. Things were never dull.

Then there was Ludwig's sailboat in Northport, Long Island. Cleaning the barnacles off his sailboat in the spring usually turned out to be fun-filled occasions. The rule was that if you didn't help get the boat spruced up for the summer, you weren't invited to go sailing. So he always had quite a few helpers who came equipped with wine bottles and various other alcoholic beverages, and it always became a "boat cleaning party." When it was time to sail the *Balaton*, named after a lake in his native Hungary, he usually had a lot of inexperienced sailors helping him. One time he told someone to throw the anchor out. Of course he meant "Drop the anchor." Well, it was thrown overboard, albeit without the rope attached. So Ludwig was out an anchor and had to buy an expensive new one. We also found out the hard way what the expression "lower the boom" meant. You better duck fast when the sail was moved, or you could wind up in the water with a big headache.

Ludwig claimed to be a confirmed bachelor and always talked about becoming a monk at the monastery of Monte Casino because of their fine wine cellar. Of course that didn't stop him from dating every pretty girl who crossed his path. As a titled single man, he was very much in demand.He once showed me a drawer full of invitations from various New York social circles, including one from the Radziwills.

Naturally there were times when the single life was much less glamorous. One nice summer weekend Margit and I decided to try a hotel we saw advertised in Lake Hopatcong, New Jersey. It was twenty dollars a night, which was not cheap for the time, so we thought it would be nice. Fred, who was home on a weekend pass from the Army, decided to join us. So the three of us set out with high hopes for a fun weekend frolicking in a nice lake during the day and in a cozy bar at night.

As we approached the lake, the ramshackle cottages along its shore made a rather poor impression. So we started to wonder what our hotel would look like, and we made jokes about our destination. One of the things we said was: "As long as the roof doesn't leak it'll be fine." It took us a while to find the place and when we did, it was a sight to behold. The grass in front of it was knee high; the "hotel" was a very run-down, large building that hadn't seen any paint for years. We should have turned around right then and there, but anxious to go swimming on this very hot summer day, we decided to make the best of it. Entering the large lobby, we saw pails sitting all over the place catching the water from last night's rainfall. So much for "As long as the roof doesn't leak." The rooms were dingy and the old mattresses leaning against the wall in the hallway didn't exactly inspire our confidence. "Well, there is still the lake," we said. So we went down to the lake on a narrow overgrown path through high grass. That was more than a disappointment; it was a shock.

The small wooden dock was in poor repair, and the water had oil slicks, rusty cans, and old tires floating in it. No way were we going swimming in that swill. That was the straw that broke the camel's back. We went back to the lobby and asked for our money back. After some negotiations they finally gave it back, and we wound up driving to Fred's family swimming hole, which wasn't too far away. So the day wasn't a complete loss. On the way home, we stopped at a restaurant/bar for a drink. We felt that after what we had been through that day, we needed it. There was only one problem. Margit, who was under twenty-one, ordered before me and used my ID, so she had a nice cool 7 and 7, while I got stuck with ginger ale. Not exactly what I had in mind!

Later that summer, Margit and I decided to try a resort in Pennsylvania. The promotional material for a place called Split Rock Lodge looked very nice, so we made reservations for a week. Our father drove us there and when we finally saw the sign for the lodge, we entered a narrow road bordered by woods on both sides. The road seemed to go on forever, and Father started laughing: "This place is in the middle of nowhere. It's so hidden in the woods that you can hardly find it. You can't possibly get into much trouble here." Although we didn't appreciate his snide remarks, we had to admit he was right. But the lodge turned out to be very nice and the lake was beautiful. So for once we thought that we had made the right decision. The only thing we didn't know was that this was a honeymoon resort. Nobody would talk to us and all the young wives looked at us askance as they jealously guarded their new husbands. Of course there was nobody to ask us to dance at night either. So we enjoyed the lake and spent quite a bit of time in the bar writing letters to Fred, who was still away in the Army. I'm sure that he was happy to get these cheerful missives from a bar in Pennsylvania. Nevertheless it was a nice, relaxing vacation, and our father picked up his two well-rested daughters at the end of the week.

In the fall, Margit and I enrolled in classes at the Art Students League of New York. The classes were good, and we learned quite a bit. Among other things, we were told was that our well-endowed model once modeled for the statue in the fountain in front of the Plaza Hotel, which we found hard to believe. We also met a few very nice people. One young man in particular was very taken with Margit. When he always offered to sharpen her pencils, we christened him the "Pencil Sharpener." After class a group of us usually wound up at the Carnegie Tavern for something to eat and a drink, not to mention a lot of laughs.

But there were some things in New York that were no laughing matter. On Saturdays we liked to go shopping on Fifth Avenue. After several hours of walking around with our loaded shopping bags, our feet really hurt. We found a very nice sidewalk café on Central Park South, a rarity in those days, and parked ourselves at one of the tables. It didn't take long for a waiter to appear to tell us: "Sorry ladies, you can't sit here!"

"Why not?" we asked.

"This is not a pickup place," we were told in an unfriendly tone of voice. What did he think we were? It seemed that the land of the free wasn't always free after all, especially not for women. Good grief, all we wanted was a cup of coffee and a chance to rest our tired feet.

Another time Margit and I went to a nearby hotel bar after class. They let us in, but women sat on one side of the room and the men on the other side. By chance a young man I had dated was there, and he came over to say hello. The maître d' was there in a flash, telling us that this wasn't permitted, because this was not a "pickup" place. We couldn't convince him that we knew each other and that this wasn't a "pickup." So all three of us were asked to leave—polite for "thrown out." We went somewhere else, and since we came in together there was no problem.

Not that public places in New Jersey were any friendlier for women. Aside from the movies, the ice cream parlor, or shopping in the department stores, you practically couldn't go anywhere as a female without a male escort. After all the freedom I had in Europe, I felt very restricted. American women must have been used to it, because they didn't seem to mind. They had grown up with it, so they didn't know any different. Ever-rebellious, I was determined to do as I pleased.

These were things I really had a problem getting used to, but despite some of the restrictions put on women, I managed to have a wonderful life as a single. Consequently marriage wasn't something that crossed my mind very often.

* * *

Chapter 45

Married Life

Even though I enjoyed my single life, I said "YES" when Fred Stoever asked me to marry him after four years of on-and-off dating.

We were married April 28, 1962 by a judge in my parents' house, because Fred's mother, a staunch Italian Catholic, objected to a ceremony in a Protestant church. Stubborn as usual, I wasn't about to take Catholic instruction and sign a pledge to bring my children up Catholic. Having a civil ceremony was an easy compromise for Fred and me, since neither of us cared where we were married. We tied the knot with only my parents, Margit, Cousin Roswitha, and Fred's parents, brother, and sister in attendance. I was so nervous at the ceremony that when the judge asked me to repeat: "I take thee Fred as my lawful wedded husband," I said: "I take thee Fred as my AWFUL wedded husband," which had everybody trying to stifle their giggles while I was hoping that this wasn't a sign of things to come.

Marriage day, April 28, 1962

Our wedding reception with about seventy guests was modest even by 1960s standards. As part of my wedding present, my boss at

Stein Tobler let me sketch the embroidery for my wedding gown, and then preempted a fifteen-yard machine to embroider my design on fine Japanese silk. I designed my own gown and my mother made the pattern and sewed it for me. Thanks to my boss's generosity and my mother's skill, I paid nothing for an exceptional embroidered wedding gown, which would cost a small fortune nowadays. My veil was also homemade and of my own design.

Instead of hiring a limousine, Fred's father simply drove us from my parents' house to the restaurant where we had our reception, and my cousin Roswitha, an experienced photographer, took all the photos. We had decided not to overspend on a wedding reception so we could save the money for a once-in-a-lifetime honeymoon trip. Nevertheless we were very careful to be sure that none of our guests were deprived of anything, and as far as I know, everyone had a very enjoyable evening.

Our wonderful three-week honeymoon started in Rome, followed by Florence, Venice, and Portofino on the Italian Riviera. From there it was on to Innsbruck, Austria, and Garmisch, Germany, the picturesque site of the 1936 Winter Olympics. Next I took Fred to see Burghausen, where I had spent some of the best years of my life after our escape to the West. We made a three-day stop in Bremen to visit Fred's grandmother, who, contrary to all the bad stories my mother-in-law had told me about her, I found to be a very nice woman. Our fabulous trip ended in Paris, where I introduced Fred to Nani and her husband Jean, who had taken such good care of me during my assignment in Paris four years earlier. Since we stayed at my former hotel, the Montpensier, Fred also got to meet Amelie, who had mothered me through my illness during the last few weeks of my stay in Paris. We arrived home with tons of photos, all the things we purchased for our apartment, and gifts for everyone.

We set up housekeeping in a brand-new, three-room apartment in Palisades Park, New Jersey. Fred continued his job in the back office of Lebenthal & Co., a municipal bond firm in New York's financial district, and I continued working as a designer for Stein Tobler. Of course I earned much more than Fred, so I paid for most of our expenses, and we still managed to save a good portion of our income.

Married life was a big change for me, mainly because I didn't know how to cook. My mother tried to teach me with limited success. Cooking just wasn't my thing. Fred was lucky he didn't starve to death that first year. One of the first things he asked when he came home from work was, "What did you burn today?" because he could usually smell it out in the hall. Surprisingly, none of the other tenants complained. In order to get the unpleasant chore of food preparation over with as quickly as possible, I turned the flame on high. That caused a lot of burns not only to the food but also to my hands and fingers. I had Band-Aids on my fingers so often that my coworkers offered to get me a pair of asbestos gloves.

One time when my frying pan caught fire the flames shot up, burning my eyebrows and the front of my hair. When I arrived at work the next day, looking like I had a bad sunburn and smelling of singed hair, there was no end to remarks like: "Look at Renate, she put herself on fire again. Maybe we should get her a fire extinguisher to go with the asbestos gloves." From then on, I kept the flame lower, exercising more patience and more caution.

Luckily my cooking improved as time passed. With my mother-in-law's Italian recipes and my mother's German dishes, my cooking eventually became a mixture of both. Although Fred wasn't a fussy eater and always ate everything I gave him without complaint, there was one occasion when he balked and complained profusely. I cooked a dinner that had been one of my favorite dishes at home. It consisted of water, white flour, bacon bits, butter, and lemon juice for flavor. When it reached a low boil, eggs were added that floated to the top as they cooked. This was then poured over boiled potatoes. Well, Fred took one look at the eggs swimming in that white sauce, looking back at him like yellow eyes in a milky sky, and said: "What the hell is this?" He acted as if the eggs were about to jump out and bite him.

"It's our dinner," I told him. "You'll see, it's delicious."

"Are you kidding? That looks disgusting! I'm not going to eat that," was his reply as he adjourned to the bedroom, closed the door, and wouldn't come out until I had disposed of that "awful looking stuff." Needless to say, I haven't made it since. Fred was definitely a meat person; vegetables and potatoes were a minor part of his diet. So I concentrated on meat dishes. Fish, or anything that came out of rivers, lakes, or oceans, was an anathema to Fred.

Our social life was restricted to Saturday pizza and TV nights with our friends Carmelita and Frank Braddock, who were also newlyweds. Frank was the nephew of James Braddock, the former world heavyweight champion who was later immortalized in the movie "The Cinderella Man," and Carmelita was a Brazilian whom I met while working at Stein Tobler. She and Frank also knew how to live frugally, and together we had a lot of fun solving all the world's problems on those Saturday nights. Too bad our government didn't have us as advisors. But then, I doubt that our policies would have been very popular, because our miserly spending habits wouldn't have been good for the economy.

I saved a lot of money by designing and making all my own clothes, curtains, and tablecloths from materials I bought at a remnants store. One dress I made for myself cost me all of seventy-five cents. In addition to saving money, it had the other advantage that my clothes were one of a kind and in the latest style. It wasn't very difficult for me, since I always had *Women's Wear Daily*, *Vogue* and *Harper's Bazaar* on my desk, and I was well informed on all the latest fashions.

Working full time, sewing, and keeping house kept me very busy, and it turned out to be more difficult than I thought, but living frugally was a cinch. I was used to that.

Never idle, Fred used his evenings to start painting in oils. He painted while sitting on our bed and I had a terrible time trying to get our sheets clean. That's when I first realized that Fred was a talented artist. His first painting was a jaguar crouching on a tree limb, ready to jump. It turned out so nice that we had it framed and hung it over the couch in our living room, where it scared the daylights out of our guests. Fred has been painting in his spare time ever since, and has produced quite a few excellent canvases. One of his paintings of a tiger won a prize and was published in *The Artist's Magazine*. He was also accepted as a member of the prestigious Salmagundi Club. Since its membership is reserved for the most accomplished artists, this was an extraordinary honor. With his intimate knowledge of wildlife, his paintings are true to nature and quite impressive.

Two years into our marriage, Fred decided to open his own investment firm with the money we had saved and small loans from our parents. Amazingly, he was able to start a municipal bond firm with less than 25 percent of what was generally acknowledged to be the absolute minimum amount of capital required. I don't know how he did it, but I remember him sitting on the bed writing out dozens of different income-and-expense scenarios night after night. So, at age twenty-seven and just over three years after starting in the mailroom, he opened his own investments firm. To honor his father, Fred took a business name very similar to the name of his father's stove business founded in 1929, Stoever Glass & Company. His first office was one small room in New York's financial district. In the beginning the objective was just to break even while my paycheck took care of all our living expenses. But in a relatively short time he did well enough to afford a very competent secretary, who later became Fred's comptroller.

Second Place
Fred Stoever
30 x 31, oil on linen

Our friend Ludwig finally seemed to be settling down too. His party group was breaking up, because a lot of them were getting married or moving away. So Ludwig braved my home-cooked dinners quite often as a welcome change to the pot of goulash he usually made for himself.

Finally he too got married.

Abdul, who had earned two master's degrees in the meantime, came to visit us one day before flying back to Cairo to get married. As was customary in the Arab world, it was an arranged marriage, and he didn't seem too enthusiastic about it. But he was accompanied by two tall Arab men, so there was no way for him to shirk his duty. Several months later, he came back to visit us with his new bride in tow. His family had chosen well; she was gorgeous and looked like the famous bust of the Egyptian Queen Nefertiti. But more importantly, she had good character and did a lot to keep him in line. Our beer-loving friend now had to walk the straight and narrow as a good Muslim should. Abdul, who used to brew beer in his bathtub, which ruined his landlady's plumbing and got him evicted, now had to hide in our kitchen to sneak a beer. I thought this absolutely hilarious.

About a year later we were watching the news when they showed Yemen's new ambassador being welcomed on the steps of the White House. All of a sudden Fred said: "Look, Renate, that looks like Abdul!"

"No way" I said. "That's probably just somebody who looks like him."

But the next day the new ambassador was on the front page of the *New York Daily News* with President Johnson. It was our friend Abdul, all right. Fred hadn't been hallucinating after all. A day later, Abdul called and greeted Fred with: "Hey, you foul ball." Abdul always called him that because Fred was a baseball player in college. Fred asked immediately: "Abdul, was that you I saw with President Johnson?"

"Yeah," he said. "I'm Yemen's new ambassador to the United States and also to the UN." Was this really my pen friend from my days in Burghausen? What a success story, and it couldn't have happened to a nicer guy.

Unfortunately around this time my mother began to have health problems. It started innocently enough with a painful elbow. What we didn't know then was that it was arthritis, which over time would spread to involve almost all of her joints. The only thing the medical establishment had to offer was stronger and stronger painkillers. Despite her affliction, she continued working in the embroidery industry. All of us, including my father, wanted her to stay home and take care of herself, but she wouldn't hear of it. Mother's iron will prevailed. This awful disease eventually left her crippled and in constant pain, but true to her character, she pushed herself to do as much as she could. One of her maxims, which I used to hear often enough while I was growing up, was: "There's no such thing as can't." She went by this all her life, and nothing was impossible as far as she was concerned. There was always a way to overcome an obstacle, but despite all of her formidable willpower, this affliction was hard to beat.

By 1968 Fred's business was thriving, which enabled him to move to a larger office and hire more people. He was doing so well that we were able to buy a fine Tudor home. It was an old house with a slate roof and copper gutters on a large property that was beautifully landscaped with lots of rhododendrons and azaleas. An impressive 225-foot-long, six-foot-high azalea hedge fronted our property, and thankfully there were at least 150 feet door to door between us and the houses on either side.

After moving there from our noisy apartment where we lived near a major highway, it felt like I was on vacation in the country, because the area had so many trees, bushes, and large lawns. When I looked out the windows and saw all the greenery outside, I felt blessed and full of wonder at my good fortune. I had come a long way from the bombed-out ruins of Plauen to a beautiful home such as this. The neighborhood was so quiet that we couldn't sleep the first few nights because we felt a bit spooked. But one thing that was really vexing was a horrible smell that emanated from the refrigerator whenever I opened its door. It smelled like a dead rat in an advanced stage of decay. Holding my nose and trying not to gag, I looked and looked, but I couldn't find the cause. To my relief the mystery was solved the next day. The former owner of the house dropped by to pick up his Limburger cheese, which he had forgotten, in a rear compartment of the refrigerator.

As is usually the case after moving into an old house, there was a lot to do. We were very busy the first year in our new house with plenty of remodeling, painting, and decorating. Coming from a three-room apartment, we needed lots of new furniture, but luckily the Limburger cheese wasn't the only thing the previous owner had left behind. He also left us some of his furniture, which filled the gap until we got our own.

* * *

Chapter 46

Jumbo Habari!

By 1969 Fred's business was very successful, so we decided to take a six-week photo safari to Africa and India, which we arranged through an agent connected with Abercrombie & Fitch. Fred's strong interest in wildlife conservation made this a dream come true. It was a time when Africa was still wild. In those days you could almost drive from Nairobi to Maasai Mara and hardly ever be out of sight of gazelles, topi, zebras, or lions, and nobody went to India on wildlife tours at that time.

Before setting out we visited Dr. Kevin Cahill, a well-known specialist in tropical medicine, to get our shots and his advice on all the dos and don'ts. We left March 5th with a group of eight others from all over the United States. We flew from New York to Athens, where we visited the Acropolis, and then on to Nairobi, which was supposed to be a six-hour flight. But about five hours into the flight we were told that Nairobi had bad weather and that we would have to land in the Sudan. When I saw lights below, I asked one of the stewards nervously running up and down the aisles if this was Khartoum. He said: "I don't know lady, I've never been there." Since I don't like to fly, his response was very disquieting. Luckily I sat there with a vodka martini, which calmed my nerves considerably. When we finally landed, we learned that we had lost an engine and that we were lucky to land safely on their short runway. Getting off the plane, we were met by some rather scary-looking Sudanese soldiers in white uniforms and turbans, with long knives in their sashes, who guided us into the airport's small building. So there we sat in Khartoum at midnight still wearing our winter clothes in the ninety-five degree heat of a tiny airport without air-conditioning. Everything was so dirty that we were afraid to drink anything, even though our throats were parched and our tongues were glued to the roofs of our mouths. Since there was no refrigeration, warm beer was the only alternative. So we hung around like half-dead flies until 6 a.m., when an Ethiopian airplane took us to Addis Ababa, from where we were able to catch a flight to Nairobi. Immediately upon arrival, several of our group were taken straight to Nairobi Hospital to get shots and malaria pills, because their doctors had neglected to tell them that they were necessary.

Nairobi was a nice, modern city. Sitting in the New Stanley Hotel's sidewalk café, it was hard to believe that this was Africa. I was surprised by its lively cosmopolitan atmosphere and the many chic stores. Wide streets with medians full of palm trees and tropical flowers reminded me a little of the Italian Riviera.

We left in four Toyota jeeps the next day for Lake Naivasha, where we stayed overnight in little cabins along its shore. I was delighted to see a big sacred ibis standing in front of our door that first morning. Luckily one of our guides was John Williams, a leading ornithologist and former director of the Nairobi Museum of Natural History, who could name all the different birds for us. The lake was a paradise for feathered folk, chock full of cranes, ibises, pelicans, storks, and all kinds of ducks. Next, we stopped at Lake Nakuru, which was so full of flamingos that large parts of the lake looked pinkish white from a distance.

Early next morning we drove to our tented camp in Maasai Mara. When we stopped on the way at a small village store, I waited outside on the porch. Among the Maasai in traditional garb milling about was a young Maasai who gave me a big smile. Not to appear unfriendly, I smiled back. All of a sudden our tour leader came charging out of the store, grabbed my arm, pulled me down the stairs, and unceremoniously pushed me into the jeep. He gunned the motor and we took off. Annoyed and perplexed, I asked, "What the hell is wrong with you?" He explained to me that the young Maasai was a "Moran," an adolescent warrior, and that my smiling back at him left us open to some possibly undesirable complications. So no more smiling at Morans after that.

From here on there were no more roads, only tire tracks, and we had to leave a good distance between jeeps because of the huge dust clouds they left behind. Every night lots were drawn to determine who would drive with whom. At first Fred was in a car with Harold, a doctor from North Carolina with a great sense of humor, so that car was dubbed the "Fun Car." As a joke, Fred was offering seats in it for a price. So the next car he was in had a sign that read "Business Car"—which wasn't quite as popular.

With great excitement we sighted our first zebra herds, giraffes, and gazelles as we headed west. It felt like we had arrived in the Garden of Eden. The Maasai villages we passed consisted of round huts arranged in a circle inside an enclosure constructed of thorn branches to keep the lions from taking their cattle at night. The men looked dangerous with their long spears and knives, but notwithstanding their appearance, they were quite friendly. Their apparel consisted of a beaded leather string around the waist and a rust-colored toga of sorts. They wore their hair in skinny braids held together with a metal clasp. Hair dyed red with ocher identified the wearer as a Moran, and I was careful to keep a straight face around them.

The women's hair was shorn, and they were adorned with loads of colorful bead necklaces, armbands, earrings, and leg bands. Some of their earlobes were so elongated that they almost hung down to their shoulders. Seeing the women carrying heavy loads of wood on their backs and a baby in a sling in the front, I became acutely aware of how lucky I was to be an American woman. I felt a strange kinship with these women, who lived such harsh lives. From my years in Germany during and after the war, I remembered how harsh a woman's life could be.

The land we traversed alternated between rolling hills and plains, teeming with wildlife. Some of the animals would come quite close, look at us curiously, then suddenly take off. The cute little Thomson's gazelles were everywhere, constantly flicking their black tails over their white behinds. They seemed to play a game of chicken with us, only jumping aside at the last minute as we approached.

Our first tented campsite was next to a dry riverbed. There we were greeted by seventeen servants, who had arrived the day before to set up camp. They cooked our food, did our laundry, and took care of anything else we needed. The dining tent was set up in the center of our circle of tents. There, tasty dinners with all the trimmings were served on snowy white linen by liveried attendants. To my sorrow, they also woke us up with a pot of tea or coffee at five thirty every morning, because early morning was the best time to see the animals. Nobody got much sleep that first night in camp because of a very noisy troop of baboons in the huge trees behind our tents. A leopard coughed in the nearby ravine, panicking the baboons into taking off for the higher branches, screeching loudly as they went. The hideous laughing sound of hyenas was ever present to rekindle the instinctive fears of our primordial past.

But after a few days we got used to the sounds of the African night, and only woke up when the ruckus was too close for comfort. That's when nobody dared leave the tents during the night to visit the toilet facility at the edge of camp. So there were a lot of jokes in the morning about ruptured bladders, and how we spent the night trying to decide whether or not to risk a trip to the latrine.

One afternoon three Maasai women from a nearby village came to visit. Since they were bare breasted, the males' eyes in our group were in danger of falling out. All of a sudden one of our attendants came running and yelling at them. "How dare you come here with your breasts exposed?" At that, the embarrassed women withdrew, and the men's faces fell when their ogling was cut short.

Serengeti National Park in Tanzania was next on our itinerary. The landscape here was flat, and the shimmering, golden yellow grass stretched as far as the eye could see under an endless blue sky. The long grasses bent under light breezes, creating an ocean of rippling, amber waves. Slowly moving clouds created a kaleidoscope of changing patterns over the vast grasslands. Lone acacia trees and bushes here and there broke the monotony of the flat expanse. The quiet was another aspect of this beautiful world; no traffic hum or airplane noise marred its calm. There was only the sound of the grasses whispering in the wind. You could take deep breaths, because the air was clear and smelled sweet. It was the Pleistocene come back to life.

On the way we encountered a ten-mile stretch where we made our first acquaintance with the infamous tsetse flies. These ugly little beasts pounce on anything that doesn't move fast enough. When we drove slower than twenty miles an hour, or stopped because Fred wanted to photograph a herd of zebra, the whole jeep was full of them in a second. They were all over us, eating us alive. We kept yelling at the driver to keep going. Thanks to Fred, we got a lot of very painful bites that left big welts, and since the tsetse flies carry deadly sleeping sickness, we were a little concerned. Our tour operator told us not to worry. "Only one tsetse fly in a thousand actually carries the sleeping sickness . . ."

"Hell, I've been bitten five hundred times, so the odds are down to two to one. Let's get the hell out of here!" Harold blurted out.

On the Serengeti Plain we found whole lion families, leopards, and thousands of other animals grazing on the great plain. A huge herd of wildebeests ran in dizzying circles around us, a group of elephants moved ponderously past our jeeps, and we tried to keep pace with ostriches running ahead of us. The adorable Thomson's gazelles that were an integral part of the scenery always kept us company.

We photographed a leopard in a tree and later came upon a family of lions that allowed us to come very close. I counted six females and fourteen little cubs. One of the cubs got up and went under our jeep, then one after another followed, until most of the cubs were under our car. That's when the mothers got terribly upset, roaring their displeasure. So we started the motor and all the cubs scampered back out and their mothers relaxed. Five minutes later, the cubs were back under the car again, so to keep the mothers happy, we had to repeat the process a few times. Then a lioness started to stalk some nearby zebras, sneaking up on them in a wide arc. But the zebras got wind of her and bolted; the lioness came slinking back looking very dejected. It was wonderful to watch.

While there, we also visited Dr. George Schaller, a world-renowned field biologist, and a best-selling author who wrote the book *The Year of the Gorilla*. Fred, who had an avid interest in wildlife conservation and in India's wildlife in particular, got a copy of Schaller's latest book *The Deer and the Tiger*, which he read several times over. When a magnificent tiger appeared on the cover of *Life* magazine, referencing Schaller's wildlife studies in India's Kanha National Park, Fred immediately decided that he would go there someday. Fred knew that Schaller was now in the Serengeti studying the African lions, so before we left, Fred got his address and wrote to him, mentioning that he would like to fund a project to help India's wildlife, and that he would like to discuss any suggestions George might have.

Dr. Schaller invited us to dinner with his family when we reached the Serengeti. It turned out to be a very congenial evening, and we left with lots of good advice and the address of Ranjit Sinh, the collector in the Mandla District in Central India where Kanha National Park is located.

From there it was on to the Ngorongoro Crater. This extinct volcano is one of the best places in Africa to see wildlife concentrated in a relatively small area. We had to navigate a steep, zigzagging trail to reach the 132-square-mile plain at its bottom that was populated by thousands of animals of all kinds. Wherever you looked, there were lions, hyenas, zebras, rhinos, and gazelles. Crossing the plain, we were chased by a rhino we had annoyed, and to escape its ire our jeeps went over bushes and holes. I saw stars when I lost my grip and was thrown against the jeep's roof. Around noon we decided to stop and have our packed lunches on a little knoll. But we had to defend our food from a flock of large black birds, which swooped down and tried to take the sandwiches right out of our hands.

A sudden rainstorm surprised us on our way out of the crater, and in seconds everything became a muddy morass, which made driving very slippery. Mud flew in all directions as we tried to get up the steep incline to the crater's rim. We all had to get out of the jeeps and help push, with the wheels churning up more mud to throw on us. So we arrived completely filthy and full of mud at our next camp, at Lake Manyara in the Great Rift Valley, where we stayed two days, which gave us a chance to recoup and clean up a little. The showers were in small canvas stalls, where attendants poured water into a pail with an attached pull string hanging from a pole. Clothes and towels hung over the walls had to be guarded because there was always somebody who thought it funny to leave you there naked, screaming for a towel and your clothes.

Elephants and cape buffalo came very close to the tents our first night there. The hysterical screeching of the baboons, the coughing of leopards, and the elephants thrashing noisily through the trees made such a racket that hardly anybody got much sleep. To be on the safe side, Harold decided to go to bed with a spear and a knife from then on.

Our last stop was in Amboseli National Park near Mount Kilimanjaro, and it was as if Africa wanted to give us a nice going-away present. A large elephant herd mulled around close to the camp, allowing us to come close enough to take some very good pictures.

On this last day, I made the supreme effort to get up at 5:30 a.m. to go on the early-morning game run. We had heavy rain during the night, which gave us a magnificent sunrise. The sun came up blood red, silhouetting the trees darkly against the sky. We watched the red glow spread, turning the horizon pink with flecks of blue and fleecy white clouds.

Later that morning we came upon a cheetah that looked like she was going to make a kill with one of those lightning fast sprints. The gazelles were jumping around in front of her as if teasing her. Suddenly the cheetah was off and running at tremendous speed, but the gazelles, taking off in a flurry of graceful leaps, managed to get away. We watched with great excitement and mixed feelings. We were glad that the gazelles got away, but also felt sorry for the cheetah, who had to go hungry for now.

When we drove out for the last time in the late afternoon, as the sun's last rays rested on Kilimanjaro's snowy peaks, we found two giraffes interlocking necks, which was fascinating to watch. Not far away a baby giraffe, still trailing its umbilical cord, ambled along with its parents. It was a wonderful, unforgettable trip of which every moment was a gift. It was much more than a vacation. It was a soul-enriching experience.

Back in Nairobi, it was a pleasure to get into a bathtub and get cleaned up for our going-away party in the hotel. I already missed the congenial evenings, sitting with a favorite drink, swapping stories around a huge campfire, with the mosquitoes falling off us dead drunk. These three weeks went so fast that they seemed like a wonderful dream, and I was sorry that it had come came to an end.

One of our group, a woman from the Midwest, failed to appear for dinner after the going-away party. When she didn't show up by 8 p.m., and it was almost time to leave for the airport, Kate, a young socialite from Palm Beach, and I were sent to her room to fetch her. We found her in a bubble bath with a wine bottle, crooning to the bubbles. We managed to get her dressed, hurriedly packed her clothes, which were littered all over the place, and delivered her to the tour operator in time for departure. It was a close call. Since we just threw everything into her suitcases and had to sit and stand on them to get them closed,

I would have loved to see the reactions of the customs agents opening her bags.

Everybody was accounted for, and they left encumbered with spears, knives, and carved statues late that night for New York, most of them in a state of happy inebriation, while Fred and I stayed behind to catch a flight to India the next day.

*   *   *

Chapter 47

Culture Shock

1969

Our flight from Nairobi to India took us to Bombay, where we switched planes for a flight to Calcutta. This was definitely not the place for a first introduction to India. It was culture shock of momentous proportions. However, as the travel company's experiment to establish wildlife tourism in India, we received VIP treatment throughout the trip. That became obvious when people came to meet us in Bombay at 3 a.m. to wait with us for our flight to Calcutta.A quick look at our tickets and vouchers confirmed it. They were all stamped "VIP."

At Calcutta's Dum Dum Airport we were picked up by two representatives of our travel agency in an almost unheard-of air-conditioned car, and driven to the Oberoi Grand Hotel. I was grateful to sit in a cool car, because even at 9 a.m. it was already unbearably hot and humid.

On the way from the airport into Calcutta, we saw cows and goats in the middle of the road, and small straw huts next to ponds overgrown with water lilies where people made their morning toilette or did their laundry. Most of them didn't wear much more than rags of nondescript color, and naked children ran around chasing scrawny chickens,

In Calcutta, the poverty and the dirt were indescribable. The Oberoi Grand, an old English hotel, was clean and very nice, but the minute you stuck your nose out the door, you were assailed by crowds of very insistent beggars. Some of them looked like they were in the last stages of consumption, and many were deformed or blind. Others had open sores festering in the tropical heat. They were a throng of pitiful, suffering humanity, holding out their hands for a few coins so they could eat and live another day. Sadly, whatever we could give those poor wretches wouldn't be enough. There were just too many of them. The scene was so unreal, it left us incredulous and at a loss for what to do. So we went back to our room and closed the door with a sense of relief, to collect our wits and assess our situation. From our window I was shocked to see people washing themselves with brackish brown water, which had collected in gutters and the broken sidewalk.

The view from our hotel room in Calcutta

At the time, it was estimated that over a million of Calcutta's people lived and slept on its sidewalks and in its alleys, but not randomly. Families had their regular places where they would roll up their straw mats against a building as they went about their daily activities. These mats and perhaps a tin cup or two comprised their entire worldly possessions. The noise was deafening, and the smells were overpowering and almost took your breath away. Since many people prepared their food outdoors, the air was full of smog from all the cooking fires, and mingled with the stench of sewage, it made the city even less appealing. Unfortunately we had a two-day stay in Calcutta waiting for the twice-weekly flight to Assam, one of India's easternmost states.

Intimidated by the sights waiting for us outside, we sought refuge in the hotel's palm court, where we met a very nice Canadian woman whose husband worked in Calcutta. Aside from a few Russians that we saw in the lobby, she was the only other European we had seen in the hotel. She sat at one of the small tables by herself with a cup of tea, so we went to talk to her, and we gladly accepted her invitation to sit down and join her. Sympathetic and fully understanding our predicament, she picked us up the next day in her chauffeur-driven car to take us to the bazaar, where we were able to find some English canned goods and powdered milk for our trip into the jungle.

Navigating a car through Calcutta's streets crowded with people and cows was quite nerve racking. We were told that it was worse to hit a cow than a person, and that there had been instances where people were burned alive in their cars by an enraged mob after hitting a cow. She and her husband treated us to dinner in their beautiful home and an interesting afternoon at the old Calcutta Polo Club which had been established by the British during colonial times. Despite Calcutta's squalor, they made our stay a pleasurable experience.

Thanks to our Canadian friends, we now had enough food to take on our trip into the wilderness, which began in Kaziranga National Park. We took a three-hour flight to Jorhat in the State of Assam, an area for which we needed special permission because of Kaziranga's close proximity to the juncture of China, Burma, and India.

On our drive from Jorhat to Kaziranga I saw women and children carrying baskets filled with stones on their heads as they were working to rebuild the road. Instead of a few dozen construction workers with bulldozers, cranes, and huge trucks, as is done in the United States, they use hundreds of men, women, and children, each equipped with a basket, shovel, and pick. The net result was the same, but probably better for India, because it gave employment to many more people. No child labor laws here!

Minding Dr. Cahill's advice, we stayed away from all raw fruits and vegetables, milk products, and of course water, including ice cubes. Only very well-cooked food was safe. We were pretty hungry most of the time, because we also had a hard time getting used to the spicy food. We usually slaked our thirst with beer, which according to Dr. Cahill was always safe to drink. Even though I wasn't particularly fond of beer, I found India's Kingfisher beer to be quite good.

The guesthouse at Kaziranga was simple, clean, and functional. We stayed there three days, going out on elephant backs every day into the lush swamps and jungles of one of India's best wildlife reserves. Fred was in his glory, taking photos of rhinos, swamp deer, some of the last wild water buffalo, elephants, and a great variety of birds.

One morning we went into the jungle on foot. A big bull elephant, seeing his territory encroached upon, threatened us with raised trunk, showing his tusks and angrily trumpeting his displeasure. He was definitely looking for trouble. Our guide quickly ripped out some dry grass, twisted it into a fagot, lit it on fire, and waved it at him. At that, the bull deciding not to tangle with us, turned, and ambled away. I was finally able to exhale.

Late afternoons, I enjoyed watching the more docile domesticated elephants, which had carried us around during the day, being fed near the guesthouse. A young servant assigned to us thought that window screens were only for the rich, and he was incredulous to learn that everyone in the United States had them. Our request to have our tea refrigerated to make iced tea was received with bewilderment. He had never heard of such a thing as iced tea, even though India is one of the world's major tea producers.

Then it was back to the Oberoi Grand Hotel in Calcutta. Things there were as hopeless as ever and we were glad to leave the next morning. We flew to Nagpur, a city in central India, where we were picked up by a car to take us to Kanha National Park, the area that provided the inspiration for Rudyard Kipling's *The Jungle Book*. It was a hot, eight-hour drive from Nagpur to Kanha on dusty roads, dodging cows, goats, oxcarts, and people. Bedding, sheets, mosquito nets, beer, food, and a cook had been sent ahead to Kanha's small guesthouse, where we were the only guests. There we were with an entire national park full of bison, leopards, tigers, antelopes, and four different types of deer all to ourselves. What a great experience.

Kanha's peace and quiet was a welcome relief and a good place to recover from Calcutta's noise, smog, and smells. It was hot there too, but it was dry heat and the nights were cool enough to sleep in a sweat suit. At this point I didn't get up with Fred at 5 a.m. anymore, for which I was given the name of "Sleep Bank" by the natives. As far as I was concerned, Fred could wish the bison, leopards, and assorted deer "good morning" for me. Sitting on the terrace in the afternoon with a cool beer, a cigarette, and Badri, our guide, I could observe the many chital, blackbuck and barasingha deer browsing in the Kanha meadow. Long-tailed silvery langur monkeys playing in the trees were fun to watch, and so were the peacocks strutting around, displaying their beautiful tails. The only noise was the peacocks' screech, the cooing of doves, and the breeze blowing dry leaves over the terrace. The natural sounds were so relaxing that I felt utterly content and at one with the world around me. Early mornings and evenings Fred and Badri went looking for tigers, but had no luck. They kept finding tracks, but the tigers eluded them. They must have heard that Fred was coming and decided to hide.

The next morning Ranjit Sinh came to meet us, and he and Fred clicked immediately. Together they made plans to rescue a subspecies of barasingha, a very large deer that was in danger of extinction. At the time there were only about sixty-five remaining, and the plan Ranjit presented was to build a one-square-mile enclosure where they could put a dozen deer to breed, undisturbed by Kanha's predators. That meant that the fence had to be a leopard-proof eighteen feet high, topped with barbed wire, and python-proof below the ground. Fred agreed to donate the funds through the World Wildlife Fund, and Ranjit, who knew Indira Gandhi, said he would use it to ask the government to do more for wildlife protection in the future. He said: "Do we have to depend on foreigners? Can't we do things like this ourselves?" I'm sure this endeavor played a part in leading to Project Tiger, the World Wildlife Fund's most successful project. Later on, Fred received a letter from Prime Minister Gandhi acknowledging his efforts on behalf of India's wildlife.

The drive back to Nagpur was another hot-as-hell, memorable trip. Just as on the drive to Kanha, we were on a constant collision course with oxcarts, cows, monkeys, people, and an occasional truck or car. The heat and the road's red dust streaming into the car made me feel like I was sitting in a blast furnace. When we finally arrived in Nagpur, we were so coated with the red dust that our sweat left streaks on our skin, making us look like red and white zebras. We were such a sight that people came to gawk at us. We couldn't wait to clean up at the Mount Hotel, but even though it was Nagpur's best hotel at the time, it only offered the minimum of basic services. The only furniture in our room was a wooden bed, a table, and a chair. The walls were painted cinder blocks and the floor was bare concrete. We cleaned up in an adjoining bathroom, where the shower was a pail of water with a tin cup. There were no dining facilities, but thankfully they had beer. We stayed there overnight, and our driver John and Badri drove us to the Nagpur Airport in the morning, where we said a sad good-bye, promising to return.

Flying from Nagpur to Bombay in a small propeller plane was also something to remember. Aside from the dozen or so passengers, the plane had crates full of chickens stored in the back of the cabin. Every time the plane hit a bad air pocket, the chickens went absolutely crazy. As a very unenthusiastic flyer, I would have liked to join the chickens, but as a "self-disciplined" human, I had to act like it didn't bother me in the least and remain quietly in my seat.

Our flight from Bombay to Rome had a stopover in Kuwait. Since it was a night flight, we could see the many flaming oil well spouts from the air. Consequently our approach to Kuwait seemed like a descent into hell, and I must admit to feeling a bit squeamish, because it evoked memories of times I wanted to forget.

We were happy to arrive at Rome's Hotel Hassler on top of the Spanish Steps, where we looked forward to some honest-to-goodness Italian food. The hotel's lovely rooftop restaurant afforded a wonderful view of Rome, which was only surpassed by its wonderful menu. Unfortunately my shrunken stomach couldn't handle much of what I ordered, and I could have cried when I had to leave most of that delicious food on my plate. Our waiter became quite upset when he saw my still half-full plate and worriedly asked: "Madama not lika our food?" I had a hard time reassuring him that the food was terrific, but my stomach wasn't.

When we arrived in the United States, the New York skyline looked mighty good to me. No matter how interesting the trip, it's always nice to be home, but the trip's strong impressions and wonderful experiences lingered in my consciousness for quite some time. I felt like I had just come home from an alien planet. We were home for a few days, yet I still lived in a world between Africa, India, and home. It seemed as if two or three different negatives merged with each other, giving me the impression of seeing all these worlds at the same time. Driving along, I could still see the cute little Thomson's gazelles, topi, zebras, wildebeests, and ostriches running before and alongside our jeeps. The thin Indian women in colorful saris carrying water urns on their heads, hungry, dirty children, oxcarts full of bamboo, water buffalo, monkeys, and goats blocking the road were still there before me.

* * *

Chapter 48

India Revisited

1970

One year later we went back to India, but this time we didn't go through Calcutta. This time we started out in New Delhi, where we landed in the predawn morning during a terrific thunderstorm. Dead tired from jet lag, we went straight to bed at the Oberoi Hotel. Unfortunately one wall of our room had a large window with a view into an aviary. The birds, beautiful and interesting as they were, had no intention of letting us sleep. Their cheerful chirping told us that the day had begun, and we soon gave up trying to sleep. From our balcony we could see the cupolas of Old Delhi glinting golden in the early-morning haze of a rising sun, a sight so beautiful and intriguing that we forgot about our tiredness. So we went for a few cups of coffee and did a little sightseeing in New Delhi, which thankfully was much nicer than Calcutta had been the previous year.

The next day, after a two-hour flight, we had to a joyful reunion with Badri and John, who greeted us at the Nagpur Airport for our long drive to Kanha National Park. On the way we passed through a small village, where it happened to be market day. We stopped because I wanted to take some photos of the colorful scene. The picture of the women in their brilliant emerald green, red, purple, and orange saris, carrying baskets on their heads, was too interesting to pass up. Many others were sitting on the ground, selling their produce or praising their wares to potential customers. As soon as I got my camera in position, males of all ages and sizes crowded around me, grinning from ear to ear, eager to have their picture taken. It was really quite funny. Consequently I never got the pictures of the women I wanted; all I got were the wide smiles of men and boys.

Kanha Park was as peaceful and quiet as I remembered it. Ranjit Sinh arrived and took us to see the enclosure he had built with Fred's financial help. The little dirt road leading to it had a sign that read "Stoever Road," and a plaque bearing our name was affixed to the fence. Over a dozen barasingha deer, safe from predators, were contentedly browsing within the enclosure. It was rather nice to see the result of Fred's donation. Once again Badri found tiger tracks in a dry riverbed. So we went there early in the morning on two elephants in search of them. We saw the tracks of a female and two cubs, but no tigers. They were around somewhere, but where? We realized that finding tigers in the wild was no easy matter, especially when you only had a few days to do so.

Looking for tigers in Kanha National Park

However, I didn't consider our search a waste of time. The country we moved through was absolutely beautiful. The early-morning sun created pools of deep shade and vivid brightness in a dense forest generously interspersed with light green, delicately feathered bamboo. Plodding along on the elephants, the only noise to be heard was the wind swishing through the trees, birds, an occasional monkey, mosquitoes, and the elephants' noise as they walked along, careless of branches whipping us riders on their backs.

One of our elephants was a little unruly, constantly stopping to eat, tearing out whole clumps of vegetation, and munching as he went. The riverbed we traversed was dry except where natural pools had formed among the rocks. Our elephant refused to get out of the shallow pools, taking up whole trunks full of water, throwing the water back, and showering us with it. The mahout had to argue with him and hit him on the head, which sounded like hitting a coconut, to get him to move on. Of course we found no tigers.

So we decided to try something different. Badri and John built a machan high in a tree overlooking a likely spot of the riverbed. I managed to climb up to the machan, only to find it too small for Fred, Badri, and me. Leaving Fred alone on the machan, Badri took me back through the undergrowth to a narrow path where we parked our jeep. On the way, we smelled the peppermint-like scent the tiger sprayed to mark his territory. Badri kept sniffing, remarking: "Tiger was here. Not long ago."

"Great," I said, "it's getting dark, we have no weapons and a tiger might be lurking behind the next bush."

When we finally reached the jeep, we heard Fred yelling: "Badri, Badri." It sounded like a distress call. Worried that something had happened to him, we ran as fast as we could to where the dry riverbed intersected with the path, working our way over boulders and rocks to the machan. Halfway there, we met Fred, who was making his way toward us. To our relief, he looked fine. The first thing he said when he came near us was: "Who's got my light meter?"

We were dumfounded! All this racket because of a light meter? Of course none of us had it. He was worried about it, because he had borrowed it from Ranjit. As it turned out he had forgotten to bring it, and it was safe at the guesthouse. With all this commotion, whatever tigers were in the vicinity probably hightailed it out of there in a hurry. Modeling for Fred wasn't high on their list of priorities, but Fred wasn't deterred. He and Badri went back to sit on the machan, while I returned to the guesthouse. Actually, I wasn't too upset to go back. The mosquitoes and assorted bugs were welcome to Fred and Badri. In the meantime, a cheerful party of Swiss tourists had arrived at the guesthouse, and I spent a very enjoyable evening with them. Fred and Badri came back late, tired and disappointed. No tiger showed his august face.

When we left Kanha, Ranjit accompanied us to some of India's famous sights, telling us about their various histories. Since he was a history major in college, we couldn't have wished for a better travel guide. This was also when we learned that Ranjit was the son of the Maharaja of Wankaner, a princely state in Gujarat, with a family tree dating back to the 1050s. Later, we found out that Mahatma Gandhi's father had been Wankaner's prime minister.

Taking the usual tourist route, we visited several Mughal tombs before we reached Agra, the site of the world-famous Taj Mahal. Built in 1648 by the Mughal emperor Shah Jehan as the last resting place for his beloved wife, Mumtaz, its beauty is unsurpassed. It was even more spectacular than any photos I had seen. Constructed completely of white marble, its perfection is mirrored in a large pool facing it. I was incredulous to see the intricately carved marble latticed window openings and the walls inlaid with thousands of precious and semiprecious stones forming delicate flowing patterns of flowering vines. It is truly one of man's highest achievements in architecture, art, and craftsmanship. We also went to see it at night, when it shimmered under the dark sky like a Fata Morgana, a beautiful image conjured up by man's creative spirit.

The nearby Agra Fort, a luxurious palace with its fountains, libraries, bathhouses, and pleasure gardens was also very impressive. This was where the famous peacock throne once stood in a beautiful audience hall, and sadly, it also contained a room overlooking the Taj Mahal where Shah Jehan was later imprisoned by his son Aurangzeb. Ranjit's Aunt Pushpa came from Delhi to join us, and she and I had a great time shopping, while Fred and Ranjit got up early to visit the nearby Bharatpur bird sanctuary.

From there we continued on to Jaipur with Razza, who replaced Badri as our guide, while Ranjit and Pushpa returned to New Delhi. The countryside in Rajasthan turned very barren and much drier, looking more and more like a desert. Camels, which thrive in this arid atmosphere, became a prominent part of the landscape. Even the people looked different; the men sported huge bright pink, orange, or red turbans and the women wore full skirts, short blouses, and long scarves over their heads that they tucked in at the waist.

On the way to Jaipur we stopped at the Fatehpur Sikri, now a ghost town, built by Akbar, the third and greatest Mughal emperor, in 1570 in honor of Shaikh Salim, a holy man whose prayers gave Akbar a longed-for son. Childless women still go there to visit the tomb of Salim to beg his help in conceiving a child. A grill on his tomb was covered with colored ribbons tied there by women as offerings. Fatehpur Sikri was the empire's capital for ten years, but it was abandoned in 1584 in favor of Lahore. Akbar was succeeded by his son Jahangir and then his grandson Shah Jehan.

Jaipur reminded me of the stories in *One Thousand and One Nights* that I had read as a child in East Germany. All the buildings were made of deep pink stucco, including the famous Palace of the Winds. A flower market in front of the palace added to its charm. There was so much to see and absorb that it was difficult to remember it all. We stayed overnight at the Rambagh Palace Hotel, the former home of the Maharaja of Jaipur. It was a beautiful building, and we were delighted with our huge, sumptuous room with an ornate balcony overlooking the formal gardens. Unfortunately the intricately carved columns and latticed marble panels between the room and the balcony had no screens, so the mosquitoes considered this an open invitation to visit. All we heard all night long was the high-pitched "srrrsssssssssee." Even hiding under the sheets didn't help much. The heat didn't help either. Needless to say it wasn't a good night's sleep.

Next morning we left for Sariska, a wildlife reserve not far from Jaipur. We took in the Amber Palace en route, another spectacular fortified palace straddling a mountaintop, reached by a ten-minute, steep climb on elephant back. It was built of red sandstone and white marble in 1592. Aside from the royal apartments, it contained formal gardens, pillared pavilions, and temples. Intricately carved marble latticework was everywhere. This was another fascinating palace where I could well imagine the bejeweled, veiled wives and concubines in the zenana, where the walls were covered with elegant frescos and marble latticed screens. Channels once carried cool water through the zenana, which surrounded a spectacular courtyard. The Divan, or private audience hall, its walls studded with panels of mirrors and latticed galleries, was most spectacular. The splendor of these rooms could only have been surpassed by the opulence of the inhabitants' attire.

We reached Sariska, the home of tigers, leopards, nilgai, and sambar, in the afternoon. Peacocks wandered the lawn in front of the guesthouse, filling the air with their shrill cries. Going into the wildlife sanctuary, we found the countryside strikingly beautiful. After traversing hilly brush country and a narrow pass carved out of the rock, we entered a valley where high, rocky cliffs fell in a sheer drop to its bottom. There, meandering, semidry riverbeds, ponds lined with palm trees, and odd thorny trees with broad leathery leaves delighted the eye. At the end of our path we found a waterfall topped by a natural bridge that the water had carved out of the rocks. We saw plenty of nilgai and even a rare four-horned antelope, but to Fred's sorrow, no tigers.

At dinner in the guesthouse's common dining room we met the United Arab Emirate's ambassador to India. As it turned out, he was a friend of Abdul's from their days together as UN ambassadors. It's truly a small world. My pen pal from another lifetime seemed to know everyone.

Razza told me the next morning that a sadhu, or Hindu holy man, who had supposedly been buried alive eleven days ago, was scheduled to be dug up today. So naturally I wanted to go. Since the sadhu didn't have four legs and a tail, Fred wasn't interested, and stayed behind. He missed an extremely interesting morning. But Razza and I weren't the only ones going to what was a big local event. We were joined by a lot of other people on the way. When Razza and I arrived there, we found that they had pitched a large tent covered with branches. Of course we were too late for the main event, the sadhu's disinterment, but after removing our shoes, we were granted permission to enter the tent. It was like a scene out of a movie. The very dignified holy man sat cross-legged on a dais in front of a large fire, surrounded by about fifty tribesmen. Even though the sadhu graciously gave me permission to take photos, it was too dark and smoky in the tent, so I gave up after a few tries. There simply wasn't enough light, and my camera wasn't good enough to capture the fantastic, dreamlike quality of the scene. On leaving, we were given some sort of candy as a blessing. Outside more men were sitting on the ground, smoking and gossiping, while the women were cooking what looked like pudding in a huge vat for their festive meal. The people looked me over in a curious, but not unfriendly, fashion. Since I was the only non-Indian present, I felt like a pink elephant.

On the way back we stopped at a tiny village. The headman and a boy came to greet us and Razza told him that I wanted to take pictures. He wouldn't allow me to photograph until he and the boy had gone to dress in their best clothes. The resulting photo was one of a dignified older man and his son. He asked us to stay and eat with them, which we politely declined. I found it very touching that, poor as they were, they would share what little food they had with two complete strangers.

Back in New Delhi, Fred still had the diarrhea he picked up in Sariska and he looked kind of green. He had eaten a lot of what was a delicious-tasting lamb ragout that turned out to be bad because, as we found out later, their refrigeration had broken down that day. The Delhi hotel doctor diagnosed it as food poisoning and gave him antibiotics, with the admonishment to eat only bland food. I thought that quite a joke. Bland food in India?

So, back in Delhi when Ranjit's Aunt Pushpa invited us for lunch, I explained the situation to her. She told us not to worry about it, and to please come. She and her husband Dr. Nagendra Singh, who later became president of the World Court in The Hague, lived in Delhi's most elegant neighborhood. Besides us, there were several other royal Indian guests. Well, lunch was served and Pushpa, true to her promise, served plain boiled chicken and rice without any spices whatsoever, not even salt. It was some of the blandest food I ever ate in my life. The other guests ate the same tasteless stuff as we did without complaint, which I thought very magnanimous.

Fred improved very quickly and we were off to Corbett National Park, established in 1936 as India's first national park. It was an eight-hour, hot, dusty ride, and I hoped that Corbett Park would be worth the pain of getting there. Once we left the arid areas behind and entered the foothills of the Himalayas, it was more than worth it.

On the way we stopped for coffee at an outdoor café in Moradabad, a Muslim city of over five hundred thousand. Looking around, I thought it very strange that I saw no women anywhere. The only living beings to be seen were men sitting at small tables, drinking coffee and smoking, who ogled me with an astonishing, almost embarrassing openness. I asked Razza about the whereabouts of the women. "They are in purdah," he said. The literal translation of purdah means screen or veil, but what it really meant was that all the women were in seclusion, shielded from public view by walls, curtains, and screens, even within their own home.

As we drove on, we passed through hilly, wooded areas, past rivers finding their way through rocky beds, and crystalline pools, until we reached Corbett Park and our encampment, consisting of several small cabins. I had a surprise that night at dinner in the common dining room. We shared the table with another couple who not only spoke German, but spoke it with the Saxon accent I hadn't heard for so long. Happy to hear the speech of my childhood, I began a conversation with them. Assuming that they were fugitives from the "Workers' Paradise" like me, I asked them: "When did you get out of East Germany?"

To my shock, the man fixed me with a cold stare and said: "We didn't."

This meant that he was a Communist government official, because the average citizen wasn't allowed to travel abroad. It felt like a cold shower, and all the fear I experienced in East Germany almost overwhelmed me. I didn't sleep too well that night.

The next day Fred and I struck out on an elephant, again following tiger tracks in a dry riverbed. Some other tracks we saw looked like motorcycle tracks, and aroused my curiosity. They were python tracks, Razza told us. Seeing their width, I was certainly glad to be sitting on an elephant. I shuddered at the thought of meeting one of them on foot. Again the tiger eluded us, but the mahout pointed out plenty of marijuana growing wild everywhere. There was enough of it growing here to keep an army high for years. Now I knew what several US "flower children" I saw in the compound were doing there. I didn't think that they were looking for tigers.

At this point, Fred was getting very discouraged. Not only didn't he see a tiger, he also didn't get the can of pork and beans we had brought along, because the cook was Muslim, and refused to handle anything with pork. Since we didn't do too well with our tiger search, we decided to look for wild elephants.

The next morning the park rangers told us that there was a herd of wild elephants in one of the park's heavily forested areas. So we took a jeep to where they had two riding elephants waiting for us and off we went, accompanied by a park ranger and Razza. After about an hour of plodding through the jungle, we spotted the herd milling around in the dense foliage. It's amazing how quietly a herd of these three- or four-ton beasts can move through such thick jungle. We pushed to within forty or fifty yards of them when they seemed to become agitated. All of a sudden all hell broke loose. The herd began to run, knocking down small trees in their path with ease, screaming, trumpeting, and making a terrible racket. A huge bull turned and stopped with his trunk raised, threatening to charge us and trumpeting his challenge. We could actually feel our elephants trembling beneath us before they totally panicked and began running for their lives in the opposite direction. Our mahouts were unable to control them, and we had all we could do to keep low to avoid being speared by branches or swept off the elephants' backs. We held on for dear life. When they had gone far enough and our mahouts were finally able to calm them, I noticed that Fred was holding his eye. Unfortunately he had been hit in the eye by a branch during our mad scramble through the forest.

Toward evening we took a ride in the jeep along the river and it was really quite beautiful. The river lay in the valley like a glittering snake, slowly turning red gold with the sinking sun. The Himalayas hovering above it, veiled in a bluish haze, looked as if they were made of smoked glass. We ran into a family of wild boars, running from us with their tails straight up in the air, and we watched them for a while. When we returned to our cabin, we found that there was no electricity. An elephant herd had come through and pulled down the poles carrying the electric wires. So we were in the dark until they got the generators going.

On the day we were scheduled to leave for New Delhi, we went to sit on a machan at 6:30 a.m., watching the large grassy area facing it.

Elephants were beating the grass to flush out a tiger. Our patience was finally rewarded when we saw a big, beautiful male tiger bounding through the clearing. Fred was happy now; he got his elephants, the tiger, and even his pork and beans. Razza, who was also Muslim, found a Hindu to make the pork and beans for Fred the night before.

Back in New Delhi, we spent our last night eating at one of the hotel's three restaurants. I had learned to like India's spicy food, so I ordered all my favorite dishes, and ate to bursting. Badri stopped by to give me a large, beautifully carved topaz as a going-away present, and John came to see us off at the airport. It was sad to leave people who we had become fond of, for who knew if we would ever see them again?

On the flight to Rome, Fred started complaining about his left eye. Now I took a good look at it and I saw a black dot on his lower eyelid. On closer inspection, I noticed that the dot had wriggling little black legs. It was a tick. It must have been on the branch that hit him in the eye during our encounter with the wild elephants.

In Rome we went to a hospital to have it taken out, because by then the tick had tripled in size. There was a red blotch on the white of Fred's eyeball where the beast had eaten itself through the lower lid. The doctor didn't know what to make of it. I had a hard time convincing him that the black thing was an animal. When I explained, he kept saying: "We don'ta hava this in Italy." The doctor held the tick between a pair of large pincers, pulling poor Fred's lower lid almost an inch off his eye in an effort to get the beast out. Of course that didn't work. We kept trying to explain that the tick had to be removed by intense heat held to its butt. Finally we were able to convince him. He heated something that looked like a slim knitting needle over a Bunsen burner, and held the red hot end to the tick's butt. After two or three attempts, the tick popped out and fell on the white tile floor. Now the nurse got upset: "It'sa gonna jump on me, find it!" she yelled, running for the door. Fred stepped on it and to everybody's relief that was it. We thanked the doctor, paid him, and off we went. It was a good thing that we got it out in time and that it didn't carry any disease.

Back in New York we went to see Dr. Cahill to make sure that nothing else had tried to hitch a ride. So ended my last trip to a fascinating place where we met some wonderful people I'll never forget.

* * *

Chapter 49

Stormy Weather

1980-1992

One of Fred's favorite sayings whenever I complained about one thing or another was: "Into every life a little rain must fall." Well, we now encountered some periods of stormy weather. There were times when it poured, and even though I thought myself a good swimmer, I sometimes thought I would drown in what was a deluge at times.

When we came home from our second India trip we were surprised to learn that Fred's father wasn't feeling well. It was very unusual for this tough, stoic man, who with a bearskin and horned helmet could have been mistaken for a Viking, to even admit to feeling sick. Over the next several weeks he kept deteriorating further, and was finally diagnosed with the big C. As the cancer progressed, it spread to his ribs and spine. He must have been in terrible pain, but true to his character, he bore it admirably. It was gut wrenching to watch, until, after months of suffering, he passed away on September 28, 1970. We weren't quite sure whether to be glad or sad. We were relieved that his terrible ordeal was over, but it was a great loss for everyone. It was a terrible blow to Fred, who loved and respected his father.

This was a man whose artist father died in Papua New Guinea at a very young age where, according to our sources, he may have been cannibalized by the natives. Consequently he grew up fatherless, and experienced the runaway inflation of post-WWI Germany. As a young iron worker's apprentice he would come home at the end of the week with hundreds of millions of marks, which was barely enough to buy food for him and his mother. Soon after he came to America in 1927, he started a stove business from scratch that was to last fifty-two years, from 1929 to 1981. Before he died he asked Fred to keep his business going until his foreman was old enough to get Social Security. Of course he didn't have to ask because Fred had already vowed to do that. So now Fred had both his Wall Street firm and his father's stove business to worry about. To help, he would take days off from his business to place bids with the Public Housing Authority for hundreds of used stoves which they rebuilt and sold to real estate managers. He paid for ads to sell stoves and sometimes he even worked there Saturdays to help carry stoves up tenement stairs and install them. That's how he managed the keep the stove business going until 1981 when his foreman was able to retire.

But even stormy weather can have breaks of sunshine. I became pregnant at the end of that same year, and to our great joy gave birth to a handsome little boy on August 19, 1971. We called him Roland in honor of Fred's father, who hailed from Bremen. According to legend, Roland, who died in the battle of Roncevaux in AD 778 in the service of Charlemagne's Holy Roman Empire, was born in Bremen, where a statue of Roland bearing the sword of justice and a shield decorated with the imperial eagle stands in the market square.

I was indescribably happy with this wonderful little boy of ours. He was everything a mother could wish for. Yes, he was a handful and full of mischief, but that was as it should be.

One of my scariest moments with him when he was a toddler was the day I was about to take him to the park. He was standing right next to me when I put the key into the electric garage door's lock. The door went up as usual, but when I bent to take Roland's hand, he was gone. I thought that he might be in the bushes, playing hide-and-seek. When I couldn't find him, I started to call him. All of a sudden I heard a plaintive "Mommy, Mommy!" I followed the sound of his voice. It came from the ceiling above the garage door. He was wedged between the door and the garage ceiling. I panicked! I restarted the door and down he came, hanging on to the door's handle. The first thing I did was to check him for injuries. Thank God there were none. Asked why he had done such a stupid thing, he explained: "I was just helping the door go up."

I still did design work at home for Stein Tobler to help my boss, who had been so good to me over the years. However, taking care of a lively little boy and concentrating to create new designs just didn't work very well, especially since Roland sometimes added his own brand of artistry to my already-finished designs. He was helping me. "I gonna help" became some of the most dreaded words in our house.

Later we joined a country club with a pool so that I could take Roland there during the summer months. One day a young woman sitting next to me by the pool introduced herself. Her last name was Osmers. I immediately remembered that this was the name of the US congressman who had done so much for us. Not really expecting an affirmative answer because it would have been too much of a coincidence, I asked her if she was by any chance related to a congressman by the name of Osmers.

"Oh, he's my father," was the astounding answer. So I told her how her father had been instrumental in facilitating our immigration to the United States in 1953. She listened, but I don't think she really understood the enormity of what her father's help meant to us. The next day her father came to the pool, and I was elated to be able to personally thank him for what he had done for us. He accepted my thanks graciously and said that he remembered my Uncle Rudy, who had approached him with requests to help us. He seemed a little embarrassed, like someone who got caught doing a good deed that he didn't want anyone to know about. This was another of my life's surprises. How often in life are you able to meet and thank a stranger who did so much for you with such life-changing results? His intercession on our behalf twenty years ago helped channel our lives in a new direction, with wonderful long-term effects. I thought him a fine man and a credit to the American political system!

That same year Fred, whose behavior had been rather erratic for some time, was diagnosed with diabetes. For weeks he had been urinating much more than normal, and losing more and more weight. Fred assumed that he had a severe case of the flu, so one Friday night he decided to have a pint of ice cream to put on some weight, and resolved to stay in bed the next day. I still see him sitting at the kitchen table, happily shoveling the ice cream into his mouth as he remarked: "Thank God I'm skinny, so I can eat all of this good stuff I want." Well it was all this good stuff that brought things to a head, practically pushing him over the brink. That night he got up thirteen times to pee, so early Saturday morning when he showed me how his thigh muscles were contracting and twitching, I knew that it was something serious. In desperation, I called Dr. Wood, a friend of ours, who graciously came within the hour. After a quick diagnosis, he immediately got on the phone and reserved a room for Fred in Columbia University's Presbyterian Hospital. Fred was in the hospital by noon and Dr. Wood arrived shortly thereafter. Fred's blood sugar level was sky high. That was quite a shock for us, who knew next to nothing about diabetes, or what it involved.

Luckily Dr. John Wood was a skilled physician, so Fred's diabetes program was properly managed right from the beginning. John advised Fred to start injecting himself with insulin rather than take pills, to give him a better chance of avoiding serious complications later on. Fred also had an excellent dietitian who advised him not to worry too much about weighing portions of the various food groups, but to be very careful in counting the daily carbohydrates.

Before he familiarized himself with the disease, Fred would have low blood sugar, or hypoglycemic, episodes, usually around 3 a.m. Sometimes they were bad enough for me to call the Emergency Medical Service, because I wasn't able to take care of it myself. Since Fred was very hard to control, they jokingly asked when I called for help: "How bad is it? Do we need reinforcements tonight?"

This too robbed me of sleep. I feared that in my exhaustion I wouldn't wake up when he was having difficulties, and I would find a dead man in bed with me in the morning. His mood swings were astronomical, and I never knew who would come in the door on any given day. Until he learned how to deal with this disease, and understood how much the sugar imbalance affects moods and thoughts, we had some very difficult times. He has learned a lot about the disease over the years, especially in how it affects his own body. Keeping the blood sugar at a fairly constant low level is a fine balancing act that is difficult to sustain, because it is affected by so many variables.

Fred now went on wildlife trips alone or with Ranjit, while I stayed home with Roland. I couldn't bear the thought of leaving my little boy with strangers for any length of time. My mother was too crippled with arthritis by this time, so taking care of a lively little boy for an extended period of time was out of the question. It used to break my heart to see her crippled hands, which had done so much for all of us, but there was nothing I could do to help her. My mother-in-law was busy with her own responsibilities, so whenever it was necessary, I relied on strangers to babysit most of the time.

I was so busy and preoccupied with my wonderful little boy that a fast-moving storm coming my way caught me by surprise. On my birthday, March 2, 1980, came one of the biggest shocks of my life. My younger sister Margit, then age forty, was killed in an automobile accident on New York's Harlem River Drive. The call from the New York City Police Department came as terrible news to me and my parents. To spare my parents from an agonizing task, I took it upon myself to identify her at the morgue.

Seeing her behind the viewing glass, her long blond hair spread around her, she looked young and vulnerable, as if she were only sleeping and might wake up any moment. I could still see the elfin child she had been when Mother and I helped her over the rubble and past smoking ruins on our flight from Plauen. She was the half-frozen little seven-year-old on our escape to the West. I remembered her as a little child trembling in the basements during the bombings, and as the agonizingly lonely teenager during our early years in the United States. Her entire life seemed to flash before me. It took a long time for my mind to grasp the fact that she was gone. I would often call her number, only to realize that she wasn't there to answer my call. Crazy as it sounds, I worried about her being cold in her grave when we had a snowstorm, only to remember belatedly that she was beyond feeling pain or cold.

Mother, already weakened by arthritis and the tremendous amount of medication prescribed by her doctors over the years, was unable to deal with Margit's death, and passed away the following year of heart failure. My brave mother, who bore the pain of her disease without complaint, who saw us to safety when it rained bombs, who managed to feed us in times of starvation, whose courage never flagged in a life that had been one long, hard struggle, finally gave up. Margit's death broke her indomitable spirit. Her motto, which I heard often enough, had always been: "There's no such thing as can't." But there was nothing she could do to bring Margit back.

Grieving over the loss of two loved ones within a short time period was immensely difficult. It was Roland and the sunshine he brought into my life that kept the dark clouds at bay.

As Roland grew up, his activities in school increased. I became a taxi driver like most suburban mothers, driving him to and from Little League, to the pool, and later to movies or friends' houses. I spent so much time in the car that when I lay in bed at night I had the strange sensation that my bed was rolling. When he got his driver's license it was a different story altogether. Like every other mother, I was worried sick when he didn't come home on time. I would wear out the floor walking up and down, praying, "Dear Lord, it's me again. I'm sorry to bother you so much, but please let him come home all right," promising to let him have it when he came home. But then when he finally was at the door and all in one piece, I was so relieved to have him home that I forgot all about letting him have it. If he was a handful when he was little, he was more than that as a teenager. We hardly ever agreed on anything. I think that every white hair I have bears his initials. But that too was normal, I was told. To become a man, he had to assert himself and develop his own personality. It is tough for a mother to let go. Letting him go off to college was just another stage that was a difficult adjustment for me. Of course that earned me the label of "overprotective mother."

When Roland was in his second year at Franklin and Marshall College, my father began to show signs of irrational disorientation. The man who used to call me every morning to give me the market reports on the world's foremost stock markets now seemed extremely confused.

Since my mother's death, he and I had become very close. I took care of my father to the best of my ability, cooking his meals, doing his laundry, and sending a cleaning lady to take care of his house, which he refused to leave. But when he sprained his ankle on the stairs, I decided that it was time to have him live with us. I was grateful to Fred, who had no objections and did his best to help. From then on his mental deterioration of what probably was Alzheimer's progressed steadily, and soon he was in and out of the hospital with heart-related problems.

It was incredibly painful to see my always mentally alert father, whom I called my voice of reason for his logical way of thinking, disintegrate before my eyes. Like my father-in-law, he grew up during WWI, under the same conditions. His mother died during the war while his father was in the army, leaving him and his eight-year-old younger brother to shift for themselves. Without relatives close by, the two young boys ate what kind neighbors gave them or in public soup kitchens. Drafted into the army at age thirty-eight, WWII ended for him in a Russian POW camp. Returning home to his completely destroyed city, he found his family alive but homeless and starving. For his generation of Germans, life was no picnic.

I felt like swiftly flowing events were sweeping me along to their inexorable, undesirable end. I hardly slept anymore, and was nothing but a bundle of nerves. My father could barely tell the difference between night and day, and sometimes he got out of bed in the middle of the night to get dressed. I was always afraid that he'd fall down the stairs in his confusion.

My father passed away on December 3, 1992, of congestive heart failure, at eighty-nine years of age. The last week of his life he was kept alive on machines, and it was absolute torture for me to see him like this. We used to think of ourselves as the four musketeers when we first arrived in the USA. Sadly, I was the only musketeer left.

It was now my responsibility to empty my father's house and ready it for sale. Giving up the house, with all its good memories, almost felt like another death with its finality. Never again would I walk up the front steps to a warm welcome, never again would I sit at the kitchen table with my parents discussing the week's events. Saying good-bye to the first real home I ever had was like saying another good-bye to my mother, father, and sister.

* * *

Chapter 50

Mato Wanagi— Sioux for Ghost Bear

While dealing with my father's declining health, I felt that I needed something to take my mind off the sadness that had invaded my life. So one day while my father was undergoing some tests, I picked up a book in the hospital store. It was a novel that dealt with the fate of Native Americans, and I was shocked to learn what had happened to them. I found it so difficult to believe that I started to haunt bookstores and libraries to verify the author's account of historical events. As it turned out, the author had done her research thoroughly, and everything she wrote proved to be correct.

My grandfather had been to the United States in 1939 to visit his two sons, and on weekends spent at our small country house in Joessnitz, he would tell us children bedtime stories of his time in America and his adventures with the Indians. Of course these stories were merely the product of his fertile imagination, but we didn't know that. As children we were fascinated with his stories and accepted them as gospel truth, so when we eventually arrived in the United States in 1953, I began asking people about the Indians. No one seemed to know anything other than what they had seen in the movies. All I got were blank looks and shoulder shrugging. So I assumed that the Indians had been absorbed by the famous American melting pot.

Western movies always gave the impression that the Europeans came to an almost-empty continent that was theirs for the taking. They were only occasionally bothered by Indian "savages" who had the nerve to try to impede our progress in confiscating their land. The Indians were shown as wild, bloodthirsty savages, not really quite human, and worst of all, they were heathens. The saying among the white settlers that "The only good Indian is a dead Indian" was taken quite literally.

Any and all means to exterminate them were acceptable. Blankets infected with smallpox given to them as "presents" wiped out whole tribes. Alcohol laced with arsenic was another popular method used to reduce their population. Plain indiscriminate murder was a widely accepted practice, openly condoned by our government. But more than anything, their mass annihilation was finally accomplished when we deliberately starved and froze them to death by killing an estimated sixty million buffalo, which were essential to them for food, warm clothing, and shelter. The Indians, of course, didn't go without a fight. They valiantly defended their land, their families, their freedom, and their way of life to the best of their ability, even though they were hugely outnumbered and way outgunned. After many battles, the survivors were locked away on reservations, which they were not allowed to leave without special permission and a pass. Conditions in those camps were deplorable; food was severely rationed, and many died of starvation. Those who refused to go on reservations were designated as hostiles, and became fair game to be shot on sight. After their final defeat, Indians became wards of the government, and weren't granted the right to become US citizens until 1925.

Remembering our days of want and deprivation after WWII, I was deeply touched by their fate. So when my father passed away, and I suddenly found myself with an entire household to dissolve, I looked in a book on reservations and chose the poorest one, which turned out to be the Lakota Sioux's Pine Ridge Indian Reservation in South Dakota.

I called the tribal office to ask if they were interested in any of my father's clothing, and I was told that they would be very happy to have whatever I wanted to send them. They gave me the address of a Mr. Marvin Ghost Bear, who would see to it that everything went to the people who needed it most. So over a period of several months I mailed many boxes filled with things that I thought would be useful. Off and on I was in touch with Mr. Ghost Bear, who was the only Native American teacher at one of their elementary schools.

In subsequent conversations I found out that he, like many Indians, was diabetic. Indians seem to have a problem metabolizing foods that we are accustomed to, like dairy, grain, and sugar, not to mention alcohol. He proudly told me that he didn't drink or smoke, but ruefully admitted that he had done his share of both when he was younger. Slowly we got to know one another, and over time a good friendship developed. I found out that Indians still had a lot of mistrust and anxiety as far as we, whom they call "Anglos," are concerned. As a German immigrant I never really considered myself an "Anglo," or as he would often tease me, "of the dominant society."

Through our friendship I was inspired to do oil paintings with Native American themes. I would send him copies of preliminary sketches, and he would advise me on apparel, feathers, etc. I also did my own research into the different tribal accoutrements, because I wanted to present Native Americans as authentically as possible. Once I sent him a sketch of an Indian on a horse riding toward the viewer. He called and told me in a choked-up voice that I had painted his father! That was news to me, for I made up the faces as I went along. Both of us thought it was a pretty strange coincidence. Painting kept me very busy, but my efforts were rewarded by many exhibits and sales.

Then one day when he told me that he and a few others were going to Washington on tribal business, I suggested that he come visit us. He had some reservations: "You know that I am brown skinned." I started laughing and told him: "As far as I'm concerned you can be green with purple dots." That settled that. So he and his companions rented a car and arrived here late on a very muggy June night. One of his friends told me that Ghost Bear was a nervous wreck about meeting us, and talked of nothing else on the way to our house. His friends then went on to New York and left Ghost Bear with us. That was our first face-to-face meeting. He was very, very shy. He later confided to me that this was the first time he had ever been invited to a white man's home, and that this was his first more-than-casual contact with "Anglos."

The next morning, over a cup of black coffee, he told me that he was as a full-blood Lakota Sioux called Mato Wanagi, which is Sioux for Ghost Bear. He was brought up from age five to seventeen in one of the government boarding schools, which was run by a Christian organization. The Carlisle Indian School in Pennsylvania, founded in 1879, was the best known of these schools, and served as a model for all the others. He said the children were stripped of their Indian names, their long hair, and their traditional clothing. The motto in those schools was: "To save the child, kill the Indian!" He told me that our government's policy was to take the children away from their parents at a young age to Christianize and mainstream them. The children were not allowed to speak their own language, and often the punishment was getting their mouth washed out with soap, so they were forced to speak English. Consequently they were often unable to communicate with their own parents when they were finally set free and returned home to the reservation. That's how their strong family ties were broken up. As young adults they no longer knew where they belonged. Neither world was home.

Freedom of religion was a major principle upon which our nation was founded, but obviously that didn't apply to what we considered pagan religions. Indians were officially forbidden to practice their religion and some of their ceremonies were even declared criminal offenses punishable by imprisonment. Another thing he mentioned was that since he grew up in an institution, he had no idea of what family life was like. Therefore he didn't know how to be a husband or a father when he got married.

We spent a few very hectic days running around New York, seeing the sights. We took in as much as we could, including the Empire State Building, the top of the World Trade Center, the Museum of Natural History, etc. The night before he was to leave, Fred thought it would be nice to give him a special treat, so he made dinner reservations at the famous Rainbow Room in Rockefeller Center. When we arrived there, they didn't want to let Ghost Bear in because he was not wearing dress shoes. He was wearing his only pair of sneakers. So our son had a short "conference" with the maître d', after which we were admitted, and it turned out to be a very nice evening after all. Ghost Bear remarked that what that evening cost us would have fed his entire family for over two months. Nevertheless he was talking about his Rainbow Room visit for the next few years, and I am sure it generated quite a few discussions among his friends on the reservation.

Before he left he invited me to visit him on the reservation for their annual powwow. Since there is no hotel or motel in Pine Ridge, I would have to stay in his trailer. Of course he warned me of their poverty, and was concerned that I might be offended by it. Little did he know that I had experienced much worse in Germany after WWII, and that I had also seen plenty of poverty on our trips to Africa and India.

We stayed in touch the next few weeks, and when I told him that I had finally decided to come, he was overjoyed and said I made his day. That really made me feel good, and now I was excited to go.

When the time came, I flew to Rapid City, where I was met by Ghost Bear and his adult daughter. The first thing we did was to buy staples like sugar, flour, oil, coffee, etc., for his elderly mother. Then he told me to buy a long garment for myself. "What on earth for?" I asked. He said it was for a sweat lodge ceremony he had arranged for me. So I bought a long orange cotton dress. He recounted an incident when some French women who were taking part in a sweat lodge ceremony came out of the changing tent buck naked, shocking the medicine man and everyone else. Obviously nobody had advised them on proper sweat lodge etiquette. But it made a good story, and most likely for a good amount of amusement. Anyhow, I was properly prepared.

On the way to Pine Ridge, we drove through the Badlands. From what I saw, they are not called the Badlands without reason. I found them fascinating and mysterious, almost like a moonscape. Arid hills created by centuries of erosion, with deeply carved, labyrinthine canyons and crevices stretched in monotonous beige into an infinite landscape, where nothing grows but stones. After dropping off the groceries at his mother's, we arrived at Ghost Bear's trailer, where I wound up sleeping on a cot. Sharing the room with me were his two older children and a little grandson, all of whom slept on the floor. The school where Ghost Bear taught provided trailers for their staff, so he was one of the lucky ones who had a job and a roof over his head. The lack of jobs and resources makes it extremely difficult for many of the people on the reservation to meet their basic needs. Unemployment runs as high as 80 percent, and the average income was only about $3,000 a year. A lot of that is derived from land they lease to white farmers in a rather strange arrangement. Instead of the farmer paying them directly at a mutually satisfactory price, the farmer pays an agency in Washington, which then sends the money back to the Indian who is leasing out the land. I imagine a lot of money gets "lost" in the process. Mismanagement of Indian accounts dating back to the late 1800s is the rule rather than the exception.

Since housing on the Pine Ridge Indian Reservation is in such short supply, most families double up to help each other out. Extended families share dilapidated trailers without electricity, running water, or sewers. To get water, they have to drive or walk to a well, which often is miles away. The water is then transported back in whatever containers they have. Some live in old, rusted-out school buses. Ghost Bear showed me the "home" of a Vietnam vet, who lived in a canvas-covered hole he dug in the ground. Food is a struggle from one day to the next. There is no public transportation in or out of Pine Ridge, so unless they have a car, they are dependent on others to give them a ride. Ghost Bear and his family drove one hundred miles once a week to go food shopping in Rapid City. I went with him to the only market in Pine Ridge, where the food was expensive. The meat looked gray; the vegetables looked dirty and half dead. That meat and those veggies certainly would not have passed inspection anywhere else.

On my first morning there, I had coffee Ghost Bear-style—that is, black and so strong that a spoon could have stood upright in it without falling over. Ghost Bear sure liked his coffee. I looked in his fridge for milk, but there was not even a drop to be found! He told me that he and his people are lactose intolerant, therefore "no milk." So I had no choice except to try Ghost Bear's black coffee, which I was lucky to survive.

He then took me on a tour of the town of Pine Ridge, which consisted of a few houses, a market that carried all kinds of other things besides food, the Catholic Church's Red Cloud Indian School, where the famous Chief Red Cloud is buried, a gas station, and that's about it. Of course, there is also the Bureau of Indian Affairs, which occupied the largest and best-kept building.

The rest of the day and evening we spent at the powwow, a yearly event on the reservation. Once banned by the US government, the powwow is not only a showcase for traditional dancing, but also an opportunity for friends and families to get together. The powwow area itself was an open circle surrounded by a roofed-over section where people could sit. Shops and food stalls for all these hungry and thirsty Indians formed a second circle around the periphery. Indians from many different tribes travel long distances for this event, where prizes are given for the best costumes and the best dancing.

The powwow opened with the Grand Entry, a colorful procession of costumed and painted dancers. "The Star Spangled Banner" and "The Sioux National Anthem and Victory Song" were played, and Vietnam vets proudly displayed the American and the Sioux flags. After a few short speeches by tribal dignitaries, the fun began. The dancing, the overwhelming sound of the drums, and the singing were continuous until well after midnight.

Some of the dancers looked like strange exotic birds in their face paint and beautiful costumes. Their feather bustles fanning out like peacock tails swayed as they moved in rhythm with the drums, simulating warriors on the hunt. They carried painted, feather-decorated shields and tomahawks. Bone hair pipe breastplates covered their chests and fur or red cloth-wrapped braids swinging with their movements hung over their shoulders. Deer-hair roaches and feather headdresses reinforced the image of wondrous, crested birds, as their moccasin-clad feet stomped out the rhythm of the drums.

The women swaying sinuously in the dance circle wore beautifully beaded dresses, with long fringes on their sleeves and hems. All of them carried feather prayer fans. One group of women wore hundreds of small metal cones made from the lids of snuff tins, which jingled cheerfully on their dresses, merging with the sound of the drums as they danced the "Jingle Dance." A kaleidoscope of swirling colors and the deep, vibrating sound of the drums enticed you to enter into its exuberant spirit. That night, lying on my cot in Ghost Bear's trailer, I could still hear the drums for a long time before drifting off to sleep.

On my last day in Pine Ridge, Ghost Bear arranged for me to take part in a sweat lodge ceremony, which turned out to be quite an experience. Its purpose is to purify oneself, to pray, and to get closer to the Great Spirit. But first we had to make prayer bundles, which was a job and a half, especially if you didn't know what you were doing. My prayer bundles looked rather sad, and I wondered what the Great Spirit would think of this offering. One-inch squares of red, yellow, white, and black fabric, four of each color, had to be filled with tobacco and tied with string into a garland. Each bundle in the garland represented a prayer.

The sweat lodge was in a clearing in the middle of nowhere, and was reached on a narrow path bordered by high grass, bushes and trees. One by one we went into the changing tent, where I put on my long orange dress. Then the leader of the ceremony came and asked me what my prayers were about. I told him, whereupon he confiscated my prayer garland, which was then hung in the sweat lodge as an offering, and off I went to be purified.

The sweat lodge was a low framework of willow branches tied together and covered with old blankets and scraps of canvas to make it completely dark inside, representing the womb of Mother Earth. According to tradition the entrance faced east toward the rising sun. Once all six of us were seated on piles of fragrant sage, red-hot stones were placed in the fire pit in the middle of the lodge. Only then was the flap closed, and except for the red glow of the hot stones, it was completely dark. Cedar and sweet grass was placed on the hot stones and sprinkled with water. Volumes of pleasantly scented steam filled the air, making everything in this confined space appear veiled and otherworldly. The leader lit the ceremonial pipe with a sprig of sage, pointed it solemnly to the heavens and to the earth, then offered it to the four directions while intoning a Lakota prayer. Then the pipe, its aroma blending with the fragrance of the cedar, was passed around for everyone to inhale. The smoke curled around us, the red glow of the stones giving it ever-changing, luminous shapes. More prayers were said and sung to rise with the smoke to Wakan Tanka. There were more prayers for the earth and all the four-legged and feathered creatures that share it with us. After that it was every individual's turn to say a prayer out loud in whatever language they were comfortable. For me it was the Lord's Prayer. In between the prayers the flap was opened three times. Each time I was ready to run for it, but "Oh nooo!"—it was only to bring in fresh red-hot stones so we could sweat and pray some more! God, was it hot in there! I must have lost a couple of gallons of water in this hellish heat. The sweat ran off me in rivers. My hair was soaked; sweat ran into my eyes and dripped off my nose and chin. Whatever bacteria and viruses my body harbored must have died a terrible death. I could almost hear them shriek.

Some of my fellow sufferers gave voice in stirring tones to their past and present problems, which were of either a physical or spiritual nature. With the assistance of all present in this prayer circle, they pleaded for God's help. I told Ghost Bear later that if I ever got started, they would all be sitting in there for a few weeks and shrivel away to nothing. After changing back into our street clothes, we went to Ghost Bear's friends' house for a traditional Indian meal of stew, blueberry compote, and their famous fry bread.

During this purification ceremony, it became clear to me that the Lakota, who we once piously called "heathens," are actually profoundly religious. They venerate and admire Wakan Tanka, the Great Spirit and are deeply aware of this mysterious force, as it reveals itself in its many different forms. They believe that everything in existence, animate or inanimate, possesses a spirit or a soul that has to be treated with respect. In their world the sacred and the worldly are tightly intertwined, and are part of their everyday lives. As they see it, life is an eternal circle without beginning and without end that is exemplified by the cyclical nature of our seasons and our lives.
Respect for the natural world and toward their fellow man are fundamental values they embrace. So are honesty, courage, and generosity.

For the Sioux, Wakan Tanka is not a punishing God they must fear. He is everywhere and part of everything; he is all good! Ghost Bear explained that they don't belief in a hell and a devil as we do. But they do have a spirit called Iktomi.
Once, when Ghost Bear teased me mercilessly, I called him Iktomi. He was highly offended and I got a lecture on what I thought of as merely an impish spirit. I learned that Iktomi is a mischievous trickster, a slippery character and shape-shifter, who can take many different forms. He is respected yet despised, because in his conceit he often outfoxes himself. He is not evil, as we understand it. We see good and evil as two opposing constantly warring forces, while Indians see things as a matter of balance and harmony.

Their faith and relationship with the earth also vastly differs from ours. They believe that we as part of creation belong to the earth. That is why all their prayers end with "Mitakuye Oyasin," which means, "We are all related to everything there is." Judeo-Christian religion teaches that we are created in God's image, and that the earth was given to us as our dominion to rule. Therefore the earth belongs to us. In the Indian religion we belong to the earth.

On our way to Rapid City for my flight home, we visited the Crazy Horse Memorial and Mount Rushmore. I admired the sculpted faces of our presidents, which were very impressive indeed.

In the meantime, all through my visit Ghost Bear kept bugging me: "Are you going to write about us?" I would look at him like he was crazy.

"Are you kidding? I'm not a writer! I'm an artist, not a writer. So stop it already!"

Back home, we stayed in constant contact. Ghost Bear had a wonderful sense of humor and teased me mercilessly. I took revenge as well as I could.

One autumn he asked me for some used winter clothing for the children. Some are so poor they can't attend school because they have no warm clothing or shoes. Many don't even have essentials like toothbrushes, toothpaste, and soap, not to mention backpacks. So I contacted my son's former elementary school, and the response was beyond all my expectations. They collected over six hundred pounds of children's clothes. When I went to help them pack, the principal's office and hallway was stacked with boxes. The clothing was wrapped in pretty paper and decorated with bows. I could see that it was done with a lot of love. They displayed the Indian's highly prized virtue of generosity admirably. It showed the American people at their best. When UPS heard this story, they sent all the boxes to the reservation free of charge.

Ghost Bear had planned to come to the school with a few youngsters to thank them and sing with the children, but before he could his kidneys stopped functioning. From then on it was dialysis three times a week. He lost his job, and with it his car and his trailer. He wound up sleeping on the floor at his mother's, but he needed a car to get to the clinic for dialysis. So my husband sent him a certified check to buy a used car. Since there is no bank in Pine Ridge, Ghost Bear had to go outside the reservation to cash the check. Three weeks later, the bank still had not cashed it, so I called the bank to see what the problem was. One of the reasons they gave me was that the check had to go back to

New York for verification first.

"What? A certified check is like cash!"

Then my husband called the president of the bank from his Wall Street office, and Ghost Bear was finally able to cash the check. That was just unbelievable, but it gives you some idea of how the Indians are treated. Anyway, he finally got himself a used car to go to dialysis, so he didn't have to rely on friends or relatives to give him a ride.

Ghost Bear went through a really bad time for about two years, staying with whoever gave him space, until he was able to get housing in a handicapped facility. True to form, he helped others who were worse off than he. He was in and out of the hospital with diabetes-related complications, but through all of this he always remained his cheerful, upbeat self, and never, ever complained. When I didn't hear from him for a while, I would scold him. So from then on, whenever he didn't catch me at home when he called, I would hear on my answering machine: "I'm OK, Mom!"

He never let me know how sick he really was, but then sadly on December 30, 2000, the telephone rang early in the morning. I saw the 605 area code and thought it was Ghost Bear, but instead it was a friend of his who called to tell me that Ghost Bear had passed away during the night. He was only fifty-seven years old. I was dumbstruck! I spent the next day making one hundred prayer bundles for him, so that his cousin Christine Red Cloud, who took care of the funeral arrangements, could place them in his coffin. I called a florist near the reservation to order some flowers and was told, "We don't deliver to the reservation." But when I told them the size of the order, they agreed that it could be done after all.

I miss Ghost Bear. We learned a lot from each other. He was what I would call "a good soul," and it was my privilege to have known him. On my birthdays he would call and sing a Lakota blessing song, when I was sick, he and his friends would pray for me in the sweat lodge. How could anyone ever forget that?

I finally fulfilled Ghost Bear's wish to write about the reservation and his people after all, when to my great surprise, my story of Ghost Bear and the Sioux was published in the New Yorker Staats Zeitung, a German-American weekly. They also used my painting of a Sioux buffalo hunt to cover the entire front page of the newspaper. Ghost Bear would have cried with joy, had he lived to see it.

Oil on linen, painting by Renate Stoever

* * *

Chapter 51

Full Circle

1993

During the summer months of 1989 I kept hearing that tens of thousands of East Germans were fleeing to West Germany via Hungary, Poland, and Czechoslovakia. To stop the exodus of their citizens, the East German authorities sealed the borders to these countries. This action quickly turned East Germany into a pressure cooker, which finally exploded. Huge demonstrations in all East German cities, including Plauen, forced the authorities to give way and open its borders to the West. Within hours, tens of thousands of East Berliners swarmed across the hated wall that divided their city. I watched them celebrate their freedom with joyous abandon at the infamous wall, the Brandenburg Gate, and the Kurfuerstendamm in Berlin.

I'll never forget that amazing day. I happened to be in a store that had the TV set on. I was stunned by what I saw and heard. I thought I was hallucinating. This situation, which had been so close to my heart, was finally resolving itself. What I and many others had hoped and prayed for came to pass at last. Of course I spent the rest of the day and evening watching the exciting, momentous events taking place in Europe. The people who had been held captive for forty years revolted and threw off the yoke of Communism. We later found out that my cousin's son, Steffen Kollwitz, was one of the principle opposition leaders in Plauen.

The next day we had to drive to Roland's college in Pennsylvania for parents' weekend. We listened to the continuous news coverage on the car radio until the signal became too weak. Sitting at dinner with the other parents making polite conversation was difficult, because my mind was thousands of miles away, worried about my relatives and possible bloodshed, yet at the same time overjoyed that they would finally gain their freedom. It was an exciting few days as country after country shook off the shackles imposed on them by the victors of WWII so long ago. Since I knew firsthand what life had been like for them, I celebrated their freedom with them. Germany's reunification a year later, on October 3, 1990, made my joy complete.

I would have liked nothing better than to get on a plane and fly to Germany, but we can't always do what we want, so I had to wait until the time was right. That time finally came in August 1993, one year after my father's death, and almost three years after German reunification, when I went back to Plauen. It was my first visit since our escape to the West on Christmas of 1947. The infamous wall separating East and West Berlin had come down in on November 9, 1989, when the Communist system proved to be the house of cards it always was. I was now able to travel there without fear.

Fred, Roland, and I took a flight to Berlin, where we spent a few days sightseeing. From there we took a train to Plauen. Passing by towns I remembered from childhood, my excitement was exponentially mounting as we neared Plauen. My homecoming after forty-six years was an extraordinary event of monumental proportions for me. When the train pulled into Plauen, my tears, which had been gathering behind my eyelids for the last hour, were starting to flow. They became a deluge when the train stopped in the station and we were met by my cousin Inge, her family, and the Plauen press, who were busy snapping pictures of this happy reunion. Inge explained to me that the City of Plauen was happy to see old Plaueners coming back, if only to visit, because Plauen had lost half of its population during the war and was now left with only about seventy thousand residents.

The next surprise was our reception at the Hotel Alexandra on Bahnhof Strasse, only a couple of blocks from where we used to live. I was welcomed in the hotel lobby by an all-male choir accompanied by my cousin Inge playing the accordion, singing the old Plauen songs I knew so well. Inge's husband Heinz belonged to a club called the Shanty Choir made up of former members of the German Navy. Heinz was one of the few sailors who survived service in submarines, where the fatality rate was 80 percent during WWII. It was this choir that welcomed us. I produced such a flood of tears, it was a miracle that the entire hotel wasn't swept away and floated down Bahnhof Strasse.

My emotions were in turmoil, with joy and grief tumbling over each other in riotous waves. There was joy to see what was left of Plauen and my family, and grief for all that was lost. All my uncles, my aunts, and my grandmother were gone in the intervening years, but I still had my three cousins Ursula, Marita and Inge. Ursula, who lives in Weimar, came the next day with her husband and son for a reunion at the Hotel Alexandra. My God, Ursula and I had grown old and gray, when our last memories of each other were as children. True, we had stayed in contact with each other with letters, but since we knew that the Communist government opened them, they only contained banalities and carefully worded, coded messages.

I had seen Inge in 1987, when she was able to come to the United States for three weeks to attend our twenty-fifth wedding anniversary/family reunion. I had to supply all kinds of notarized documents and affidavits to Plauen's Communist police before she received permission for the trip. I fondly remember the Englewood, New Jersey police department producing a very impressive document when I told them its purpose and destination. Inge's husband and son were not permitted to leave, of course. They were kept as hostages to ensure Inge's return.

When she got here, Inge was amazed at the amount and variety of merchandise in our stores, especially in our supermarkets. Shelves stuffed full of all kinds of food elicited her excitement and admiration. I had to take lots of photos of her at the meat counters, Inge holding a ham, Inge holding a leg of lamb, Inge holding a turkey. "Otherwise," she said, "nobody at home would believe me." The butcher at our supermarket obliged us by holding up a string of sausages, with Inge next to him grinning from ear to ear. The rest of the time we spent sightseeing in New York and Washington. It was a happy, whirlwind three weeks and she was very unhappy when she had to leave to go back to her depressing reality in East Germany. The 1989 change of government couldn't have come soon enough for her and her fellow countrymen.

Fred and Roland were finally able to meet what was left of my side of the family. I showed them our apartment house in the center of Plauen, which was still standing, by the way. The other houses on our block that had burned down during the bombings had been replaced with ugly, new, Communist-style structures. What had been our grassy, park-like playground looked uninviting and resembled a junkyard. Standing there, I could see myself as a child looking up to what had been our kitchen windows. The years faded away and I almost expected my mother to open the window and throw me a sandwich.

We found that my paternal grandfather's apartment house, which I had aptly named our "Ice Palace" during the two terrible winters we spent there after the war, was boarded up, and sadly, we couldn't go inside. No repairs had been made since the government had taken it over years ago, and it looked as if it was in danger of collapsing. Its derelict, wretched appearance made me want to cry.

If the house could speak, it could tell of my grandparents' struggle to stay alive and of their terror when they found themselves entombed in its basement by tons of rubble when bombs took down the rear wall. It could also talk about our desperate survival inside its ice-covered walls and the grim winters when our emotional state was as icebound as our "Ice Palace," mirroring the frozen wasteland that was our city. The lots next to it and across the street where buildings once stood were now fenced off. Almost fifty years after the war the area still looked empty, compounding the feeling of abject desolation of a once-nice neighborhood.

Not far from our hotel in Plauen was the cave where we had spent so many terrifying days and nights in abject misery, waiting for the next bomber squadrons to arrive, wondering if we would survive the next few hours. The entrance was bricked over now, but it was still there as a mute reminder of those grim times.

Heinz took us on a day trip to Dresden. That tragic, once-beautiful city presented a forest of cranes. Rebuilding was in full swing. Its famous Frauenkirche was still a ruin, but right next to it were long shelves with numbered pieces of rubble corresponding to numbers on the plans they used to rebuild it. The Zwinger, a complex of royal buildings, had been repaired in the intervening years to some extent, but the scaffolding told us that much more was being done. Since we only had one day in Dresden, we tried to visit as many of the city's most important features as time allowed before driving back to Plauen.

While the cities of the capitalist West had been reborn in a flurry of rebuilding within a relatively short time, Communist East Germany was left behind in a painful past where shortages of every kind were still the norm. I used to send my relatives everyday essentials like toothpaste, toothbrushes, and other items like coffee and tea that for them were financially unaffordable. Coffee, for instance, cost three east marks for an ounce. Every one of my letters also contained dollars for their special stores called Intershops, where those who had western currency were able to buy otherwise unobtainable merchandise.

The Communist maxim, "From each according to his ability, and to each according to his need," certainly proved to be irrelevant. Communist rule actually made everybody poorer—with the exception of the Communist officials, of course. They were more equal than everyone else in a state that claimed to be a prime example of equality for all.

It was ironic that Plauen and Saxony had become Communist. Some of the young men who fought to oust the armed Communist cadres that had disarmed the police and taken over the city in bloody fights after WWI lived to see them take over again after WWII. I thought it a cruel twist of fate that the young men who successfully battled to save their city and its people from Communist agents like Rosa Luxemburg and Karl Liebknecht now faced Communist control again. So Plauen and Saxony were saved from Communism after WWI, only to suffer the same fate after WWII, and this time there was no escaping it. Russian occupation and the Stasi, East Germany's secret police, kept everybody in line, stifling any and all voices of protest. The only way out was suicide or an attempted flight to the West, which meant almost the same thing. Plauen's overall dismal appearance mirrored the depressed mental state of its population.

I once complained in a letter to Inge about crime in the United States. She answered me with facetious flair: "Why don't you come to live here? You'll be very safe, because the secret police are following you at all times, and no one has enough time to commit a crime since we have to continuously stand in line for all kinds of consumer goods. This is very good planning because our government always knows where we are. We're all waiting in lines." A dry, acerbic humor helped them to survive otherwise unbearable conditions and tolerate their city's sad condition with equanimity. But she did tell me that suicides were common, and that several of her friends decided to end the misery in which they found themselves.

Fred and Roland stayed for one week and then returned home to go back to work. I stayed on for another two weeks. I spent a lot of that time walking around Plauen, wishing that my parents and Margit could be with me to see it once more. I tried to find places I remembered, but many were gone. Whole streets and neighborhoods were missing, and more often than not replaced by weeds and bushes. The houses in some neighborhoods stood empty because no repairs had been made since the end of the war; their facades' broken windows intensified the sad and forlorn feeling pervading those streets.

Only parts of Bahnhof Strasse, the main thoroughfare, had been rebuilt and were in acceptable condition. Many of the destroyed buildings had been replaced by ugly boxy structures looking completely out of place between some of the older, ornate buildings that were rescued from demolition. The area around the train station, which had also been heavily bombed, was almost unrecognizable, with rows of standard nondescript buildings replacing the houses that once stood there.

Lots of building was going on since the fall of Communism and I could see huge cranes everywhere. Even our hotel had been completely rebuilt, with all the amenities you could wish for, and to my astonishment, Plauen already had a McDonald's. Lacking the famous arches, it looked rather elegant in a nice building with large glass windows overlooking flower beds. With McDonald's here, I saw that progress was being made, and that it wouldn't take long for Plauen to undergo a dramatic transformation. That thought did a lot to soothe my anguish over its dilapidated state.

I was happy to see Plauen's streetcars plying the streets again, as they went up and down Bahnhof Strasse. At least one thing that I remembered from better times was still in existence. Hopefully these beloved conveyances wouldn't fall victim to progress.

Of course we also went to see our garden property in Joessnitz. Again, we were only able to see it from outside its gate. Even though it was American property, and protected by international law, the garden had been taken from Inge and given to good Communist Party members.

From our vantage point at the gate, I could see that the garden looked like nothing I remembered. Most of the many trees were missing, and neglect was obvious. The apple tree we sat under during our interrogation with the American officers, which had such a miraculous ending, was gone too.

At this point I wondered if our family would ever be able to get the property back. It would be a big problem to get the Communists to leave what they still considered theirs. Final resolution and its return was awaiting the legal system. The same problems existed in all the former Communist states, and it would take years to unravel ownership titles.

My maternal grandparents' house distinguished itself only by its derelict wretchedness. The church that had given me the wonderful memory of Christmas in 1942, having weathered the war and an atheistic political system, stood in a state of dismal neglect.

I spent two days with Cousin Ursula and her husband, who took me to Markneukirchen, which I had visited countless times as a child. We stayed in her parents' former house overnight. Since that too had been confiscated, it was also in a state of incredible disrepair. It boggles the mind what a bad political system can do to a people's way of life.

We went into the forest where we had such wonderful times picking blueberries a lifetime ago. Only now those same woods looked sickly. A lot of their rich, green needles were brown and drooping from naked branches. Even the wonderful scent I remembered was gone. The corrosive effects of air pollution had claimed the beauty that had once been theirs. It was a sad thing to see. It had never been so clear to me that we are killing our planet in our suicidal mad rush to progress, and with it ourselves, because we are of the earth. Communist East Germany's concern for the environment had obviously been zero. They had polluted and destroyed the heritage of future generations without restraint. I couldn't help wondering how long our planet would tolerate our destructive activities.

We also took a day trip to Bad Elster, a well-known spa in Saxony, and later we had dinner in a grimy country restaurant in Czechoslovakia that served us abominable food. Czechoslovakia seemed to be in dire straits, despite the fact that it had usurped all the wealth and properties of their expelled German population after WWII. Incredibly, East Germany, although run down, was one of the wealthier Communist countries.

Ursula and her husband took me to the area where we crossed the border on an icy, snowy Christmas morning so long ago. On this beautiful summer day the scene looked serene and bucolic. The wooden watchtowers had been replaced by more menacing concrete structures, and the woods had been cut down to remove all cover for would-be escapees. A sign warned us not to go beyond the watchtowers, because too many mines remained in the innocuous expanse of grass. Thank God they hadn't mined the border yet when we crossed in 1947. I sadly wondered how much tragedy, tears, and desperation this innocent-looking strip of land had witnessed over the years. I realized how lucky we had been to flee the "Workers' Paradise" before all these "improvements" took place.

Left to right, Ursula, Inge, Marita and me

Back in Plauen, reporters from Plauen's weekly newspapers came to interview me, and they wrote some very nice articles about the visiting native who now made her home in America. To my everlasting surprise, my homecoming had created quite a stir, and my city of Plauen had received me with warmth and open arms. I had come full circle.

* * *

Chapter 52

Mother Comes to Visit

Mother's visits are rare and unannounced, always catching me off guard. I never know when she will decide to make an appearance, which is rather unsettling, because it always leaves me surprised and unprepared to tell her how much I miss her. Usually I can't grasp what she is trying to tell me. Occasionally her message is clear enough for me to understand, but most times comprehension comes only after time has passed. Then there are the mornings when I wake with a vague memory of one of her visits, but no matter how hard I try, recall remains elusive.

Unfortunately, dreams are not concise, and present themselves as a series of disjointed, unintelligible symbols, leaving us frustrated in our attempts to interpret their meaning. So it is with Mother's nighttime visits, when my befuddled mind often forgets that she has left this earth for a well-deserved rest.

Sometimes Mother comes to visit me looking young and vibrant, as she did in her youth. She is usually dressed in gaily-colored summer clothes, and appears happy and relaxed in a way I can hardly remember. Maybe these dreams are wishful thinking on my part to see her well and happy, to have death give her what she was denied in life.

But usually I see her as careworn and pain ridden, as she was for most of her life.

Mother's life was very hard, to say the least. She grew up during the First World War with all the ensuing misery of its aftermath—starvation, runaway inflation, and rampant unemployment, followed by bloody social unrest between the Communists and the Nazis. That produced Hitler, resulting in more misery and death for millions of people. WWII and its after affects gave her more of the same in spades. Only this time she had two young children to protect while her husband was away in the army. Fighting life alone turned her into a tough, war-hardened veteran who was not easily rattled.

I wish my mother could come to visit in actuality, for there is much I would like to ask her. Only she could answer questions about things in the past that I don't remember, or was too young to understand.

In a lot of ways she is still with me as a permanent houseguest. I see her every time I look in the mirror, because I look a lot like her. Even my small hands are exact replicas of hers, except that her hands were worn from hard labor, and for the last ten years of her life, her hands were severely crippled by arthritis, which left her in constant pain. Those poor hands told the story of her life, and showed how much they had done for us and for everyone else who needed her help. I remember her as the most courageous human being I have ever known. Despite her small stature and slight build, she had a will of iron, which refused to bend to misfortune. I can still hear her telling me "There is no such thing as it can't be done" when I balked at something she told me to do. It was the motto she lived by, and expected me to follow. I'll never know if I would have had the courage and fortitude to follow her example, for my life has been much easier than hers. I never had to risk my life for my family or worry about how to feed my children.

It was Mother who saw my little sister and me through the terrible times of WWII, when bombs fell day and night. I see Mother carrying my little sister as we desperately run for our basement bomb shelter while the firebombs suck up the air around us. I feel her arms around us as she shields us with her body to protect us from the chunks of plaster falling from the ceiling as the concussion bombs shake the building.

Haunting my dreams to this day is the night we fled the burning city with nothing but the clothes on our backs, and Mother's desperate struggle to shepherd us to safety in the countryside, where we had a small summer cottage. In a place where dreams mix with memories, I see her trying to spare us the trauma of seeing the bloodied bodies and body parts in the rubble by hiding us behind her and telling us not to look. Suppressed in daytime, the memories come at night to stalk me in dreams, in which Mother and I run and hide in the ruins to evade the specter of death reaching for us with long bony fingers. Just under the surface of my consciousness, the things we experienced together are impossible to erase.

I see Mother giving us what little food she begged from farmers while she did without during the years under Communism, when we almost starved to death. We survived the war, but barely survived what followed.

Some nights she takes me back in time to when we fled Russian-occupied East Germany and shows me a white expanse of snow, edged by a dark line of forest stretching along the horizon. I feel the icy wind sweeping us along; I see my mother, who is skin and bones, dressed in nondescript rags as she manages to get us across the border through ice and snow to the American-occupied West. When my sister and I are completely exhausted, and sit in the snow not wanting to continue our thirty-hour ordeal, Mother's powers of persuasion urge us on: "Come on, you must be brave. Only a little further and we'll be in the clear." I wake up snuggled under my warm blankets, glad it was only a dream. These decisive thirty hours changed our lives.

I see us arriving in the West frozen to the bone, so covered in snow and ice that we were barely recognizable as human beings. The American GI who caught us yielded to Mother's pleading and let us go. Thanks to Mother's courage we were free to live our lives without fear, and could join our father, who had fled to the West six months earlier.

Sometimes she's in the primitive barracks of a refugee camp in the West, sewing away to augment my father's meager earnings and to keep us clothed and fed. She is making our clothes from the best parts of old clothes, so we were always clean and well dressed, no matter how poor we were.

Then there are the other nights when Mother stops by, which always leave me feeling content, because she takes me back to my early childhood. Together we walk through the forest I remember so well, once again delighting in its mysterious beauty. She takes me through flower-covered meadows under clear blue skies dotted with white clouds. The flowers, ruffled by a light breeze, grow in abundance and reach to my knees. I pick as many as my hands can hold, marveling at their beauty. We reach a quiet lake with a little cottage at its edge. Delightfully, in this dream all the pear and apple trees are blooming in the garden surrounding our cottage. This enchanting vision fills me with wonder and joy. Is she telling me that the once-broken and charred trees, which were emblematic of our lives, would recover? I like to see it that way.

I see my mother in the good days before our lives were ripped asunder by the war, trying to explain to me why the stork brought me a baby sister when I asked for an older brother.

Rarely confrontational, Mother's disapproval usually took the form of a gentle rebuke couched in positive terms. A master of the diplomatic approach, she never forced her opinions; she left it to me to think about whatever the problem was, and allowed me to sort it out for myself. It usually turned out that she was right. Her common sense always steered me in the right direction. I often wished that she were here to give me advice on some of the everyday problems. All I can do is draw on memory, and ask, "What would she do? How would she handle the situation?"

In my dreams I see life dealing Mother her worst blow of all when my younger sister Margit was killed in an automobile accident. I can still see her devastated and heartbroken, sobbing uncontrollably, and rejecting all consolation in her grief. It was more than she could bear, finally breaking her dauntless spirit. Sadly, she followed my sister within the year.

Many of my recollections resurface in dreams in which Mother is alive and well. Sometimes her presence is so real that I'm filled with feelings of regret and disappointment when I realize that it was only a dream.

All I have now are her infrequent visits in the depth of night when we wander the labyrinth of the past together, a past in which dreams and memories mesh in faraway places that seem at once familiar, yet strange.

She gave so much of herself to all of us that sometimes it's like she never left. Her love and what she taught me by example will always remain with me.

* * *

For sales, editorial information, subsidiary rights information
or a catalog, please write or phone or e-mail

IBOOKS
1230 Park Avenue
New York, New York 10128, US
Sales: 1-800-68-BRICK
Tel: 212-427-7139
www.BrickTowerPress.com
email: bricktower@aol.com

www.Ingram.com

For sales in the UK and Europe please contact our distributor,
Gazelle Book Services
White Cross Mills
Lancaster, LA1 4XS, UK
Tel: (01524) 68765 Fax: (01524) 63232
email: jacky@gazellebooks.co.uk

CPSIA information can be obtained at www.ICGtesting.com
Printed in the USA
BVOW06*1348120715

408373BV00006B/217/P

9 781596 879812